YELLOWSTONE DENIED

YELLOWSTONE DENIED

The Life of Gustavus Cheyney Doane

Kim Allen Scott

UNIVERSITY OF OKLAHOMA PRESS : NORMAN

Library of Congress Cataloging-in-Publication Data

Scott, Kim Allen, 1954–
    Yellowstone denied : the life of Gustavus Cheyney Doane / Kim Allen
    Scott.
        p. cm.
    Includes bibliographical references and index.
    ISBN 0-8061-3800-9 (alk. paper)
        1. Doane, Gustavus Cheyney, 1840–1892. 2. Explorers — West
    (U.S.) — Biography. 3. Soldiers — West (U.S.) — Biography.
    4. Yellowstone National Park — History. 5. Judith Basin (Mont.) —
    Discovery and exploration. 6. Snake River Region (Wyo.-Wash.) —
    Discovery and exploration. 7. Indians of North America — Wars —
    1866–1895. 8. Arctic regions — Discovery and exploration. 9. Mayors —
    Mississippi — Yazoo City — Biography. 10. United States. Army.
    California Cavalry Battalion (1862–1865) — Biography. I. Title.

    F594.D627S36 2006
    910′.92 — dc22

                                                    2006044698

                1 2 3 4 5 6 7 8 9 10

Contents

Illustrations

Maps

Photographs

Unless otherwise indicated, all photographs are courtesy of the Merrill G. Burlingame Special Collections, Montana State University Libraries, Bozeman, Montana

Preface

Taking the measure of a man from the documentary residue of his life is a responsibility that I have not taken lightly. The biographer's charge is to condense the activities of a lifetime, as recorded on letters, journals, reports, and reminiscences, into a single volume; yet regardless of the dearth or abundance of such material I find myself haunted by the possibility of doing the subject a grave injustice. When I first became aware of Capt. Gustavus Cheyney Doane and his important connection with the early exploration of Yellowstone National Park, I became curious as to why the extensive personal papers the officer left behind had not resulted in a comprehensive biographical study. The more I examined the reasons, the more I became convinced that Doane's life, as well as his legacy, had been the victim of what William Shakespeare's *Hamlet* described as the "slings and arrows of outrageous fortune." An incredibly gifted man whose exploits had consistently placed him within tantalizing reach of lasting fame, Doane nevertheless seemed fated to be denied widespread recognition during his lifetime and regulated to a brief historical footnote after he died.

Whether Doane created his own misfortunes or simply fell victim to incredibly bad luck, the following pages provide the reader with ample support for either viewpoint. My major concern in telling his story was finally to bring a wider notice to a man whose historical obscurity did not seem entirely the result of his own actions. If I have succeeded in this task, my work has not been in vain.

Acknowledgments

I have many people to thank for their help during the research for this book, but Ed Barnett of Chico, California, deserves special mention. In 1999 I contacted Ed to ask about his family's papers. Ed's ancestor, Walter Cooper, had been a pioneer entrepreneur of Bozeman, Montana, and the Montana State University Library was interested in adding to its collection of Cooper materials. Entirely by chance, I discovered that Ed possessed not only additional Cooper documents but also a rich cache of letters, photographs, and reminiscences that Doane's widow had bequeathed to Ed's grandmother. This fortuitous discovery, along with the generous decision by Ed and his brother, Cooper Barnett, to donate all of the papers to our library, helped to resolve many unanswered questions regarding Doane's checkered past. This incident also convinced me that my luck in telling Doane's story would be substantially better than any that the captain had experienced in his own attempts to achieve recognition.

Some of my investigations were financed by a Research and Creativity grant sponsored by the Montana State University Vice President for Research, Creativity, and Technology Transfer, for which I am deeply grateful. The funding from this grant allowed for travel to the National Archives in Washington, D.C., where there are too many helpful, professional, and knowledgeable staff members to list individually. Other people who assisted in the gathering of Doane information include John Hollinger and Elizabeth Williams, Hollinger Corporation, Fredericksburg, Virginia; Robert Krick, Jr., National Park Service; Lee Whittlesey, Yellowstone National Park; Ed Frank, University of Memphis; Donald Walker, University of the Pacific; Janie C. Morris, Duke University; Larry Rogers, Concord, California; Jack Hawkins, Bozeman, Montana; David Eckroth, Billings, Montana; Jim Doane, Daytona, Florida; Sharon Pohlman, Seeley Lake, Montana; and Steve and Kelly Russell, Bozeman, Montana. Most of all I would like to thank my wife, Jayne, for her patience and encouragement during the years I have worked on this project. I could have accomplished nothing without her.

YELLOWSTONE DENIED

CHAPTER 1

"You said they were spoiling the country"
Early Life

Montana representative John M. Evans may not have spent much time personally handling the hundreds of individual case files that came to his Washington office in the early weeks of 1930. Like most congressmen during those terrible early months of the Great Depression, Evans probably had a secretary to shuttle to their appropriate offices the myriad requests for seed packets, government publications, and special relief. However, one case that winter seemed to be particularly insistent: the Bozeman writer proved determined to get a satisfactory answer. Mary Lee Hunter Doane, the seventy-one-year-old widow of Capt. Gustavus Cheyney Doane, needed money desperately, and she turned to a government that she felt had been particularly neglectful of her late husband. In a carefully worded three-page letter, she demanded from the United States government the exclusive privilege of copyrighting the 1870 report written by her husband on his reconnaissance of the country that later became Yellowstone National Park. The report, published in 1871 in pamphlet format and out of print for decades, had long been recognized as a major factor contributing to the legislation establishing the park in March 1872.[1]

Mary presented her case in the manner of one who felt an obligation had been denied, using a well-worn myth to bolster her argument. She recounted again the colorful fable of a campfire discussion involving her husband, Cornelius Hedges, Nathaniel P. Langford, and Henry D. Washburn during their expedition and how the men reached a resolution that the land be reserved as a public park. Quoting from a recent *Saturday Evening Post* article that described the imaginary scene, she wrote:

> To me that camp fire at the junction of the Firehole and Gibbon rivers is one of the most touching and stirring episodes in American history, and I never pass its site — which I often do — without thinking of that little group of men which, fifty-nine years ago, on that frosty night, dreamed a splendid dream, achieved a great act of renunciation, and left as proud a tradition and as proud an actuality as we possess. May I not have your help, so that I may at this late date, receive some financial benefit from the sacrifices made at that time?[2]

Evans found the argument compelling enough to take action and made inquiries on the widow's behalf to Herbert Putnam, the Librarian of Congress. The request eventually landed on the desk of William Brown, the acting register of copyrights, who was obviously unimpressed. Brown sent a terse reply to Putnam for his answer to the Montana congressman, stating that Captain Doane's report "was not subject to copyright then, and could not be copyrighted now under any process of existing law."[3] Evans could do no more than enclose the memo with a short letter to the widow, stating: "I regret the information is so discouraging, but I have done the best I could do to help you."[4]

If Congressman Evans thought that the Doane case file could be safely retired after sending his apology, he had not counted on the persistence of his petitioner. In a few weeks he got another letter from Bozeman showing the determination (if not the desperation) of Mary Doane. "Is there not some way in which I could secure the exclusive right to publish this?" she asked. "I have had many requests for this report, but I hesitate in publishing it unless I can have the exclusive right to do it. I feel that as Captain Doane's widow I have a better right to this than anyone else. Will you not go into this matter a little more for me and see if a way cannot be figured out?"[5] There is no record of Evans's final reply to Mary, but it is safe to assume that a tactful explanation of copyright law became yet another addition in a long line of disappointments for Captain Doane's widow in her efforts to keep his memory alive.

Refusing to be satisfied with Evans's efforts, Mary fired off a duplicate of her original request to Senator Thomas J. Walsh, obviously hoping that the added weight of senatorial pressure would secure her prize. Walsh duplicated Evans's efforts, once again writing to Herbert Putnam, who in turn sent the copyright question to the apparently exasperated William Brown. Before sending on Brown's second brusque assessment of federal copyright law, Putnam at least dug through the stacks to find a duplicate copy of the original pamphlet for Senator Walsh to return to Mrs. Doane. A reminder of her husband's ephemeral celebrity as an explorer was a poor consolation to a woman who wanted to establish a more lasting notice and make some money in the process.

The contradictory strategy of using an altruistic argument to achieve a self-serving goal does not seem to have occurred to Mary Doane in her correspondence with the government. She had emphasized the heroic sacrifice that her husband made in renouncing a claim to the region he allegedly discovered, only to insist that the act of renunciation justified her own desire to profit from his heroism. The sense of entitlement conveyed by her request provides an interesting parallel to the attitudes and actions that her husband had exhibited throughout his military career. Gustavus Doane had always displayed in his writings an expressed or implied demand that he deserved special consideration as an explorer, a scholar, and a soldier. When that consideration was not forthcoming, he allowed its absence to embitter his outlook and poison his relationships with his brother officers and superiors.

Many officers in the post–Civil War frontier army shared Doane's frustrations over the limited opportunities for advancement and recognition. The cumbersome system of promotion based on attrition and seniority held many line officers in junior rank during the entire length of their careers. According to one estimate, a second lieutenant starting his service in 1877 would have to remain in the army twenty-four to twenty-six years to reach the rank of major. Congress did not pass legislation specifying promotion by branch of service and examination until 1890.[6] For officers like Doane, who hungered for fame as much as for advancement, the situation was doubly intolerable. Some, like Nelson A. Miles, became so obsessed with self-promotion that they lost the respect of their peers in a ruthless climb to the top of the command chain. Others, like Frederick Schwatka, were savvy enough to court the popular press and eventually abandon the army altogether in order to establish their names as famous men. Doane chose a different path, however. Incredibly inept in picking the right superiors to help him in his quest for lasting fame, Doane refused the option of cultivating sources outside the military for his goals and ultimately railed in fury against the honors he felt had been denied. His headstrong and stubborn nature, along with a callous tendency to concern himself with his own career before considering others, continually placed obstacles between himself and the glory he so desperately craved. The pattern of approaching the brink of fame only to be subsequently disappointed began for Doane at an early age.

Solomon and Nancy Doane called their gray-eyed, dark-haired son "Cheyney." The first surviving child born to the Galesburg, Illinois, couple on May 29, 1840, Gustavus Cheyney Doane did not much care for his Christian name and never answered to it. Other inheritances from his father, including a restless spirit and an outrageously poor business sense, would be harder to deny as the boy grew to manhood; but at least in his choice of names Cheyney

Doane could demonstrate the stubborn independence that was his and his alone.

Solomon Doane had a pedigree that extended back to the Plymouth Colony in 1629; but like other descendants of Dean John Doane, Solomon had traveled far from the family's original home on the Massachusetts shoreline to seek his fortune in the West. By the late 1830s he had settled along the Illinois frontier and married a bright, educated young woman named Nancy Davis. The couple's first attempts at starting a family both ended in miscarriages. When Cheyney survived his infancy, his mother doted on him, teaching him to read at an age when most children barely learned the alphabet.[7] Solomon, who worked as a carpenter and furniture maker, did not initially take an active role in educating his son other than imparting to him an incurable case of wanderlust, because the family never settled long in one place. In the 1840s the little lead mining town of Galesburg already served as a point of departure for the prairies of Iowa and Minnesota, and the steady departure of immigrants west constantly fed the elder Doane's natural inclinations. During the first few years following the birth of Cheyney, Solomon also heard stories of the fabulously rich farming land to be obtained cheaply in the Oregon Territory, which only grew more enticing after he moved his young family to St. Louis in 1844. He practiced his trade for another two years in the Missouri city before gathering enough resources to move again, this time in a much more ambitious journey along the Oregon Trail.

The spring of 1846 did not produce as many overland trail emigrants as the previous year had, but it would be the time of departure for some of the most famous travelers ever to brave the dangers of the journey. Among the 1,700 pioneers who left for California or Oregon that year were the ill-fated Donner party and the most famous chronicler of the migration, Francis Parkman.[8] Solomon Doane and his family also joined the ranks of pioneers who left Independence, Missouri, that spring. While it cannot be precisely determined which particular group they traveled with, the general outline of their journey can easily be reconstructed. The first Oregon-bound train left western Missouri in April. Equipped with cumbersome ox-drawn wagons and essential household goods, families like the Doanes pushed west along the trail that roughly paralleled the Platte River across Nebraska. The parents of such families recorded their feelings in diaries and letters, relating the incidents of the trail in monotonous entries that illustrated among other things their desire for the familiar while constantly encountering the strange.

For emigrant children like Cheyney, however, the experience of the Oregon Trail was entirely different from that of their parents. Without the breadth of their parents' experiences, children could view the adventure with a special clarity that helped them strongly identify with the new land. "This environment, after all, helped shape and define reality itself— those ideas of what was possible and expected in life—among children taking their first steps toward mental maturity."[9] The impact of this overland journey on Cheyney Doane must have been profound. As he gazed out on the limitless expanse while trudging alongside his parents' wagon all the universe likely seemed to him a mystery awaiting discovery, and the conversations around the campfires at night regarding the imagined danger of Indian warriors constantly poised to steal away wandering children tempered his wonderment at the land with an ingrained loathing of its Native inhabitants. These early impressions would remain with the boy the rest of his life.

Solomon Doane and his family reached Oregon later that year and took up a land claim near Oak Grove, a small settlement south of Portland. A school had been established in the area. Nancy made sure her son attended as often as her husband would allow his absence from farm chores, but other circumstances soon interfered with Cheyney's early education. The summer of 1848 brought the news of the rich gold discoveries in California, and the restless Solomon simply could not resist the siren's call. Caught again by the gambling spirit, he disposed of his property and with Nancy, Cheyney, and the family's newest addition, James, arrived in San Francisco, May 8, 1849, on the English ship *Janet*. Doane found the gold camps already crowded and the riches elusive, however, and again turned to farming, becoming one of the early settlers in the Santa

Clara Valley, just south of San Francisco. There the family grew, with the births of four more children: Anna ("Annie"), George, Charles, and John. Solomon Doane continued to gamble with his family fortunes in Santa Clara, displaying a woeful talent for buying dear and selling cheap, consistently miscalculating the price of land he purchased. His initial acquisition had been made under the advice of John Charles Frémont, the famous explorer and army officer so influential in bringing California into the control of the United States. It is unknown whether Cheyney actually met the "Pathfinder" as a boy, but he certainly heard the admiring tales of Frémont's adventures while growing up.

As the oldest son, and blessed with a powerful physique, young Cheyney reluctantly submitted to the dull, restraining farm work on the outskirts of the growing town of Santa Clara. Here too he began to display a remarkable mechanical aptitude, probably gained from working alongside his father at carpentry chores. "It seemed he could make anything he saw anyone else make," remembered his brother George years later; and his father encouraged this talent more than any to be learned from books.[10] Solomon Doane strictly enforced the work ethic among his six children, demanding obedience to his orders and hard labor to coax a living from the soil. Nancy Doane's priorities differed from her husband's; she worked instead to educate her brood in order to free them from the backbreaking life of husbandry. The conflict between the couple only grew worse as the years passed, but Nancy shrewdly manipulated her husband's never-ending schemes for riches to advance her own ambitions for her children, especially Cheyney.

The trip across the plains, the years in Oregon, and the expanse of fertile valley in his early years left a deep imprint of the frontier upon Cheyney. Each year he became more restless as he found his path cluttered by newly erected fences and farmsteads. "Even when a child," his mother wrote him many years later, "you resented the people settling around us at Santa Clara. You said they were spoiling the country."[11] He nevertheless found some time to attend local schools and demonstrated a bright mind with a promise for greater achievements if properly cultivated. When an opportunity to encourage that cultivation appeared in the guise of an investment, Nancy Doane acted.

The Methodist Church of California had founded an ambitious school at Santa Clara in 1851 dubbed "The University of the Pacific." By 1853 the coeducational college had two buildings (a male and a female institute) and began a full course program in the liberal arts for a combined enrollment of 145 students.[12] The annual tuition for the school program, with additional fees for languages and music, put the school out of reach for the Doanes' modest income. But by 1854 a new fund-raising scheme to build an endowment for the school came into play. For a mere $100, a bond could be purchased by any interested investor that would guarantee six years' enrollment, enough time to complete all degree requirements for an undergraduate diploma. In addition, the bond could be transferred by the purchaser.[13] The possibility that the bond would rise in value as standard rates of tuition increased over time made a compelling argument for purchase, and Nancy convinced her husband to invest. Although the college eventually refused to accept the bonds at full face value, the Doanes' purchase had opened the door for Cheyney's escape from the life of a farmer.

In 1857, the year the infant university graduated its first full class of ten, Cheyney enrolled at the college and did well. As a first-year course he took classes in algebra, Sallust, Ovid, Xenophon's *Anabasis*, Historical Greek Testament, general history, and the Bible. Years later he would claim that he quickly tired of the school's curriculum and petitioned California's Senator William M. Gwin for an appointment to the United States Military Academy at West Point. In the absence of any documentary evidence, Cheyney's further assertion that Gwin denied the application due to the student's uncompromising antislavery position makes the story highly suspect. None of his surviving college essays could be considered abolitionist in nature.

In spite of his alleged early military ambitions, Cheyney's life at the infant University of the Pacific must have been a completely new world, introducing him to ideas and concepts that in some ways allowed his restless spirit to soar and in other ways reinforced his resistance to authority. The school maintained a strict study regimen and vigorously enforced a separation of the girls' and boys' sections. During his first year, Cheyney had to adjust to rules regarding his speech ("students will be required to abstain from all obscene and profane language"), his hygiene ("habits of personal cleanliness will be required of all members of the institution"), and his attitude ("they will be expected to maintain a gentlemanly deportment towards the teachers and one another").[14] All of these rules went against his natural disposition, for Cheyney became well known in later life for a slovenly appearance and language that would hardly bear repeating at a proper Methodist gathering. His aversion to discipline would be demonstrated at the school as well.

In January 20, 1858, at the beginning of his second term, Doane joined the Archanian Literary Society, an early fraternal organization that required its members to participate in readings, essay writings, and debates. The Archanians published a small handwritten serial called the *Archanian Clarion,* and Cheyney became an enthusiastic contributor to its columns. Writing under the pen name "Wanderer," the young student began to develop a talent in composition that would serve him well in later years.

Conditions at the new college remained quite primitive as Cheyney pursued his education. The benches the students sat on had no backs (a feature that observers other than Cheyney found easy to criticize), and the recitations were often stupefyingly boring.[15] Mandatory church services held every Sunday, with an additional moral or religious lecture delivered by the faculty in rotation, were the only occasions when Cheyney and his fellow male scholars could consort with members of the Female Institute. Cheyney began to welcome these tiresome exercises the longer he remained in school, and he wrote many verses of admiration to the young ladies who suffered along with him each Sunday on those hard benches.

The young student may have remained at home during his first year, but eventually Cheyney boarded with two other boys in a house near campus. One of the poems he composed during this time described their Spartan living quarters as filthy and complained:

"our chairs are by courtesy empty nail kegs, and the floor and the dishes a foot deep with soot."[16] Other writings left by Cheyney during his college years give even darker hints about the conditions of his personal relationships. He often found himself estranged from his fellow students, sharply noting the class differences between himself and more well-heeled young scholars. In one article he wrote for the *Clarion,* Cheyney intemperately described his classmates: "Collected together from all parts of the country and from all stations in society, having different dispositions, different classes and different objects in view, the acquaintances formed are merely nominal and generally of the most formal and heartless kind, having merely self-interest at stake, and rivalry at the bottom, and between the two there is lost all real friendship."[17]

The lessons of superficiality in friendships and cultivating people only for the sake of his own advancement were the darker conclusions of Cheyney's education at the University of the Pacific. He quickly mastered the chameleon-like ability to adapt to almost any social setting, appearing as a polished gentleman or as a rough-hewn farmer's son depending on his audiences and their ability to assist him achieve his object in life. One of Cheney's closest friends among the students at the college seems to have been chosen primarily for this purpose. Richard Ellet, a member of an Illinois clan that boasted one of America's most famous civil engineers, became Cheyney's companion. From the other end of the social scale he chose George W. Towle, another Santa Clara farmer's son. Both of these young men were members of the college's preparatory school during Cheyney's years at the college and two years younger than him.

Other essays that Cheyney wrote demonstrated his inability to keep his mind on classical studies or social contacts. He returned again and again to describing the wild country that he remembered from his childhood and the freedom that it represented. "Who can traverse the solitudes of a dense, dark forest," he asked in one of his essays, "and see the monarchs of the vegetable world standing as they have stood for ages without feeling a kind of reverence for the old trees that have so long withstood the winter storms and have silently been living witnesses of so many changes and events?"[18]

Even more telling of the young man's inclinations are remarks that he gave at a senior oration on December 3, 1860, entitled "The Eloquence of Solitude": he asserted that a "new and more blissful existence seems to open up before us" when man encounters the wilderness.[19]

Cheyney's appreciation for the natural world should not be confused with an embrace of the simple, solitary life or a rejection of the need to climb society's corrupt ladder of success. His view of the natural world became more akin to John Charles Frémont's than to Henry David Thoreau's, valuing the landscape more for its potential for individual glory than for its romantic preservation as a primeval soul restorative. Having been raised on tales extolling the great "Pathfinder's" accomplishments, Cheyney concluded that the natural panorama he admired also held the key to the acceptance he craved. Accordingly, his essays showed as much appreciation for things military as for things natural. "It is our duty to preserve the martial spirit of the people," he once wrote; "the policy of crying down war and discountenancing the military spirit, though it may afford an excellent theme for the contemplation of would-be philanthropists and Quakers, will not work well when applied to practice in so material a world as this, in which success belongs to the quickest and the bravest."[20]

If Cheyney ever found aversion to discipline a cause for trouble at college, it came from his membership in the Archanian Society. The weekly meetings always held programs of readings and debate, but sometimes youthful passions got carried away. The issue of slavery proved to be a violent debate topic, and most of the members harbored sympathies for the peculiar institution. Intensity of feeling caused the minority antislavery faction to leave the society in 1858 to form the rival Rhizomian Society.[21] Cheyney remained with the Archanians and at one point tried to express his position on the topic in a largely unsuccessful humorous essay called "Familiar Lecture on Geology as Connected with Political Science." He spent most of the work building a case to consider the African people distinct from and inferior to the human family by a facetious review of geological evidence, concluding that it was "inevitable that as man has dominion over the fishes of the sea and the fowls of the air, and the beasts that walk thereon, he must also have dominion over the Negro race."[22]

The problem with Cheyney's ridicule was that taken at face value it seemed like a poorly reasoned defense of slavery rather than a satiric critique of the institution. At a time when the issue split the very church denomination that operated the college, slavery could hardly be seen as a subject for laughter. "The Bible has also been introduced so deeply into the conflict," Cheyney observed, "that it has become a matter of serious question whether the scriptures were primarily intended as a plan of salvation, or merely a collection of arguments pro and con, as to whether the normal condition of Black humanity is slave or free."[23] Publications like Cheyney's essay simply exacerbated an already tense situation between the students of the Archanian and Rhizomian societies and a corresponding concern of the school's administration regarding the propriety of the student groups' activities. The faculty of the college took disciplinary action against the Archanian Society in March 1860, temporarily suspending several students who were members.[24] Exactly what had occurred may never be fully known, but certainly Doane's mocking essay did little to foster the confidence of the teachers in the student society. The Archanians eventually resumed their activities, but this happened after Doane had graduated.[25]

Doane completed his final year at the college first in a class of five in Greek, Latin, and mathematics and second in general scholastic rating. His course work had included classes in geology, navigation, geography, astronomy, botany, and zoology, as well as the Greek and Latin readings he found so tiresome. On June 13, 1861, the graduation exercises took place at the University of the Pacific. In a ceremony tedious for participants and spectators alike, each of the students receiving degrees had to deliver a lengthy oration, which was interspersed with musical interludes. Doane had the honor of going first, delivering a two-page Salutory in Latin followed by a nine-page speech entitled "The Laurels of Learning," which may have netted him the loudest applause from an audience subjected to a ceremony that would last the better part of the afternoon. A spectator at one such graduation exercise at the college complained that "three hours' application to a hard bench, with no rest for [my] back, is not conducive to a condition of mind fitted to enjoy even the most eloquent of discourses."[26] The applause he enjoyed after the speech, the warm congratulations he received, and the future he must have contemplated that day would prove all too fleeting. With degree in hand, a polished writing style, an opportunistic view of friendship, and no particular calling to follow, Doane realized the necessity of returning to his father's farm.

CHAPTER 2

"An appetite which required at least two men's rations to satisfy"

Civil War Years

W hen Cheyney Doane graduated in the summer of 1861, California, like the rest of the nation, was in the midst of intense political upheaval and social unrest. Many Southerners had participated in the gold rush of 1849 and had become prominent members of the state's citizenry. In some areas their influence outweighed their numbers, San Francisco being an excellent example. While many Union sympathizers in California varied greatly in their support of Abraham Lincoln and the Republican government, San Francisco secessionists worked both openly and secretly to bring their remote state into the Confederate fold as a "Pacific Republic."[1] As a result, the call for volunteers issued in the metropolis of the Golden State was made for the local replacement of departing regular army soldiers rather than for actual service in the war back east. Doane counted himself among those Unionists who longed to see action in Virginia, more out of a sense of adventure than from true patriotism; but he initially settled for the lackluster prospect of garrison duty in Santa Clara County.

After his return home from college, Doane labored with plow and ax, chafing under his father's harsh rule. When a volunteer company of home guard soldiers recruited in the nearest town, Doane eagerly enlisted. He began infantry drill with the San Jose Zouaves in early 1862 and attended their musters whenever he could, but the drudgery of farm work always called him home. In the fall of 1862, however, the opportunity for service in the East finally arrived for Doane.

For over a year Brig. Gen. George Wright, commander of the Department of the Pacific, had been sending proposals urging the use of California volunteers in the Army of the Potomac to the secretary of war. During that time other Union states that had seen a decline in enlistments became desperate to meet the quota of soldiers imposed by the Lincoln administration. Massachusetts governor John A. Andrew asked that any Californians desiring eastern service be assigned to his state's requirement. The city of Boston in particular wanted these men credited to its quota and raised a bounty of two hundred dollars per recruit to assist any Californians with their transportation and equipment expenses.[2] In San Francisco, former Bay Stater James Sewall Reed became the agent through which the people of Boston would receive their California recruits. As soon as the Boston money was pledged and the War Department gave its approval to the scheme, Reed appointed himself captain and began to raise the company for the Second Massachusetts Volunteer Cavalry, a company that would become known as the "California Hundred."[3]

Prior to his recruiting effort in San Francisco, Reed lived in Fremont Township, where his wife taught school for the younger Doane children. When Reed finally got the authorization to raise the company for Boston's draft quota, he asked Doane to assist in recruiting the Hundred at his headquarters on the corner of Post and Kearney Streets.[4] Doane, old enough to leave home without his father's permission, knew that the promised bounty money from Boston for transport also freed him from the need to secure his parents' financial blessings. After he had joined Reed in the city, Doane began the work of helping to select the men who would join their "elite equestrian corps." Although a good number of young men proved eager to enlist in the new company, Reed felt he needed to be quite selective in choosing those physically worthy of membership and insisted on a competitive process to fill the ranks. When Doane's old schoolmate George W. Towle wrote in October to ask about joining the company, Doane callously replied that Reed desired larger and older men. During the intervening weeks the rigorous physical examination screened out far more recruits than were accepted. Ironically, Doane himself failed to pass the doctor's scrutiny; but Reed reassured his assistant by promising to find a less exacting physician once they arrived in Massachusetts.[5] Towle decided to ignore Doane's advice; he traveled to the company's headquarters to see if he could join the unit and was accepted.[6]

Another of Doane's old school chums managed to convince the doctors that he possessed the stamina to join up. Richard Ellet had his own reasons for wanting to get into the fight back east. His nineteen-year-old cousin Charles Rivers Ellet had just been promoted to colonel, assuming command of the Mississippi Ram Fleet, a special marine force authorized by secretary of war Edwin M. Stanton and ostensibly under army command. The Ram Fleet had been organized by Richard's uncle, Charles Ellet, Jr., who died leading the ships to victory in the Battle of Memphis. Richard's other uncle, Alfred Ellet, received a promotion to the rank of brigadier general with the Ram Fleet; and Richard's older brother John also served as an officer in the command.

By mid-December the Hundred finally reached its full complement of men and prepared to leave San Francisco for the eastern seaboard. Even though he had literally failed to pass muster, Doane marched with his comrades down to the wharf on the morning of the eleventh and boarded the steamboat *Golden Age*. A large crowd had gathered to see the patriots off on their adventure, and Captain Reed had the men stand in formation on deck as the ship steamed off for Panama. Unfortunately, the rigorous physical requirements had absolutely no bearing on the volunteers' ability to stomach the hazards of ocean travel; shortly after their ship passed the Golden Gate, many of the would-be heroes parted with their breakfast.[7]

Doane's first military experience provided reinforcement for his tendency to expect preferential treatment from his superiors, and the unit he had joined mirrored his personal resistance to authority when that special treatment was not forthcoming. Although Doane had no official status with the company, Reed assured him a set of sergeant's stripes; and he was likely considered a noncommissioned officer by the volunteers as they received their first orders aboard the *Golden Age*. Once the ship reached the open sea, some of the men complained about the rations of rancid salt pork and hardtack, and Reed's inability to do anything about the situation seemed to some a positive unwillingness to act. On December 16 the *Golden Age* stopped at Acapulco, where some of the troopers managed to get on shore and purchase fruit. From there the ship continued south to Panama, where the entire company disembarked, boarded railroad cars, and traveled to the Atlantic side of the isthmus and their next ship, the *Ocean Queen*.[8]

The bad food on the *Golden Age* was nothing compared to the rations on board the *Ocean Queen*. Wormy rice, rotten salt pork, and ship biscuits filled with weevils were served to the men with unrelenting regularity. A riot occurred one morning: the volunteers overturned the galley tables and dumped most of their meal on the floor. The captain of the ship confronted the Californians and threatened to put them in irons. "If you think you have men enough to do it start right in," cried the mutineers, "but we propose to have something to eat and if you do not furnish it we will proceed to take it."[9] The captain stormed away from the men and complained to Reed, who abused his soldiers by shouting at them: "Now I will see you all damned and in hell before I will ever help a God damn one of you again!"[10] In spite of both captains' bluster, the *Ocean Queen* promptly stopped at a port in the Florida Keys to take on fresh provisions for the protesting passengers, a concession that may have bolstered the Californians' mistaken perception that their unique volunteer status merited special treatment.

When the *Ocean Queen* reached New York on January 3, 1863, Doane and his comrades temporarily forgot their unpleasant introduction to military life in their first warm rush of welcome from eastern politicians. Sumptuous meals served up between patriotic ceremonies did much to improve the Californians' attitude, and their later arrival at Camp Meigs outside of Boston started a whole new round of grateful public expressions. Doane, like the other volunteers who became the subject of so much Boston publicity, basked in the comfortable realization that he had become a hero without any more effort than donning a uniform and taking an unpleasant ocean voyage.[11]

Amidst all the flattering attention a cloud of uncertainty settled on Doane regarding his future with the now famous California Hundred. Forced into submitting to another medical exam before he could officially enter the regiment's roster, Doane passed the inspection on January 8, 1863, only to find himself placed as a private in the ranks of Company I with a group of local Massachusetts recruits. It took Captain Reed more than a month to untangle the paperwork and get Doane transferred back into Company A, the official designation of the California Hundred. As promised, the captain promptly rewarded his protégé with a warrant for the rank of second sergeant on February 11. Doane proudly displayed the yellow chevrons on his sleeves during the unit's final weeks of training.[12]

The month's delay in officially joining the company may have cost Doane the chance to receive a decent mount. George Towle described Doane years later as "a tall, rawboned individual, not very tidy in his appearance with an appetite which required at least two men's rations to satisfy and a very dry wit. He rode a pinto horse that was the smallest in the Company, in riding which his feet would come very near the ground."[13] Even on his diminutive horse, Doane learned to share a unit pride in the California Hundred that grew toward a collective conceit. They maintained their distance from the other companies of the Second Massachusetts and visually distinguished themselves by adopting a unique cap badge.[14] They wove outlandish tales during their off-duty visits to Boston, adopting a verbal swagger that may have appeared humorous in newspaper stories but gave veiled indications of continued discipline trouble to come.

On February 12, 1863, Doane and his comrades boarded railroad cars for their journey to the war. Instead of finding the smoke-clouded battlefields of honor that they had expected, the Hundred arrived at a miserable wind-swept spit of land jutting into the York River across from Yorktown, Virginia. "Camp California" on Gloucester Point would be their home for months. The army command could not have chosen a better location to foment dissatisfaction among the troopers. After a brief stint in the hospital due to a fever, Doane rejoined the company and took part in one pointless scout after another that spring, periodically exchanging shots with concealed snipers but otherwise seeing no more of war than could be experienced on occasional chicken coop raids. This sort of action was exactly what the Californians expected had they stayed at home; and their bitterness, fueled by idle camp routine, increased daily.[15] Ugly rumors began to circulate regarding Captain Reed's handling of the bounty money paid by the city of Boston. Some of the enlisted men believed that Reed never offered a satisfactory accounting of exactly how much money remained in the company fund and wrote letters to California newspapers condemning their commander. A few of the published complaints regarding Reed seem absolutely peevish on closer examination. For example, Reed imprisoned eight troopers after they refused to clean up some trash because they said the captain "had plenty of Negro servants and hostlers lying around doing nothing."[16]

Doane kept a close watch on the rebellious members of company, and his loyalty to his commander earned him contempt from some of the men. "I will not say that all have lost their respect for him," wrote one trooper of the captain, "for in the whole company there are sergeants now who would crawl around him and be offended at nothing, just for the sake of the offices they now hold."[17] A few troopers began playing a dangerous game of bluff with their noncommissioned officers, which almost resulted in their court-martial. A small group of complainers huddled together on the afternoon of May 25, 1863, to plant a story testing Corp. Edward R. Sterling's trustworthiness. They concocted a wild tale of organizing the company to desert en masse and form a guerrilla force to join the Army of the Potomac. As anticipated, Sterling went directly to

Captain Reed, who then hurried off to report the conspiracy to his superiors. Unbeknownst to Doane and the other noncoms, the commanding general at Yorktown took the threat seriously enough to dispatch a small army to surround the camp of the California Hundred shortly after midnight. The entire complement of enlisted men was marched off to prison, while Doane and the other noncoms were confined to their tents. The investigation that followed exposed the entire hoax, and the men were eventually released; but the gulf of distrust grew between the officers and enlisted men in Company A. The only thing everyone could agree on was that combat action would cure the growing insubordination. "Could the boys once get into battle, they would make the biggest kind of fight," wrote Pvt. Charles P. Briggs to a newspaper back home. "In fact, they don't care for five times their number."[18]

As it turned out, the Californians had to settle for an enemy one-fifth the size of their number when they finally got into battle. In late June, while the rest of Lincoln's army prepared for an epic duel with the Confederates in Pennsylvania, Maj. Gen. John A. Dix proposed a more modest assault on the rebel capital in Virginia. The California Hundred, together with troopers from the Eleventh Pennsylvania and Twelfth Illinois cavalry, were placed under the command of Col. Samuel P. Spear and ordered to destroy railroad bridges north of Richmond. The combined force of over 1,050 men would attack only a handful of reserve Confederate units assigned to guard the bridges.[19]

On June 24 Spear ordered his expeditionary force loaded on boats at Yorktown, steamed up the York River to its confluence with the Pamunkey, and continued to White House Landing. The transports made it to White House at 7:00 A.M. the next morning, and it took eight hours for the expedition to disembark and destroy some abandoned Confederate gun emplacements nearby. The raiders first struck at a small rebel picket force in the hamlet of Tunstall's Station about four miles from the river. Capturing one of the Confederates and scattering the others, Spear's force cut the telegraph lines and burned a few buildings before pushing on into the rainy night. After a few hours' rest the column continued at dawn along the south bank on the Pamunkey River, with Doane and his comrades in the advance. Close to noon they came in sight of a large mule train parked about a half mile from Hanover Court House. They captured the train and cut telegraph wires then pushed on to their objective, the Virginia Central Railroad bridge spanning the South Anna River.[20]

About forty North Carolina infantrymen had been posted to guard the bridge, under the command of Lt. Col. Tazewell L. Hargrove. The Rebels occupied two strong earthwork redoubts flanking the railroad tracks on the south side of the river, but these fortifications had been built to defend against an attack expected to come from the north.[21] As soon as he saw the enemy advancing in force from the south, Hargrove realized the redoubts would be exposed to enemy fire from that direction and withdrew his men across the bridge to the north side of the river. There another contingent of infantry hustled south from Taylorsville reenforced the Confederates, bringing the total number to about ninety-four effectives. Hargrove distributed his tiny force in a series of rifle pits dug along the east side of the tracks but continued to concentrate most of his firepower on the bridge itself. Doane and his comrades dismounted to advance through a cornfield to the abandoned redoubts, and the excellent cover allowed the Union artillery to deploy and pound the Rebel infantry on the north bank. With bullets from the North Carolina sharpshooters thudding uncomfortably into the earthen walls, however, Colonel Spear could not send any soldiers out to begin setting fire to the bridge; he needed to eliminate the enemy force to complete his mission.[22]

Union scouts eventually brought word that a narrow bridge of fallen logs a few hundred yards downstream would allow them to cross the river and flank the redoubt. Spear ordered the California Hundred down to the logs, and one by one the soldiers made the perilous crossing as stray Rebel gunfire zipped around them. Doane made the passage unscathed; but when Richard Ellet attempted to follow, a bullet ball smashed through both of his thighs. He fell screaming to the ground. This first combat casualty seemed to galvanize the Hundred; along with some troopers of the Twelfth Pennsylvania, they stormed the defending Rebels with their pistols and sabers in a vicious hand-to-hand assault. Many of the Confederates suffered saber cuts and close-range powder burns before Hargrove surrendered.[23]

The Yankees had little time to celebrate their victory. An attempt to burn another bridge two miles upstream was turned back, and the entire expedition rushed back to the waiting river transports at White House Landing. En route the soldiers managed to capture Gen. Robert E. Lee's son, Brig. Gen. William H. Lee, who was found recuperating from a leg wound at a Wickham family plantation home, Hickory Hill.[24] Although the Union high command discounted the results of the raid because only one bridge had been destroyed, the Hundred took justifiable pride at having made such a valuable capture on their first combat mission and their safe return to base with their prize. For his own part, Doane made sure Richard Ellet made it back with the rest of the column and saw him safely evacuated to a hospital near Fortress Monroe, Virginia.

The combination of their first battle and their assignment to join the rest of their regiment near Centerville, Virginia, on August 6, 1863, seemed to quell the grumbling of the Hundred. By that time Doane and most of the company's other noncommissioned officers had an opportunity to review the various letters that had appeared in the California press accusing Captain Reed of malfeasance and responded with a letter of their own, warmly praising their commanding officer.[25] During the weeks following the battle at South Anna Bridge the California Hundred had reconciled themselves to the demands of military discipline, and the assignment of Reed to acting major of the first battalion removed one of the most immediate sources of irritation for the majority of the complainers. But Reed's promotion was a disaster for Doane personally because Capt. Francis Washburn, a Massachusetts officer, took temporary command of the Hundred on Reed's departure and apparently did not indulge in the favoritism that the sergeant had come to expect.[26]

Fortunately for Doane, no immediate return to camp routine

occurred. The portion of northern Virginia that the Second Massachusetts had been assigned to (the corridor outside Washington, D.C.) had proven to be a vulnerable area for the Union due to small bands of rebel partisans posing as peaceful farmers by day and operating as raiders and arsonists by night. As a result of the depredations, the Californians drew the unenviable assignment of dealing with the partisan rangers commanded by the famous guerrilla Col. John Singleton Mosby. Like all others who had tangled with the "Gray Ghost," Company A learned quickly that Mosby earned every bit of his fearsome reputation.[27]

The Union high command seemed unable to come to terms with Mosby's hit-and-run methods, and the Californians continued to patrol the roadways in neat vulnerable columns while the guerrillas set up ambush after ambush at points most convenient to their purpose. Some of the enlisted men with frontier experience resented their ongoing status as moving targets and begged to be allowed the option of "bushwhacking" themselves. Dismounted patrols sneaking through the woods in Indian fashion, they argued, would be the only effective way to combat the guerrillas. As autumn progressed the Hundred received their chance to demonstrate their prowess as counterinsurgent fighters.

Doane ached for the opportunity of advancing to an officer's rank. He, like many other noncoms in the regiment, toyed with the idea of applying for a commission with a rumored black cavalry regiment said to be forming in Massachusetts in the winter of 1863–64. White noncommissioned officers could instantly be awarded a lieutenant's bars if they would agree to transfer to a black regiment; but the rumors about the Third Massachusetts Cavalry turned out to be false. Richard Ellet's experiences merely exacerbated Doane's anxiety. After a few weeks in the Chesapeake General Hospital, Richard succeeded in exploiting his family connection to get both a discharge from the Hundred and a promotion. Richard's uncle, Brig. Gen. Alfred W. Ellet, had received special permission from Secretary of War Stanton himself to recruit convalescent Union soldiers for service in the Mississippi Marine Brigade. Richard Ellet's status as a wounded veteran made him an ideal candidate for the procedure, which allowed General Ellet to arrange his official discharge from the Hundred and subsequent commission with the marines. It would take time for Ellet to heal enough to join his new command; while lying in the hospital at Fortress Monroe, Richard began making solicitations to his relatives on Doane's behalf. Meanwhile, for Doane, there were patrols to perform, picket duties to endure, and a long wait for an opportunity to advance.

On September 27, 1863, Doane left on a scouting expedition under the command of Capt. William R. Rumery. With a small mounted patrol in advance as a decoy, Doane and others of the Hundred followed along on foot through the woods. Their tactics finally paid off. Sergeant Doane and privates Frederick J. Quant and Henry H. Fillebrown managed to capture one of Mosby's officers and three other partisans, all of whom reportedly claimed that they would have fought to the death had they known their captors were from the hated Second Massachusetts.[28] Before Doane had a chance to bask in his prowess as a guerrilla hunter, he was ordered to mount up and accompany another patrol to Leesburg and Snickersville, right through the heart of the country that by this time had earned the sobriquet "Mosby's Confederacy."

No one thought to bring out any extra rations to Doane before he was sent out again, and his horse also suffered from a lack of proper feed. Assigned a place in the advance of the patrol column with 2nd Lt. John W. Sim, Doane and his little pinto had a hard time keeping up the first day out. The horse had thrown a shoe and, on the second day of the march, gave out entirely from exhaustion. By this time most of the command had gone ahead, and as night fell Doane had difficulty even keeping up with the very rear of the column, a detachment of German-speaking troopers from the Thirteenth New York Cavalry. During the night he left the horse and tried to find Sim, stumbling around camp after camp in the dark with no success. Worse yet, by the time Doane got back to where he had left his horse, he found that the animal had strayed. It took several more hours to find it. When daylight came and the column moved out, Doane rode along with the New Yorkers, half-famished and exhausted from a lack of sleep. At ten o'clock they stopped in a cornfield. Doane, noting smoke rising from a nearby farmhouse chimney, announced to the German troopers his intentions of going to get something to eat. Without bothering to get permission from their officers, a sergeant named Manderson, a corporal, and several enlisted men from the Thirteenth accompanied Doane to the farmhouse, but the enlisted men returned to the column long before the noncoms. They reported that when they had left the house Doane "had in front of him a very large loaf of bread and a crock of butter which they had no idea he would leave until it was all consumed."[29] The officer in charge of the company ordered the missing men's horses led along; so by the time Doane, Manderson, and the corporal returned to the cornfield they found themselves forced to follow on foot.

Hurrying along the road, the trio overtook a mounted civilian and commandeered his horse. Doane and Manderson told the corporal to mount up, overtake the column, and bring back their horses as quickly as he could. The two sergeants walked along at a more leisurely pace after the corporal disappeared around a bend in the road ahead, enjoying the October morning with full stomachs to console their aching feet. They had gone a mile or so along the deserted road when, about twenty yards ahead, they saw a man in a Union overcoat partially concealed in the edge of the woods. Doane pulled out his pistol in a flash, but Manderson convinced him to put it away because he thought it was the returning corporal. "Have you got our horses?" called Doane, but in answer the man turned around and pointed a pistol at Doane's head. From behind came the ominous click of a revolver hammer, and when Manderson turned he saw that another Rebel had stepped out from the woods to the roadbed in back of them. A tense moment followed as the sergeants raised their hands and the guerrillas came forward to relieve them of their gun belts. The Rebel in the Union overcoat gruffly demanded to know the Yankees' regiments as he stripped them of their weapons. Doane, quickly thinking back to the partisans he captured earlier in the week and the hatred they expressed toward the Second Massachusetts, answered in a false German accent, "Thirteenth New York!" Satisfied that their captives were nothing more than a pair of "dumb Dutchmen," the partisans contented themselves by kicking Doane and Manderson and allowing them to proceed down the road without further abuse. The two sergeants hurried along at a breathless run until they overtook the column and regained their horses, probably thanking their good fortune that they were not on their way to a Richmond prison.[30]

Doane found his troubles from this brush with the enemy just beginning. When the column returned to the regiment's winter camp at Vienna, Virginia, Captain Washburn lost no time filing charges against Doane for "conduct prejudicial to good order and military discipline." Washburn had Lieutenant Sim and Sergeant Manderson both testify in support of the three specifications on October 16, and Doane had no choice but to plead guilty to all of them. Stripped of his chevrons and reduced to the rank of private by order of the regimental commander on October 22, Doane had within the span of one week gone from enjoying the glory of capturing an enemy officer to enduring the disgrace of being captured himself.

Fortunately for Doane, Richard Ellet had been released from the hospital at Fortress Monroe and spent the month of October at the Ellet family home near Bunker Hill, Illinois. While there, he convinced his uncle Alfred to use his influence with Secretary of War Stanton to get Doane transferred to the Mississippi Marine Brigade. On November 3 Richard reported to his brother, Lt. Col. John Ellet, on board the ram *Autocrat* at Cairo, Illinois, and assumed his duties with Company B of the cavalry battalion a week later. During their time together the brothers agreed on the text of a letter sent to their uncle requesting Doane's transfer, making several suggestions to speed up the process by recommending that Brig. Gen. Alfred Ellet offer as a justification for the request the recent death of another officer in the battalion.[31]

In the winter camp at Vienna, Doane managed as best he could. Little occurred that December to break the monotony of camp life, since the winter had deprived the trees of foliage and the partisans of their cover. Occasionally patrols would go out hunting guerrillas, and a few were killed or brought in, but for the most part the only excitement for the Hundred came in the form of camp gossip. Rumors about the formation of another new black regiment held no interest for Doane; his new status as an enlisted man barred even that remote possibility for advancement. The only hope he had for reinstatement as a sergeant with the Hundred lay with whatever friendship he maintained with Capt. James S. Reed, who now acted as a major in command of the Second Massachusetts first battalion. Unfortunately for Doane, even that slim chance would soon disappear.

Captain Reed had not been missed by some in the Hundred. His new duties kept him removed from daily contact with the unit he had recruited. Taking advantage of his temporary higher rank privileges, Reed brought his wife down from the Massachusetts to join him in early February. Doane had no opportunity to see either one of them, because military etiquette kept him far from battalion headquarters. Even if Mrs. Reed felt inclined to plead for their old family friend it was too late to do Doane any good: her husband lost his life in an ambush on February 22, 1864. Mosby's partisans shadowed a patrol led by Reed for several days along a Virginia turnpike and waited until the Yankees had reached an ideal spot about three miles from Drainsville. The short fight cost the Union cavalrymen seven soldiers in addition to Reed, with another seventy-five captured.[32]

When Hattie Reed returned to Boston with her husband's remains, she also carried away Doane's last hope for a promotion with his present unit. The events set in motion by Richard Ellet finally bore fruit, however, and Doane's future in another regiment would surpass anything he could have expected in the Second Massachusetts. On March 22, 1864, Special Orders 71, Department of Washington, arrived in the hands of Col. Charles R. Lowell, the commanding officer of the Second Massachusetts Cavalry. The order commanded Pvt. Gustavus C. Doane immediately to sever his connection with the California Hundred and report as a first lieutenant to the Mississippi Marine Brigade at their station south of Vicksburg.[33]

Although he could have left the regiment at once, Doane could not help reveling in his good fortune a bit before shipping out to his new command. He made a quick trip to Washington, D.C., where he promptly presented himself at a military tailor shop. Once outfitted in his fine blue frock coat with the important lieutenant's straps securely in place, Doane rode back out to Vienna, ostensibly to bid his comrades farewell. However, George Towle, Doane's old college mate, had deduced the real reason for the visit. Doane had come back to the Hundred "so that he might have an opportunity to rub up against and rasp Captain Washburn as an equal," said Towle. "With us, he was the same old Doane, although the contrast in his personal appearance was somewhat startling."[34] After savoring the final moments of his triumph, Doane departed for a fresh opportunity to find the glory that had so tantalizingly eluded him thus far in the war. A few troopers in the Hundred genuinely hated to see him go. "Doane is a good soldier and a clever gentleman," wrote one admirer, "and this promotion could scarcely fall on more worthy shoulders."[35]

Doane's service record with the Mississippi Marine Brigade proved to be an interesting repetition of his experiences with the California Hundred. The marines also billed themselves as an "elite" unit, and many of the organization's members acted as if they believed their status entitled them to special treatment. The brigade originated as an afterthought to a special naval force created by Charles Ellet, Jr., a civil engineer with absolutely no military experience who contacted Secretary of War Stanton in 1862 with a plan to build and command a fleet of swift, lightweight vessels equipped with iron-tipped ramming prows. Ellet argued that these rams would help clear the Mississippi River of Confederate gunboats with greater efficiency than heavily armored vessels, and Stanton eventually agreed with him. He offered Ellet a commission as colonel, authorized the purchase of the boats, and essentially established a naval force on the Mississippi River that answered directly to his office in March 1862.[36]

Fortunately for Doane, nepotism and favoritism played a key role in the recruitment of officers for the organization that Charles Ellet, Jr., had established. He began recruiting for the Ram Fleet by securing the transfer of his brother Alfred from the Fifty-ninth Illinois Infantry. Alfred brought along his son Edward and his nephew John when he reported for duty; and Colonel Ellet added his own son,

Charles Rivers Ellet, to the ranks of the new flotilla. The first major battle of the Ram Fleet occurred on June 6, 1862, when the Ellets successfully attacked Confederate gunboats on the Mississippi guarding Memphis, Tennessee. Unfortunately Colonel Ellet lost his life in his first battle. This caused a shakeup in the organization of the Ram Fleet and a stair-step series of promotions for the surviving members of the Ellet family. Alfred became a brigadier general, in command of both the fleet and a brigade of marines, an entirely new unit that he had been authorized to recruit. Charles Rivers Ellet, a mere nineteen years old, replaced his deceased father as colonel in immediate command of the Ram Fleet; and John Ellet, whose brother Richard had joined the California Hundred with Doane, became lieutenant colonel.[37]

The newly formed Mississippi Marine Brigade consisted of a ship-based strike force of infantry, cavalry, and artillery specifically for the purpose of combating guerrillas along the river and interfering with Rebel commerce. General Ellet received permission to arrange for the discharge of any convalescing soldiers to facilitate their enlistment in the brigade; but even with the promises of "no trenches to dig" and "always a chance to sleep under cover," soldiers who had been maimed in combat did not find the prospect of signing up for more fighting attractive. The traditional naval custom of distributing prize money to volunteers for capturing enemy ships, however, eventually helped convince enough adventurers to start the unit, although they never enlisted in sufficient numbers to reach the brigade's full quota.[38] The quality of these recruits, whose motivation was based partially on personal gain, began to tell almost immediately.

By the spring of 1864 the soldiers of the Mississippi Marine Brigade had literally demonstrated their willingness to steal a red-hot stove,[39] and their reputation as wanton thieves made the outfit notorious to commanders north and south. By the time Doane arrived at his new command in Vicksburg on April 21, 1864, the Mississippi Marine Brigade had been raiding up and down the river for months, burning homes of Rebel sympathizers and seizing cotton by the ton.[40] Union officers from many other regiments indulged in profiteering from the Mississippi cotton traffic during the war, but the Marine Brigade elevated the liberation of lesser Rebel property to a high art, carrying off so much from private homes and smoke-houses that they actually operated their own trading post in Louisiana for a few weeks in March 1864.[41]

While the marines traded their booty to friend and foe alike at their makeshift Louisiana store, Doane got his transfer from Virginia and spent a few weeks at Benton Barracks outside of St. Louis. On April 21 he traveled downriver to join the fleet on board the ram *Fairchild* with 1st Lt. Edward C. Ellet, the general's son.[42] Assigned to Company B of the cavalry battalion, Doane had no time to acquaint himself with his new command before being sent off on a raiding mission downriver. The rams *Fairchild* and the *Raine,* both carrying the cavalry companies, landed at Rodney, Mississippi, where they confiscated grain for their horses and exchanged shots with some Rebel pickets. Both ships then returned to Vicksburg to help transport troops under the command of Brig. Gen. John McArthur for an expedition up the Yazoo River in search of a Confederate brigade operating in the area.

The regiments that General McArthur led to Yazoo City moved along a land route while the Marine Brigade ascended the Yazoo River in four rams. Doane's company disembarked at Satartia, Mississippi, and formed part of a shore reconnaissance by scouting the countryside around Yazoo City, eventually quartering themselves in the nearly deserted town once the rams arrived. On the morning of May 7, 1864, Doane led a small patrol along a narrow road east of Yazoo City and spotted a woman riding a mule a hundred yards ahead. The lieutenant called for her to halt several times; but when she failed to do so, Doane galloped forward, grabbed her bridle, and prevented her from proceeding. The woman vehemently denied any knowledge of Rebel movements in the area; but as Doane and his men accompanied her down the road toward her home, a detachment of Confederate soldiers opened fire on the Yankees from the rear. Doane first had his men dismount and return fire, but he panicked when he considered the possibility that more of the enemy might be blocking the road ahead. The situation, uncomfortably reminiscent of Capt. James Reed's fatal encounter a few short months ago along another country road in Virginia, convinced Doane that he faced the possibility of repeating the disaster. He ordered his men to remount and then led them galloping across a cotton field in a wide arc around the Rebels to regain the road back to Yazoo City. In that headlong rush to safety, Doane lost only one man and one horse wounded but also effectively started his career as a combat officer by running away from the enemy.[43]

The very next day cavalry battalion commander Maj. James R. Crandall repeated the results of Doane's ignominious command debut. Crandall led the four companies out from Yazoo City to Benton, a small town ten miles east, to deliver dispatches to General McArthur; but when the marines arrived at the town they discovered McArthur's force had moved still farther to the east in search of the enemy. Doane and his comrades pushed on after McArthur, observing ample evidence that a running battle had occurred along the road earlier in the day. Darkness fell as the troopers jogged wearily along, and around ten o'clock they saw the welcome glow of campfires ahead through the trees. Crandall, riding at the head of the marine battalion, answered a picket's challenge with his unit's name and, even though the unseen sentinels fired in response, ordered his men forward. The major's fatigue and consequent eagerness to reach the comfort of those campfires almost resulted in disaster, because once the leading marines in the column entered the firelight they discovered that they had stumbled into the main camp of the Rebel force. Before the startled Confederates could react, Crandall ordered his troopers to wheel about and gallop rapidly off into the darkness. That night, as Doane careened in his saddle while plodding the twenty exhausting miles back to Yazoo City, he consoled himself with the fact that his commanding officer had ordered a flight just as readily as he himself had done the previous day.[44]

Doane's first experiences as an officer must have been very disappointing. He had departed from Virginia with every reason to expect fame and promotion, but he found in Mississippi only a continuation of the conditions he had left. Just as during the first months of the California Hundred at Gloucester Point, the unruly malcontents of Doane's command fought a shadow enemy in nasty little bushwhacking forays. Instead of inspiring a battle-hardened company of veterans in honorable combat, any chance Doane had of gaining military distinction depended on his leadership of slovenly warriors engaged in backwater brawls.

Those slovenly warriors may have shared Doane's frustrations, but their reaction to the disappointment took a much more sinister turn after the marines returned from Major Crandall's scout to occupy Yazoo City. While in garrison a rumor of enemy atrocities circulated that helped fuel the soldiers' resentment of the local citizenry on May 16. An unconfirmed story about the hanging of two soldiers from the Eleventh Illinois Infantry seemed all the more credible to the marines, especially because just a month ago near Vicksburg they had discovered the mutilated bodies of three white officers from a black Union regiment similarly treated by the enemy.[45] The rage generated by the rumored execution of the Illinois privates built throughout the day, and that night several intentionally set fires swept away Yazoo City's courthouse and business district. The behavior of the troops during the conflagration did little to endear them to the town's civilians. Some marines worked desperately to save citizens' belongings from the consuming flames, but others purposely sliced the water hoses to continue the destruction. The people of Yazoo City had ample cause to remember these blue-clad vandals for some time to come.[46] Fortunately for Yazoo's civilians, events farther up the Mississippi would soon call the Yankees away from their ruined town.

Even though river traffic along the Mississippi moved freely from St. Louis to New Orleans during the year following the fall of Vicksburg, sporadic raids by swiftly moving Rebel artillery occasionally disrupted shipping. One point on the river, a hairpin turn opposite Greenville, Mississippi, proved particularly troublesome in the final week of May 1864. The soldiers of a Confederate battery attached to the command of Col. Colton Greene discovered that they could fire on boats coming down the river from a point on the north side of a narrow neck of land, limber up, dash a short distance to the south side, and then deploy to fire more shells at the same boat as it passed by that position. Greene's artillerymen began their campaign on May 24, and by June 3 the Southerners had effectively blockaded the Mississippi. On June 4 Maj. Gen. Andrew J. Smith led an expedition that would include Ellet's Marine Brigade to drive the enemy away from the river.

Twenty-four transports, conveying over ten thousand soldiers, made up the avenging Union force, the largest combat army that Doane had ever seen. The next afternoon, after the *Fairchild* pulled to at Sunnyside Landing, Arkansas, Lt. Col. George E. Currie led the marines along a muddy road that paralleled the southern bank of Lake Chicot for a few miles until they encountered some enemy horsemen. After a brief firefight the marines returned to the landing to report the skirmish to General Smith. During their absence the general had managed to land an additional three thousand men from the other transports—more than enough, in the general's opinion, to shoo away Colonel Greene's small force of Rebel guerrillas. While the soldiers of Union army prepared to make camp that evening the darkening sky began to pelt them with a steady rain.[47]

The next morning the marines mounted up in a downpour and splashed down the road beyond the site of yesterday's encounter. They found that the enemy had reenforced his line along the west bank of a wide, sluggish watercourse. Ditch Bayou flowed north into Lake Chicot, and only one bridge spanned the muddy channel close by its junction with the lake. The retreating Confederates had tried to burn the bridge in spite of the drenching rain and succeeded in partially destroying it, making Ditch Bayou a virtual moat that prevented the Yankees from closing on them.

During the ensuing battle the Union forces lined up along a low embankment on the eastern side of Ditch Bayou and exchanged volleys with the Confederates, but the Yankees found themselves unable to advance or stop the murderous fire of their enemies. The marines eventually took advantage of covering fire to withdraw from the embankment, regain their mounts, and ride farther south along the bayou to find some way across. Because the smaller Rebel force could not match the southern extension of the Union line, Doane and his company plunged their horses into the mucky bottom of the bayou and floundered across in relative safety. Colonel Greene knew that his command would be unable to prevent their eventual envelopment should the Union force find a way across the bayou to the south, so he ordered a hasty retreat after a few more defiant volleys. By the time the marines had gained the enemy's former position in the tree-line the Rebels had vanished. The fight had cost the Union forces 180 casualties, and the determination of the Confederates to avoid annihilation or capture made the battle of Ditch Bayou little more than a mid-distance shooting match with no clear victor. The weary Union troops slogged their way to a small town, where once again they acted on their frustration by robbing civilians and burning their houses. Like the civilians of Yazoo City the previous month, residents of Lake Village and Columbia, Arkansas, would long remember the visit paid them by the vengeful Yankees.

In this ugly arena of war there could be no glory for Doane, just more raids into the hinterland for plunder. By now the young lieutenant had begun to reconcile himself to the alternative that many in the brigade had already accepted: the pursuit of fortune over fame. The richness of the country in which they operated, and the opportunity to gain from the misfortunes of war, proved to be a temptation that few in General Ellet's command could resist. Doane's company actively participated in the thievery, but he made sure all his reports emphasized the military, rather than the illicit, results they achieved. His literary talents, honed by all the college essays he had written at Santa Clara, now served him well; and his assumed comportment as an educated gentleman impressed his commander. "He makes a very good officer," wrote General Ellet to his wife. "I like him very much. He has right good sense and can send in a better official paper than any officer of his battalion."[48]

Neither Doane's talent with a pen nor his ability to adapt his personality to mirror his colleagues would lead to his lasting fame while serving with the marines. Instead of duplicating the literary achievements of his boyhood hero, Maj. Gen. John Charles Frémont, Doane abandoned the thought of following in the footsteps of the great Pathfinder in favor of a more immediate, and brutal, possibility for gain. He and fellow lieutenant Richard Ellet relaxed their control of the men when an opportunity for plunder came their way, and even General Ellet found their activities distasteful. "Unfortunately they have the greatest set of villains in their company that were ever before banded together," he wrote. "Regular finished highwaymen, who do not hesitate to put a pistol to the head of any man they find and demand 'his money or his life,' or seize a woman and throw her down and search her person for jewelry, or violate her if so inclined. They are certainly the most reckless fiends that I ever heard of."[49]

When the marines returned to their base at Vicksburg after the Arkansas raid they spent the next three weeks in relative idleness. Doane and Edward and Richard Ellet used their time to flirt with the local women, freely spending the money that they had gained from their operations. On July 2, 1864, the marines moved out on their final campaign: another raid into Mississippi from the river but with no clear objective or purpose. General Ellet failed to inform his subordinates of the expedition's mission, telling them only that they (accompanied by a black Union regiment and a caravan of empty wagons) were to march inland from Rodney, Mississippi, on the road to Coleman's Crossroads. On this raid Doane came closest to losing his life by again leading his company straight into an ambush that killed one of his men in the first volley. A series of small pitched battles developed over the next two days, but General Ellet's indecisiveness prevented the marines from participating effectively beyond a few brief rearguard actions. The entire botched affair, including the inept direction of the Union forces by Ellet, so disgusted Col. George Currie that he began to contemplate resigning his commission.[50]

As it turned out, officers other than Currie grew disgusted with General Ellet's military incompetence and the marines' ongoing property confiscations. Maj. Gen. Edward R. S. Canby, commanding the Military Division of West Mississippi, became weary of the endless complaints involving the Mississippi Marine Brigade and decided to act. On July 31 the marines were ordered into camp at

Omega Landing, Mississippi, and told to prepare for a general inspection by Maj. Gen. Napoleon J. T. Dana. The inspection occurred on August 7, and Dana's report pointed out that the Marine Brigade "is now so insufficient in number when all together that it is not sufficient of itself to compose any important expedition." The inspector also reported that the serviceable horses of the marines were of suspiciously good stock and that a recent discrepancy between the costs paid and received on a shipment of cotton entrusted to the care of Ellet's men could not be explained. The formality of the inspection accomplished its purpose, and Canby informed General Ellet on August 10 that the marines would be disbanded.[51]

At first it seemed that the men might be allowed to go home on a technicality. General Canby initially decreed the marine rank and file would have to be sent back to their former regiments, but he had misunderstood their terms of enlistment. Members of the Marine Brigade had not "transferred" to the outfit: they had rather been completely discharged from their former regiments and enlisted anew in the marines. After becoming aware of their status, Canby realized that the marines would either have to be sent home immediately or be retained as a distinct unit. When the general settled on the latter option, the trouble really started. On August 26, 1864, General Ellet announced to the marines that Canby had ordered that they become a land-based infantry regiment, reorganized under the command of Lt. Col. John Ellet and posted in garrison at Vicksburg. The cavalry battalion was dissolved; Doane and the other officers were assigned to one or another of the ten newly created infantry companies.

As Doane tried to take his place as a first lieutenant with Company H, the anger of the enlisted men exploded. Just as the California Hundred's insubordination had led to their arrest in Virginia, the marines' resistance would result in their own brush with court-martial in Mississippi. They snarled that they had not joined for land service and refused to serve in any capacity that required them to leave their comfortable shipboard billets. The Ellet family in particular became the target of their wrath, because the men felt they had been betrayed by the clan that commanded them. Doane, well known to be socially connected with the hated family, found what little authority he had over his company completely compromised.

The situation grew quite ugly on the afternoon of August 27. Most of the men on board the flag ship *Autocrat* refused to leave when ordered, and Lt. Col. John Ellet ran ashore to ask for help in putting down the mutiny. Col. Frederick A. Starring of the Seventy-second Illinois Infantry called up two regiments of troops and positioned them along the levy before he boarded the *Autocrat* to confer with the Ellets. Maj. David Tallerday temporarily replaced Col. John Ellet as commanding officer. This change seemed to calm down most of the resisting soldiers, who shuffled down the various gangplanks in grumbling obedience. One squad of twenty-three men said they would not go unless they went under guard, and a few others who resisted were gathered with them. The die-hard mutineers were dutifully arrested and hauled off to prison while the rest of the jeering, insolent masses marched off to their camp. Along the way Doane had to endure the insults of his own men, as they loudly accused him of selling them out to recruiting officers for kickbacks and stealing cotton.[52] After the whole incident was over, Colonel Starring acidly summarized the effectiveness of the newest regiment in the Department of Western Mississippi, describing them as "demoralized, insubordinate, undisciplined, and grossly ignorant."[53]

The men of the Mississippi Marine Regiment reconciled themselves to their new role as garrison troops only as far as the nearest lawyer's office. Outraged at their handling by the army and the Ellet family, the troopers of Doane's company joined with others to engage the services of James H. Purdy, attorney at law. For the lucrative fee of a $500 retainer and the promise of $15 per applicant, Purdy agreed to take the men's case as far as necessary to secure their honorable discharge.[54] They reluctantly set up a camp outside of Vicksburg to await the results of Purdy's efforts, and Doane spent the time in uncomfortable isolation. Gen. Alfred Ellet had left for Philadelphia to await further orders, which, to no one's surprise, never came. The rest of the Ellet family made themselves scarce around camp, and any chances Doane may have had to consort with

John or Richard had to be when he could go into the city itself. During these visits the friends would naturally discuss their postwar plans, made all the more critical for Doane because his military experiences had done nothing to advance his peacetime prospects. Quite naturally, the men turned their attention to their surroundings and the possibilities for profit that lay at their doorstep.

CHAPTER 3

"You have not told us what kind of business you are in"

Reconstruction Mississippi

By January 1865 Doane's military career had in many ways strengthened his long-standing resistance to authority and his desire for special consideration and recognition as an educated gentleman. Service in two units whose disappointed sense of entitlement had erupted into mutiny should have taught Doane the value of military discipline and obedience, but instead he grew to share in the resentment of his comrades. By currying favor with Captain Reed of the California Hundred and the Ellet family of the Marine Brigade, Doane had initially received preferential treatment; but after his benefactors were no longer in a position to help him, his discontent grew with a simmering intensity. Toward the end of his stint with the Marine Brigade, avarice began to take the place of the distinction that Doane craved. After he returned to civilian life, he continued his pursuit of financial gain along with personal recognition from his fellows. When riches and fame were not forthcoming, his indignation would eventually build into an impetuous anger.

Lawyer James H. Purdy succeeded in getting the entire Marine

Brigade an honorable discharge, which was completed by the end of January 1865.[1] Instead of returning to California, Doane followed John and Richard Ellet to their uncle's family home in Bunker Hill, Illinois. Here he spent the remaining months of the war, further ingratiating himself with the Ellets and taking a keen interest in Gen. Alfred Ellet's daughter, Elvira. During this time Doane got letters from California bearing news of his family's dismay at not hearing from him. He had never been a prolific letter writer since joining the army in 1863, and his sister, Annie, felt the silence more keenly than his parents or brothers. Her missives coupled her reports on the family's continuing financial decline with plaintive questions on how Cheyney could be so thoughtless.[2]

Cheyney had his mind on a destination other than California that summer. John, Richard, and Edward Ellet convinced Doane to return with them to their wartime haunts in Mississippi to invest with Alfred Ellet's friends in a mercantile operation and a cotton plantation in Yazoo County. Their decision was hardly unique; so many men from Bunker Hill, Illinois, joined the exodus to Mississippi that the local press referred to them as the "Yazoo Brigade."[3] Even those who stayed at home participated in the enterprise by investing capital that their more adventurous relatives would directly oversee in the South. In early May 1865 Doane and the Ellets traveled down the Mississippi, perhaps with carpet bags in hand, to establish their fortunes in Yazoo City.

Arriving at the bustling town ninety miles northeast of Vicksburg, the "Yazoo Brigade" returned to help build a town they had burned to the ground less than a year before. Doane and his friends stepped off the steamboat into a community literally rising from the ashes, accompanied by the music of hammer and saw ringing out across the dusty main street. A sudden infusion of Northern capital spent by ambitious Northern agents gave Yazoo City the look and feel of a frontier boom town of the far West. The atmosphere should have seemed familiar to Doane, whose childhood memories of the California gold rush could find many parallels in the heady optimism of the recent arrivals and the discouragement of the older settlers.[4]

The postwar economic opportunities in Mississippi held as much promise for financial ruin as for success. While idled plantations could be leased or purchased at a bargain, the labor to operate them grew scarce and expensive. Former slaves unaccustomed to their new status as freedmen found their services in high demand and were reluctant to commit to one employer for very long. Many freedmen believed a rumor that the federal government intended to issue forty acres and a mule to each family at the end of 1865 as a sort of Christmas present. They would become reluctant to sign contracts guaranteeing their labor for the coming year, and planters who depended on them took various measures to retain their labor. When Edward Ellet and his partner Philip Howell leased a local plantation, they offered their hands quarterly cash payments and extra rations to keep them on the job; but other landholders considered harsher measures. They patrolled the roadways to intimidate freedmen from traveling during the summer. When the first provisional state legislature met in November, it decreed anyone without a labor contract could be arrested for vagrancy.[5]

Some Northerners who arrived at Yazoo City alienated the white natives by working hard to gain the freedmen's loyalty. Albert T. Morgan (a former officer in the Sixth Wisconsin Infantry) and his brother Charles leased "Tokeba," the plantation of J. J. B. White, and quickly became the most notorious newcomers in Yazoo County, due to their close relationship with the black people hired to work Tokeba. Aside from earning the contempt of the racially sensitive white natives by working in the fields themselves, the Morgans added to local tensions by establishing a school for black children. For merchants in town the economics of race relations took a different form. Freedmen who had contracts but were short on cash needed extensive credit with Yazoo City merchants, and the recent arrivals from Bunker Hill varied in their response. Thomas Van Dorn refused to trade with any freedmen in his store, but Doane and Richard Ellet's silent partner, "Major" P. C. Huggins, insisted that their firm buy and sell with both races. With thirteen new stores established in the early summer of 1865, competition for business, white or black, remained fierce.[6]

By deciding to do business with all citizens, the firm of Doane, Ellet & Company linked its prosperity to the success of the new order of racial and economic boundaries arising in Mississippi. Freedmen who drew wages would have money to spend; and if local planters could hold their employees to labor contracts those wages would provide a steady income for Doane's new store. The whole situation bewildered his family, who could not understand his refusal to return to California in favor of a mysterious business venture in the faraway Delta country. "But Cheyney you have not told us what kind of business you are in," Annie wrote him that May. "Explain what the 'Contraband' trade is."[7] Business pressure allowed scant time for an explanation. By August the number of stores in Yazoo City had more than doubled, and Doane, Ellet, & Company found itself hard-pressed to keep its shelves stocked.[8] If the prosperity of that heady summer could only continue, the future looked bright indeed.

Along with the economic boom the resentment of the town's white natives grew. To see the business district flourish under the direction of those who had destroyed it in the first place was for many whites almost as irritating as being forced to coexist with their newly freed slaves. On October 5, 1865, elections were held for all civil offices in Yazoo County under the auspices of a provisional state government authorized by President Andrew Johnson. Many former Confederates gained offices, including the postmaster, mayor, probate judge, and sheriff; but the local agent of the Bureau of Refugees, Freedmen, and Abandoned Lands retained authority over matters relating to racial relations and continued to insist on equal treatment for blacks.[9]

Edward Ellet and the Morgan brothers worked their leased plantations without interacting with anyone other than their own fellow Northerners. Had the weather cooperated, their industry in planting and generosity toward their employees might have resulted in prosperity. Unfortunately the winter of 1865–66 proved unusually wet, and the cotton crop fell far short of the carpetbaggers' expectations. Many of the new mercantile establishments in Yazoo City did poorly as a result of the cotton famine, including

Doane's fledgling enterprise. Richard Ellet took advantage of the slow trade to return to Bunker Hill for a visit in November. Upon his return, Doane made the trip back to Illinois himself. Based on hints in Edward's letters home it appears that Doane may have courted his partner's sister, Elvira, during his stay at Bunker Hill; but if so, she refused his advances: he returned alone to Yazoo City in February 1866. Business continued to be poor during the spring of 1866. The rain was still heavy, and many riverside plantations such as Edward Ellet's and Albert Morgan's flooded out almost completely.

If Doane ever considered going home during this time the mail from California quickly changed his mind. Nancy Doane wrote her son with the news that Solomon had squandered the family savings on a failing San Francisco mercantile operation and had been forced to seek work as a common laborer. "You remember, Cheyney, that he used to say he would rather die than to be reduced in circumstances as to have to work by the day," said Nancy, "but he has come to it and you may judge of his feelings."[10] Alarming descriptions of the postwar depression in California filled the letters from home and helped convince the young carpetbagger that his future remained in Mississippi.

Romance may also have helped in his decision to stay in the South. Ever since his unsuccessful flirtation with Elvira Ellet during his visit to Illinois, Doane had sought alternative prospects for his affections among the eligible female residents of Yazoo County. Amelia Link, the pretty nineteen-year-old daughter of planter Noah D. Link, became Doane's next objective. A Canadian by birth, Noah Link settled in Yazoo County in the 1830s and by 1860 had amassed a fortune in property and slaves. The land remained after the war, even if the human property necessary to work it had been lost, giving the Link family the appearance of Old South aristocracy that appealed mightily to Doane during that wet spring of 1866. While he courted Amelia, his mercantile firm made some changes to improve business. When Thomas Van Dorn (the Bunker Hill native who refused to trade with the freedmen) abandoned his storefront on Main Street to return to Illinois, the Doane firm made plans to lease the place. Even though the rent exceeded what they could afford, they set up shop in the finest "stand" in town on June 10, 1866. Business continued to be poor, but Doane gave the appearance of a man of means and used the illusion to press his suit for Amelia's hand. On July 25, 1866, the couple married. In one important way the union turned out to be a perfect match: Amelia, just like Doane, had only the appearance of wealth.

As the summer of 1866 slipped away into autumn, the fortunes of Doane, Ellet & Company continued their downward spiral. Short crops and low cotton prices combined with the higher rent to put an unbearable strain on the company's finances. Even the steady draws that Edward Ellet's plantation made on the store (covered by Alfred Ellet's generous drafts) could not stop the relentless slide into bankruptcy.[11] In desperation Doane and his partners sold too much on credit and received too little in cash payment. In addition to the impending collapse of his business, Doane's peace of mind was disrupted by more bad news from California. His sister Annie wrote that one day in the latter part of June their father, while cutting some firewood on their new farm, accidentally chopped off his big toe with a rusty ax blade. His face began to stiffen on the very day of Doane's wedding in far-off Mississippi; after ten more days of excruciating torture, Solomon died a painful death from lockjaw. "Cheyney, can you not come home and see us?" Annie begged. "Oh how I wish you could even if it were only for a month."[12]

Even if Doane realized that as the eldest son of his widowed mother it fell to him to take up his father's responsibilities, his financial situation would not allow him to leave Mississippi. On November 15 he was forced from the partnership by P. C. Huggins, who promptly reduced expenses by abandoning the Van Dorn storefront. Doane had no choice but to move with Amelia to her father's plantation and return to the life of a farmer — the same fate that he had left California to avoid. While Doane spent the winter of 1866–67 trying to wrest a living from Noah Link's acres, political events occurred that offered a means to escape from a life of drudgery.

On March 23, 1867, the United States Congress passed the Radical Reconstruction act over the veto of President Andrew Johnson. The act established military control over the former Confederate states and demanded the registration of voters to elect delegates for state constitutional conventions. Although all local civil authorities in Mississippi temporarily retained their respective positions, their authority was effectively gutted by a provision in the law that decreed that military commanders could remove any such officer at will.[13] One set of new civil officers, the registrars of voters, needed to be filled by loyal Union men to make sure the newly enfranchised freedmen were recorded as legitimate voters for the constitutional convention delegates.

In Yazoo City the new assistant subsuperintendent of the Freedmen's Bureau, 1st Lt. Daniel M. White, took on new importance as the eyes and ears for the military government of Mississippi. As the preparations for selecting the three registrars for Yazoo County got underway, White reported that "the civil authorities in this city have shown no disposition to protect the freedmen."[14] White accused Yazoo City mayor David Jones of charging freedmen a license fee for the privilege of living in the city limits and arbitrarily confiscating firearms from black citizens. If troops could be once again posted to Yazoo City, argued White, it would ensure the fair treatment of freedmen and help ensure a smooth operation for the voter registration effort.[15]

While the growing tensions between white and black natives fermented, Doane sensed an opportunity that could once again free him from the life of a farmer. The tenure of all current Yazoo County authorities would be brief once the new state government formed, and any ambitious Union man stood a good chance of making a career out of the resulting political vacuum. The most logical first step would be to register voters, since the meticulous process of visiting each and every adult male freedman within a given district would allow the sort of personal contact necessary for any future political race. Accordingly, Doane applied for one of the open registrar's positions, but local justice of the peace Samuel Gallinger secured it first. Gallinger could not swear the "ironclad oath," however, a proviso that any officeholder had to swear he had never borne arms against the United States. On May 18 the judge was removed, and Doane was appointed in his place.[16]

For a brief moment it looked as if Doane could embark on a political career, but he was soon disappointed. Joshua W. Bourne, a former officer of the Seventh Missouri Infantry and another recent transplant from the north to Yazoo County, protested Doane's appointment by hinting that certain wartime irregularities made him an unsuitable candidate for registrar. Bourne's motivation is not at all clear (he himself already had an appointment, and he never recorded the nature of his allegations against Doane), but he prevailed in his request. The appointing board reversed its decision, revoked Doane's commission, and replaced him with Francis P. Hilliard, a loyal Union man who also had applied for the job.

Doane's loss of the position that he felt entitled to resulted in an outrage that clouded his better judgment. On May 26, 1867, he called on Albert Morgan, whose Tokeba plantation bordered the Links', and asked him to bear the following note to Joshua Bourne:

> Capt. Bourne — Sir: I have heard from undoubted authority that you have traduced my character in public and before the Board of Registration of this State. Whoever has the effrontery to prefer *lying* charges should have the courage to substantiate them. My Friend, Col. Morgan, is authorized to confer with you in regard to an early meeting. Respectfully, G. C. Doane.[17]

Not to be outdone, Bourne showed that he too could play the part of the Southern aristocrat when it came to the code duello and understood quite well the rules of this deadly game of dare. After asking his "friend," J. M. Sublett, to act as his second, he took the prerogative of the challenged party to send a reply on June 2:

> Col. Morgan — Dear Sir: In behalf of Capt. Bourne, I have to say that he will be pleased to meet your friend, Mr. Doane, at Beattie's Bluff, Big Black river, on the Madison county side, on Thursday, the 6th inst., at 4½ o'clock P.M. — Weapons, double-barreled shot guns loaded with buck shot, sixteen to the barrel. Distance, five paces. Respectfully, J. M. Sublett[18]

The chilling implications of Bourne's response should have so-
bered Doane, who in spite of all his past disappointments had never
before allowed his temper to get away from him. Now, as a result of
his own impetuousness, he faced the reality of sure death should
the proposed duel be carried out under Bourne's choice of weapons. Anxious days followed the receipt of Bourne's note. When
Doane nervously pointed out that fighting at Beattie's Bluff would
violate the laws of Mississippi, Bourne coolly replied that they could
meet at Young's Point, a sandbar on the Mississippi River opposite
Vicksburg. The morning of June 6 arrived without either man back-
ing down. Doane nervously boarded a skiff at the Vicksburg wharf
with Albert Morgan and Edward Ellet to begin their journey to the
Louisiana shore. A blistering sun beat down on the three men as
they rowed across the river, and they arrived at the sandbar at about
twenty minutes after four o'clock in the afternoon.

Meanwhile, Joshua Bourne had troubles of his own. He had left
his home at Deasonville two days earlier to pick up his second, J. M.
Sublett. But once Bourne arrived at Sublett's home he found that
his second had been called away on business. Doubling back to
Yazoo City, Bourne telegraphed another acquaintance named Johnson in Vicksburg to ask him to act as his second. Unfortunately, he
missed the last boat out from Yazoo that day; so Bourne began
cantering on horseback down the Vicksburg road late on June 5,
riding all night and changing horses twice during the journey. He
finally reached the city at noon the next day, met with Johnson, and
then procured a shotgun for the coming ordeal. Once the pair
finally began to cross the river in their own rowboat, the appointed
time for the duel had already passed.

When Doane consulted his pocket watch and saw that the dreaded
hour had come and gone, he could not believe his luck. He had kept
an appointment with sure death and yet had been given a wonderful
reprieve. With the all important testimony of two witnesses that his
adversary had failed to show, Doane left Young's Point for Vicksburg
shortly before five o'clock. Bourne arrived at the place seven minutes
after the hour, only to find that Doane had gone. Immediately the
Missourian regained his own boat and rowed furiously back over to

the Mississippi shore. Once they arrived in Vicksburg, Johnson, as Bourne's second, delayed going to the Prentiss House Hotel until ten o'clock that night, time enough for Doane and his party to plan their next move. When Albert Morgan received Johnson's request for a new meeting time, he claimed "the old affair was over and a new one must be commenced" and refused to accept Bourne's note of explanation, because Johnson had no "written authority."[19] Doane had the upper hand at this point because Bourne's hasty replacement of J. M. Sublett with Johnson allowed Albert Morgan honorably to refuse communication with Bourne through a second party that had not been previously involved with the challenge exchange.

Bourne was no coward, though. Cited for gallantry during the battle of Raymond, Mississippi, on June 29, 1863, the Missouri officer had served with distinction during the war and faced far more enemy fire than Doane had.[20] Bourne simply would not allow the matter to rest until he followed it through to the end; he sent Johnson back to the Prentiss House the next morning to confront Albert Morgan with the proper credentials. Johnson did so and demanded a new location for the duel, but this time Morgan declared that he considered this a brand-new challenge, which could not be honorably considered until the old affair was settled. Disgusted with this slippery interpretation of the rules of dueling, Johnson loudly denounced Morgan as a "poltroon and a coward" and stomped out of the lobby. Although the narrow brush with death should have taught Doane a valuable lesson in controlling his temper, he rashly claimed victory in the duel and published at his own expense a full column consisting of all the duel correspondence in the Vicksburg newspaper the next day to crow over his bravery. Bourne's reply the following week laid out the facts in more detail; but from the standpoint of anyone familiar with the code, Bourne had lost on a technicality.[21]

The moral victory brought Doane nothing as far as political advancement was concerned. He still remained an outsider, while Bourne and the other registrars worked that summer making sure that every adult freedman in Yazoo County signed the precinct books for the upcoming election. The effort met with considerable resistance from white voters, though. Reports of floggings and other means of coercion being employed to keep blacks from registering made their way back to the Vicksburg headquarters of Maj. Gen. Edward O. C. Ord, commander of the Fourth Military District.[22] Bourne and his fellow registrars reportedly faced threats of physical violence for their pains, a consequence of service that Doane ought to have been glad enough to avoid. A roving band of horse thieves conducted their operations in Yazoo County that summer too, showing a marked preference for the stock of Northern newcomers over Southern natives. The situation got so bad that on July 4 Ord dispatched Company E of the Fifth United States Cavalry to garrison Yazoo City.[23]

More trouble arrived for members of the Yazoo Brigade that spring. Flooding along the Yazoo River submerged the bountiful cotton crops planted by Doane, Edward Ellet, and the Morgan brothers.[24] Doane and Ellet watched their hopes for fortune drowning beneath the muddy water that flooded the fields, but Charles and Albert Morgan fell first in the catastrophe. Their landlord, J. J. B. White, foreclosed on the Morgans for back rent due and directed Sheriff William M. Dyer to attach all property at the Tokeba Plantation for collateral. Edward Ellet, who had several thousand board feet of cypress logs at the Tokeba Landing sawmill, sought an injunction against the sheriff, but Dyer would not honor it. After displacing the Morgan brothers he sold all the movable property at Tokeba at auction. The incident convinced other Northerners that none of the current city or county officials would give them justice.[25]

With the elections for delegates drawing near, and the perceived bias of the local government growing, Doane decided to reenter the political arena in anticipation of changes in Yazoo City's municipal government. A large political rally had been planned for the upcoming constitutional convention, and Doane prepared an oration that he hoped would make his reputation. He worked on his manuscript, summoning up all the lessons he had learned in rhetoric, political economy, and grammar from the University of the Pacific. The result was a massive, thirty-two page treatise that dwarfed the speech he had made at his 1861 graduation, a testimony to his ambition and his frustration at the circumstances that prevented him from achieving his due. He used the classic debating technique of setting up a straw man by presenting an argument of ten Southern assumptions and then refuting them point by point. His tenor was grandiose, his attitude patronizing, and his presentation hardly designed to appeal to a population resentful over what it considered a foreign rule. For example, he argued that the task of the times was "the regeneration of a people, stripped of resources, exhausted in conflict, and weighed down by the terrible incubus of a dead barbarian, whose carcass has not yet been removed from the face of the land."[26] Overall, the speech showed with painful clarity how Doane's ambition interfered with his ability to empathize.

On the morning of September 21, 1867, Doane prepared to make his debut as a leader to be reckoned with. The day dawned sunny and warm; as the streets of Yazoo City began to crowd with freedmen and poor white farmers, mayor David Jones and town marshal Patrick McGinley watched the growing mass with suspicion and fear. Earlier in the day Jones had received a note from 2nd Lt. Daniel Hitchcock, commander of the local army garrison, offering military assistance to quell any potential disturbances in the town.[27] As Doane mounted the speaker's platform and prepared to deliver his dissertation to the masses, some Southerners positioned behind a high board fence began to pelt the crowd with rocks. During the ensuing disturbance, Mayor Jones called for help. Bedlam broke out as the soldiers arrived to clear the streets; Doane sadly watched his audience, and his political debut, melt away in a mass of shouting, swearing confusion.

If the riot had temporarily dashed Doane's ambitions for a political career, within a few months the forces of nature would come to his aid. An epidemic of yellow fever in early October struck down dozens of citizens, and anyone who could afford to abandon Yazoo City for the perceived safety of the countryside did so without hesitation. After Mayor Jones and most of the city council left town, 1st Lt. Daniel M. White, the Freedmen's Bureau agent, sent headquarters an urgent note to report the complete breakdown of civil government in Yazoo City.[28] White's note was quickly followed by a report from another officer dispatched from the adjutant general's office in Vicksburg, which detailed the unfair treatment meted out to the Morgan brothers and the "total unfitness" of David Jones for the office of mayor.[29] The combination of these two reports, along with some gentle prodding from Doane, eventually produced the desired results. On December 6, 1867, Special Orders Number 199 from the headquarters of the Fourth Military District named Gustavus Cheyney Doane as mayor of Yazoo City, Mississippi.

Doane's appointment provided a new method for making money. Marshal McGinley resented his new superior and refused to cooperate with any orders Doane issued except for one: the confiscation of weapons carried by freedmen. The crop failure of the summer had reduced many black people to desperate poverty, and some began purchasing firearms to protect themselves.[30] A freedman caught in town with a pistol in his waistband would have the weapon confiscated and be forced to pay a five dollar minimum fine in the mayor's court. McGinley shared in the profits, so he complied with Doane's orders to collect those fines. The practice became so remunerative that Doane applied for a vacancy as a justice of the peace for Beat Three of Yazoo County just a week after taking office as mayor. As a magistrate, his authority to collect fines would extend beyond the city limits. As long as the practice of confiscating weapons remained restricted to the freedmen, the enforcement attracted little notice; but when Doane decided to expand its application to white citizens, serious trouble began.

Doane was saddled with Marshal McGinley for the town enforcement, but he managed to get the constable of Beat 3 removed in early February and Edward Ellet appointed in his place. "It was a lucrative place if the holder was active and on the job," Ellet recalled years later; "the pay was in fees . . . and we collected what was coming to us with a ruthless hand. I made twenty-five dollars a day for the three months I stayed on the job."[31] It appeared at first that the headquarters of the Fourth Military District would sustain Doane's intention to enforce the concealed weapons ban on whites. On January 4, 1868, General Ord's adjutant general wrote Doane that "the blacks, who are imitative in their habits, will quit the practice of carrying arms, as soon as they see the whites whom they imitate have ceased or are prevented from doing so."[32] Doane reported on his progress two months later and suggested expanding his operations to include vagrancy because, he argued, "so little labor is accomplished by both blacks and whites that it is often difficult to determine where vagrancy ends and industry begins."[33] The mayor pushed too hard shortly afterward when he tried to get Marshal McGinley fired and interfered with the county court charges against Nathaniel Vancleave, both errors that would lead to the end of Doane's political career.

Vancleave, a local planter, made the mistake of bringing a concealed revolver into town one morning in early March and was arrested by the constable for justice of the peace Samuel Gallinger. As he was locked into the county jail, Vancleave found out he faced over five hundred dollars in fines in Gallinger's court but only fifty-five dollars in Doane's court. He agreed to be released to Doane's jurisdiction when the mayor sent a note demanding that the county jailer surrender Vancleave to the custody of the Yazoo municipal court. Before Vancleave paid the fine to the mayor's office, however, someone (most likely Marshal McGinley) convinced him that he could avoid punishment altogether if he challenged Doane's authority in Judge Robert B. Mayes's county probate court. Judge Mayes issued a writ of habeas corpus on March 17, but Doane not only stubbornly refused to set Vancleave free but also sentenced the planter to time on the chain gang until he could produce the fifty-five dollars. Mayes warned Doane that he had overstepped his authority and presented his case directly to Maj. Gen. Alvan C. Gillem, the new commander of the Fourth Military District. Doane had no jurisdiction in this case whatsoever, argued Mayes, and the outrage over sending a white man to work on a chain gang would lead to widespread civil unrest.

Perhaps Doane realized too late how dangerous an enemy Judge Mayes would prove, and the mayor desperately tried to backpedal when he knew his action would not be sustained by headquarters. He ordered Vancleave released on March 27 by telling the jailer the prisoner had "satisfied in full" the judgment of his court. Vancleave, in return, agreed to sign a statement handwritten by Doane that "he was persuaded by certain persons, whom he now believes to have been acting from motives of personal gain, alone, to sue out a writ of habeas corpus involving useless and expensive litigation, and further that he verily believes from his knowledge of the facts, that he has been used in the hands of evil disposed and designing men with a view to stir up strife between the Federal and Civil Courts."[34] As expected, General Gillem's adjutant wrote to Doane the next day, informing him that Judge Mayes's position in the matter would be upheld. Doane may have been disappointed, but at least he felt the matter would now be forgotten and he could return to business as usual.

Judge Mayes was far from finished. The judge pointed out to General Gillem that Doane could be held in contempt of court for releasing Vancleave before the jurisdictional question was settled. Doane nervously circulated a petition among Yazoo City leaders expressing their support for his actions. Mayes eventually withdrew his threat to pursue the contempt charges after Gillem requested it by stating: "I am glad that the necessity of performing that duty is removed by the General Commanding, which by defining the duties of the several officers with sufficient clearness to prevent future conflict will effect all at which I would aim by imposing the penalties."[35] Only a day after setting aside the indictment, Mayes issued a bench warrant to rearrest Vancleave on the original charge. Vancleave, understandably outraged that the case against him continued, filed suit against Doane for false arrest and imprisonment. The mayor begged for help from headquarters, noting that "if my understanding of the views of the general commanding be correct, no further steps were to be taken in the above case."[36] By this time so many factors had combined to erode Doane's credibility—including his simultaneous attempts to have Marshal McGinley removed from office, the rumors of his profiteering from the firearms violation fines, and his intentional defiance of the probate court—that Judge Mayes knew he had the upper hand in the matter. He wrote a lengthy legal treatise to Gillem, which expressed in no uncertain terms his court's authorization to prosecute Vancleave based on the general's earlier letter confirming that jurisdiction.

Judge Mayes ruthlessly attacked Doane in the letter, destroying what little credibility remained for the mayor's administration, and in the process created an interesting summation of Doane's self-destructive character traits. Mayes described Doane as "one who is unsettled in his views of the principles and forms of law, yet quite as settled in his purpose to force through his crude conceptions." Doane's pride would not allow him to accept a decision reversal, Mayes claimed, and he warned that appeals from the mayor's office "are apt to be frequent, and reversals almost as numerous; but he . . . is unable to account for the correction of his errors other than attributing it to prejudice or to some equally unworthy influence; and he keeps himself in a fever of excitement without any reason beyond his own combined ignorance and obstinacy."[37] Anyone could see Doane's tenure as mayor rapidly coming to an end. His court's authority had been demolished, Edward Ellet resigned as constable, and the lawsuit pressed by Vancleave threatened to take all Doane's profits, if not his very freedom. It would only take one more mistake to finish off the mayor, and it arrived very conveniently one afternoon in the guise of a favor to a friend.

After their eviction from Tokeba Plantation, Albert and Charles Morgan began carrying pistols to deal with the numerous overt and subtle threats that resulted from their involvement with the freedmen. One afternoon Charles came into town to get the mail and was accosted by a crowd of toughs who pushed and insulted him all the way down the main street to a waiting flatboat. Morgan had held his temper through most of the abuse; but when the crowd rushed him, he coolly drew his pistol and leveled it at the nearest man and stopped their advance. When he returned to town the next day, Charles was arrested by one of Sheriff Dyer's deputies and charged with carrying a concealed weapon. Charles knew he would be found guilty and did exactly as Vancleave had done by requesting a trial in the mayor's court. Even though he could see the trouble ahead, Doane heard the case, fined his friend twenty-six dollars, and declared the incident over. The *Yazoo Banner* knew better, however, and confidently crowed that "the mayor had no right to punish for the unlawful exhibition of a deadly weapon, which is an indictable offense . . . when the grand jury meets Morgan will learn that there is some little law yet left in Mississippi."[38]

Doane quietly resigned his office as justice of the peace on May 18 and as mayor on the following day. With Amelia in tow, he fled Mississippi for Bunker Hill, Illinois, with a rumored haul of nearly four thousand dollars.[39] Edward Ellet waited a few days after Doane left before stealing down to the Tokeba Landing, bribing a deputy with whiskey, and hijacking a huge load of his impounded cypress logs.[40] Ellet sold the logs in New Orleans for a handsome profit and, like Doane, fled the country. The Yazoo Brigade ended their Mississippi sojourn as fugitives.

CHAPTER 4

"A solitude peopled with fantastic ideas, an empire of shadows and of turmoil"

Reenlistment and the Yellowstone Expedition

The post–Civil War army seemed to be a poor arena for anyone who hungered for fame and distinction. By 1866 the United States government had discharged almost a million volunteer soldiers and began a series of legislative measures that steadily reduced the size of the regular army.[1] Once the national secession crisis had been settled on the battlefield, some politicians questioned the need for a large standing army, even though the uses for that army gradually increased as migrating settlers inevitably clashed with the Native peoples of the western plains. Despite the expanding demands of the western territories for a military presence, Congress in 1869 reduced the army to just 37,313 men to perform the unpopular duties of policing the frontier and continuing the Reconstruction occupation of the southern states and in 1870 again cut the forces to 30,000.[2] In addition to creating an army with undersized organizational units at the regimental and company level, this government policy created a surplus of officers whose careers were stymied by a promotion system that allowed advancement only by vacancy within an individual's regiment.

The officer corps of the army evolved into a competitive conglomerate of Civil War veterans who had, in most cases, accepted a lower rank in order to stay in uniform. The practice of awarding brevet ranks (honorary promotions usually given for meritorious service) added a confusing element to the promotion system: many lower-grade officers were informally addressed by their higher brevet rank and could, in come cases, use the title for preferment in assignments. By 1869 a full 1,000 officers in the army had a higher brevet rank, and a perception arose in the military that those who lacked such distinction must somehow have failed in their Civil War duties. A civilian wishing to gain an officer's commission without having achieved a brevet rank during the war would face stiff competition for the limited positions available; even though the regulations stipulated that first and second lieutenant vacancies were to be filled by veterans who had served creditably for at least two years, political patronage also played a role. Appointments for these junior officers were apportioned to the various states based on the number of troops they provided during the war, with California, Nevada, and Oregon being the exceptions.[3]

When Doane made up his mind to reenter the army in the spring of 1868, he had two immediate obstacles to gaining an officer's commission. His dismal record during the war and as the military mayor of Yazoo City had not earned him the notice that would have earned a brevet rank; nor could he claim to have been an officer who had served creditably for two years. His court-martial in Virginia while serving with the California Hundred had reduced him to the ranks, and the Mississippi Marine Brigade had been dissolved before Doane could claim even ten full months as a lieutenant. Regardless of how discouraging the chances of getting a commission seemed, Doane realized that the army had been his only source of even modest success after failing at business, farming, and politics, and he used what little influence he had to get back into uniform.

After fleeing Mississippi with Amelia, Doane went to the Ellet family home in Bunker Hill, Illinois, where he waited on the results on his plan to get an officer's commission. As his situation in Yazoo City had begun to deteriorate, Doane had written to Senator John Conness of California to remind the politician of a wartime promise. Apparently Doane had ingratiated himself with Conness during his visits to the capitol while still serving with the California Hundred; and in 1865 the senator had written, "If anything I could say could benefit you I would gladly say it and be of service to you."[4] Doane had carried the letter for three years, and while it lacked the status of a brevet commission it at least represented a favor that could be used in an emergency. Now Doane recalled the offer for assistance, and Conness accordingly wrote to Maj. Gen. John M. Schofield, secretary of war, recommending Doane for a commission on April 15, 1868. Because California was exempt from the quota that other states had to observe regarding the appointment of volunteer officers, the senator's recommendation for one of his state's veterans had the desired impact. Ten days later Doane got the welcome invitation to attend an examination for officer candidates at Carlisle Barracks, Pennsylvania.[5]

The examination proved mostly a formality and included both physical and mental tests that Doane passed easily, compiling a score of 78.5 out of a possible 84.[6] His university education again had given him an advantage, but it also gave him the expectation that he would gain promotion and distinction based on his intellectual abilities. The problem of stagnation in the army line of promotion should have been obvious to anyone contemplating a career in uniform, but Doane believed that he could beat the odds and gain a higher rank through his college training and writing skills. He also had vague ideas of participating in the last great reconnaissance of uncharted territories in the American West. The exploits of Maj. Gen. John C. Frémont still held appeal in the popular imagination, and especially in Doane's. Even if most of the major features of the West had already been traversed, Doane knew that his natural talents with a pen and his instruction in the sciences could assist him in making a career as a self-promoting explorer. As it turned out,

Doane's writing skills would indeed bring him a national reputation during his first years in the army, but he would find it to be a mixed blessing as he continued his practice of cultivating the wrong superiors for preferential treatment.

Doane received his commission as a second lieutenant in the Second United States Cavalry Regiment on August 1, 1868, and orders to report to Fort McPherson, Nebraska, shortly thereafter. Amelia accompanied him, which showed how dependent on him she was and how thoroughly she felt alienated from Yazoo City. As a second lieutenant, Doane should have been assigned living space consisting of one room and a kitchen; but it is unlikely that those amenities were available for newcomers at Fort McPherson that summer, because the post lacked adequate housing for more than a quarter of the officers stationed there.[7] Amelia endured the primitive living conditions until Doane was ordered on to Fort D. A. Russell, Wyoming Territory, on August 18. At least here she would have a roof over her head, but she often had no husband to share it with. Having no more than arrived at the Wyoming fort, Doane was sent out with his first command on a sixty-mile chase across the plains after some Indians who had raided nearby Cheyenne City.[8] Amelia saw little of her husband even after his return from this unsuccessful three-day mission. Doane was assigned to Company H and on September 14 ordered back into the field, this time under the command of Lt. Col. Luther P. Bradley, scouting along the Republican River. He would not return to Fort Russell and his wife for nearly three months, and his next assignment did nothing to bring him the distinction he craved.

In the eyes of the army, Doane's education in California and experiences in Mississippi suited him for a quartermaster's duty. His only modest accomplishment during his first year on the frontier was fighting a blizzard to deliver some emergency rations to a distant post. Toward the end of his life, Doane would claim that his nine months of inactivity at Fort D. A. Russell allowed him to propose his first exploration expedition, a trip down the Colorado River. He even hinted that Maj. John Wesley Powell may have absconded with his idea, but the facts do not correspond with Doane's memory. Powell had publicly announced his intention to explore the river on December 18, 1867, before Doane even left Mississippi, and wrote to Gen. Ulysses S. Grant with his proposal on April 2, 1868. If the idea of advancing his career by volunteering for exploration ever occurred to Doane during this dreary period of his life, it happened during the spring of 1869 when his company formed part of a battalion ordered from Fort D. A. Russell to Fort Ellis in Montana Territory.

The transfer marked a new beginning for Doane, but to Amelia it represented yet another journey to widen the gulf between herself and her Mississippi home. She would be the only officer's wife to accompany the cavalry on its 600-mile march to Montana, again demonstrating that she had no option but to follow her husband, regardless of the hazards involved. Doane, however, looked forward to the trip and wrote a letter to Edward Ellet, inviting him to come along to do some big-game hunting. Ellet, who had been visiting and drinking with old army comrades in Philadelphia, was ready for any sort of adventure and made immediate preparations to visit his friend.

On May 15 four companies of the Second Cavalry under the command of Lt. Col. Albert G. Brackett boarded freight cars on the Union Pacific line at Cheyenne City and began their journey. The railroad took the men and horses as far as Carter's Station, a point just east of Fort Bridger in southwest Wyoming Territory, where they disembarked and began the march north. Edward Ellet did not reach the place until three days after the troops left, but Doane had left a horse for him. After two days' hard riding Ellet caught up with the battalion. The march to Montana turned out to be a real adventure vacation for Ellet, and Doane somehow managed to get permission to accompany his friend on hunts while the command rested a day or two in camp. On one occasion the friends wandered over fifteen miles away in pursuit of bighorn mountain sheep. Doane managed to bring down a fine ram; but when the pair attempted a shortcut along a steep mountain cliff to bring the meat back to camp, Ellet was attacked by a pair of eagles whose nest he had tried to raid. Doane, who had gone ahead, managed to frighten the eagles with a few rifle shots before they clawed Ellet from the face of the cliff. The two badly shaken adventurers made it back to camp long after dark.[9] Undaunted by this misadventure, Doane and Ellet continued their hunting forays, once even bringing a live badger back to camp, much to the amusement of Colonel Brackett.[10]

Amelia's loneliness continued once the command arrived at Fort Ellis on July 1, 1869. The outpost consisted of a few rude barracks surrounded by a log stockade with blockhouses. Although a few laundresses lived at the fort, Amelia was the only officer's wife at the post that summer and was forbidden by the rules of etiquette from consorting with enlisted men's spouses. The nearby town of Bozeman offered few female residents for socializing either, and it would be months before three other officers brought their spouses to Fort Ellis. To make matters worse, Doane was ordered away from the post within two weeks of arrival, assigned to help map a route from the fort to the mouth of the Musselshell River, an assignment that kept him away until September 9. The journey proved to be fortunate for Doane. Edward Ellet, whose money had run out after accompanying a prospector on a fruitless journey to the upper Yellowstone, returned to Fort Ellis just after Doane's patrol had left. Ellet intended to borrow money from Doane to get back home but could not wait until the Musselshell detail returned to the fort. As a result, Ellet had no choice but to make his way back to Illinois without the aid of this friend's Yazoo City profits.[11]

When the Second Cavalry arrived at Fort Ellis, Colonel Brackett set the men to tearing down the stockade and building more barracks with the salvaged logs. This work continued while Doane was out on the Musselshell expedition; and, after his return, he briefly supervised some of the work himself. Within a week of being reunited with Amelia, however, Doane was off again, this time to the District of Montana headquarters at Fort Shaw, where he remained for a month's detached service and again demonstrated his talents as a skilled writer of reports. By the time Doane returned to Fort Ellis, Brackett had been replaced by a new commander who would prove a valuable ally to the lieutenant in advancing his career. Maj. Eugene Mortimer Baker had graduated from West Point in 1854 and served with distinction throughout the Civil War, having been cited for gallantry at the battles of Williamsburg and Winchester. A heavy drinker and personable officer, he recognized early on that Doane's ability to write a good report made him a valuable asset to the command. This became all the more important when the Fort Ellis troops became involved in their first campaign against the Indians in Montana Territory.

The federal government's handling of Montana's Indians in 1869 provided a field test of President Ulysses S. Grant's "Peace Policy." The army had insisted for years that management of all the western tribes should be within its purview and advocated the transfer of the Bureau of Indian Affairs from the Department of the Interior to the War Department. Corrupt civilian agents who were engaging in profiteering at the Indian's expense, argued the military establishment, were the root cause of friction on the frontier, and army officers could be trusted best to deal fairly, but firmly, with the Native peoples. When Grant took office in March 1869, he adopted a compromise of sorts that kept the Indian Bureau under civilian control but allowed army officers to serve as superintendents and agents for many tribes of the northern plains. Grant's "Peace Policy" intended that Indians would be confined to reservations and managed by the agencies, while the army would confront those Indians off the reservations as "hostiles." Military forces could only interfere with Indians on a reservation by the direct request of the Indian Bureau officials.[12]

When a rash of horse thefts occurred in Montana Territory that summer, the Montana superintendent of Indian affairs, Lt. Col. Alfred Sully, received numerous calls from outraged settlers demanding that the perpetrators be punished. A few attacks on white settlers added to the public outcry, most notably the August 17 killing of Malcolm Clarke, a prominent citizen of the Prickley Pear Valley.[13] Clarke, married to a Piegan woman, had been murdered by several of his wife's relatives and his son seriously wounded as a result of a family feud, but the frontier press used the incident to further their assertions that a general Indian uprising was in the making. Sully wrote to the Bureau of Indian Affairs in Washington,

D.C., on August 3 asking it to involve the War Department in providing more soldiers for the territory, and followed up with another letter the day after Clarke was killed, claiming the situation had deteriorated to "a state of war."[14] Although the military commander of the District of Montana, Col. Philippé R. de Trobriand, initially downplayed the perceived threat during the ensuing weeks, the Interior Department formally asked the War Department to intervene. The stock raiding continued throughout the fall. In late December Sully decided to try a combination of diplomacy and threat by traveling to the Teton River Agency and demanding from the Piegan tribal leaders the killers of Malcolm Clarke and a return of all the stolen livestock. On January 1, 1870, Sully gave the Piegans a two-week deadline to deliver Mountain Chief and four other Piegans accused of Clarke's murder. When no compliance seemed forthcoming, Lt. Gen. Philip H. Sheridan, commanding the Military Division of the Missouri, telegraphed an order to his subordinates that was chilling in its brevity. "If the lives and property of the citizens of Montana can best be protected by striking Mountain Chief's band," wrote Sheridan, "I want them struck. Tell Baker to strike them *hard*."[15]

Colonel de Trobriand ordered Major Baker to take all four companies of the Second Cavalry at Fort Ellis to Fort Shaw on January 6, 1870. Doane, now in command of Company F, may have looked forward to his first opportunity to lead men into battle on the frontier, but the weather certainly dampened the ardor of any would-be warrior. Bitter cold plagued the column before it reached Fort Shaw on January 14, and the cavalrymen had to rest a few days at the outpost to thaw out and receive their final orders. Although de Trobriand gave Baker wide discretionary powers, the colonel specifically ordered that the villages of Heavy Runner and Big Lake "should be left unmolested" and that only the camp of Mountain Chief would be the soldiers' legitimate target.[16] Fifty mounted infantry from the garrison joined the expedition; and on January 19, in subzero weather, Baker set forth with a column of over three hundred and fifty men. Horace Clarke, the son of the murdered Malcolm, rode along with the troops, as did Joe Kipp, a mixed-blood Piegan who had scouted several Indian camps along the Marias River just two weeks earlier.

Doane suffered along with the rest of Company F on a grueling night march on January 22, wrapped in blankets and buffalo robes in an attempt to ward off the freezing temperature. At daybreak, the column reached the first Piegan camp on the Marias, a small cluster of five lodges. After surrounding the camp and rousting the surprised occupants from their sleep, Kipp informed Major Baker that they had captured the band of Grey Wolf, who told Kipp that Mountain Chief's village could be found about six miles downstream.[17] Baker ordered Doane's company to take the advance. After following the trail about four miles, the troopers met and captured four Indians without resistance. Doane left the prisoners in charge of a sergeant and continued to ride east along the Marias River, which was hidden from view in a deep ravine. The soldiers came in sight of a large herd of ponies on the edge of the bluffs, and soon the smoke from the Indian village appeared just below. Doane detached a sergeant with six men to cut out and drive the stock away from the village. The rough ground posed particular risks for their efforts, and one of the troopers' horses tripped in the narrow ravine, breaking three of its legs.[18]

Doane sent several men to report to Sgt. Thomas Anderson with instructions to ride down the bluffs above the village, cross the stream, and deploy on the other side, while the lieutenant led the rest of the company along the ridge between the village and herd of ponies. As Company F picked its way down the slippery, snow-covered terrain Doane could see Anderson's men crossing the river above the village. The sergeant deployed his men along the slope on the opposite side of the river, and in two minutes the Indians were completely surrounded. At this point Baker and the rest of the command came forward and dismounted with carbines at the ready.[19]

Peering down into the sleeping village, Joe Kipp suddenly recoiled with horror. He recognized the designs painted on the side of the tepees to be those belonging to the band of Heavy Runner, one of the chiefs who had attended Sully's New Year's Day council and who had been given a written safeguard by the general. "Wrong village!" shouted Kipp to the major. Baker would hear none of it: he ordered the scout restrained and told his men to shoot Kipp if he uttered another sound. The positioning of so many soldiers, along with Kipp's shouting, caused enough noise to wake some of the sleeping Indians. Heavy Runner stepped out from his lodge, waving Sully's safeguard over his head as he called to the soldiers to hold their fire. He only advanced a few yards before a bullet tore through his chest. All along the line, Baker's men opened fire down into the tepees below. The screams of the wounded and dying Indians mixed with the blasts of gunfire as bullets ripped indiscriminately through the thin hide covering of the lodges.[20]

Doane had placed Sergeant Anderson's men in a very precarious position on the bluffs opposite the main column, but the only real danger they faced were the bullets from their own comrades, who were "firing in their direction constantly."[21] Even though they risked death by friendly fire, the men of Anderson's squad stood their ground and poured volley after volley into the village. The Piegans who attempted to flee in that direction were shot down, and several had to be chased high up on the slope and killed with revolvers. Some of the Indians managed to escape the hellish fusillade by hiding in the brush, however; and in spite of the soldiers' best efforts, a few survivors escaped to warn other villages downstream. The awful firing continued until Baker ordered Doane to mount his command and ride down and continue the carnage at close range. Doane led his men forward. As they swept through the village to complete the work he watched his men pause in front of lodges and fire into doorways to silence the screams of the occupants. Not all of the soldiers could stomach the slaughter, though. Some of Doane's men held their fire to capture hysterical women and children who poured out of the perforated lodges and herded them together into a bunch.

While Doane's men secured the village, Major Baker ordered the rest of his command down to the river bottom to assist with the mopping up. One hapless trooper received a bullet in the back of his head, fired by a warrior concealed in a tepee. It was the only death recorded on the army's side that day. Joe Kipp informed the major that some of the captives said that the village of Mountain Chief, the actual target of the raid, was another sixteen miles downstream. Baker left Doane in charge of the village with Company F while he led the balance of the command in pursuit of Mountain Chief. Doane completed the destruction by having his men pull down the lodges, stack dead bodies and foodstuffs on top of the collapsed tepees, and set fire to them. The work of destruction continued all day; and as night fell Doane posted a guard around the 140 women and children who had escaped immediate death. "Sergeant O'Kelly was on guard that night and is entitled to great credit for his energy and alertness," Doane would recall years later, "the camp being full of wounded, the sentinels firing at intervals all through the night, which was made hideous by the groans of the wounded, the howling of the dogs, fire breaking out in the woods, and the stampeding of the pony herd in a tremendous wind storm."[22] According to hearsay evidence, even darker events may have occurred that night. Pvt. Daniel Starr recalled to a comrade years after the event that eight warriors had been captured with the women and children, and during the night two made a desperate bolt for freedom into the freezing darkness. Starr claimed that after troopers recaptured the warriors, Doane lost his temper and ordered all eight of the men executed. When the troopers prepared their carbines, Doane said, "No, don't use your guns. Get axes and kill them one at a time." Starr admitted that he and the other guards quietly dragged the prisoners out from the tepees they shared with the women and children and obediently performed the gruesome duty.[23]

When Major Baker returned the next morning after a failed attempt to surprise the camp of Mountain Chief, Doane simply reported the official tally of the raid: 173 Indians killed, of which 53 were women and children. The lieutenant also reported the disconcerting fact that he had discovered smallpox among the 140 survivors. Baker, unprepared to deal with prisoners anyway, ordered all the captives released and gave them several boxes of hardtack and bacon for their sustenance in the freezing cold. The entire command then marched upstream to a trading post, where Baker met with representatives of the Blood Indians and threatened them with similar treatment if the horse stealing raids did not stop. The military force returned to Fort Shaw on January 29 and to Fort Ellis on February 6.[24]

The white people of Montana applauded the work of Major Baker and his troops in punishing the Piegans, but the incident proved to be a public relations disaster for the army. It took Baker more than a month to file an official report on the battle. During the interim eastern newspapers quoted Colonel Sully's charges that only twenty or thirty of the Piegan dead were actually adult male warriors and that Baker had destroyed a camp of friendly Indians. Several members of the United States Congress loudly condemned the raid and even went so far as to suggest that all the soldiers involved should be driven from the service. As a result of Sully's accusations and the congressional outcry, Gen. William T. Sherman, the army's commanding officer in Washington, D.C., had to press Baker for clarification in his report regarding the "sex and type of Indians killed" on March 12, 1870.[25] Perhaps by that time Baker had called on Doane's talents in writing; but if so the supplemental report had none of the lieutenant's trademark verbosity. The document merely provided the official body count, with the sex of the slain identified, but also took the extraordinary step of demanding an official investigation of the campaign to clear all of the involved officers' reputations: "Less than this cannot, in justice, be conceded to them."[26]

If Baker was making a calculated bluff by demanding an investigation the strategy worked, because the army never called an official board of inquiry into the Marias River incident. The flurry of charges and countercharges, however, resulted in lasting repercussions for the army's desire to take a more active role in managing the western tribes. Congress had seriously considered the transfer of Indian Affairs to the War Department prior to the Baker Massacre, but afterward legislation not only retained the office in the Interior Department but also forbade army officers from ever again serving as Indian agents or superintendents.[27] A more important result of the controversy for Doane came in gaining Baker's complete trust. Doane's official report gave ample credit to his noncommissioned officers and, with some clever verbiage, made the fight seem like an actual battle where resistance was offered.

Doane's stubborn loyalty to his comrades showed how completely insensitive he had become to anyone's opinion beyond that of the frontier military. When asked by "an anxious settler" quoted in the Deer Lodge *New Northwest* if he thought the Montana tribes would remain peaceful as a result of the massacre, Doane replied, "Well, I can't say, but there are certainly 173 very good arguments in favor of their remaining quiet, laying out on the Marias!"[28] That callous statement may have been applauded by the frontier citizens of Montana, but it did nothing to endear Doane or his comrades to the rest of the nation. General Sherman shared Doane's loyalty to the army regardless of the political consequences and wrote General Sheridan: "You may assure Colonel Baker that no amount of clamor has shaken our confidence in him and his officers."[29] Sustained by his superiors while condemned by the eastern press, Baker had ample reason to reward Doane for his fidelity. An opportunity would come in an assignment that would mark the height of the ambitious lieutenant's career.

The possibility of emulating his childhood hero, Maj. Gen. John C. Frémont, likely occurred to Doane during the 1869 march from Fort D. A. Russell to Fort Ellis. The route traveled by the soldiers took them around the edge of the last remaining unmapped regions of the United States, the area today known as Yellowstone National Park. The land had already been "discovered," first by the Indians who inhabited it and next by the fur trappers who visited the upper Yellowstone in search of pelts during the early decades of the nineteenth century; but as late as 1869 the country had yet to be accurately described in print or reliably mapped. It would be a springboard to glory for the first person to do so; and by the summer of 1870 Doane, with Major Baker's assistance, determined to be that person.

Exploration of the Yellowstone region had been attempted several times during the 1850s and 1860s by both the government and civilians. From the stories of Jack Baronett (a member of a party that had visited the region in 1863) the surveyor general of Montana

Territory, Henry D. Washburn, became interested in exploring the region.[30] Washburn proposed an expedition in 1869; but after he cancelled his plans, two members who had planned to make the trip, David E. Folsom and Charles W. Cook, determined to go alone. They left Diamond City with a third volunteer, William Peterson, on September 1, 1869, and traveled through the region, visiting the falls on the upper Yellowstone River, the Grand Canyon of the Yellowstone, Yellowstone Lake, and the Lower Geyser Basin. On their return, Folsom and Cook wrote an account of the trip published by a Chicago literary periodical of limited circulation, the *Western Monthly,* in July 1870. Without the means or inclination to follow up their publication with other publicity, however, Cook and Folsom had not achieved national recognition as the first reliable visitors to report on the wonders of the Yellowstone. Folsom visited Helena after the article had been submitted and spoke with Washburn about what he and his friends had seen, which rekindled the surveyor general's interest.[31]

The Cook-Folsom-Peterson party had left the Fort Ellis area for Yellowstone on September 8, 1869, the very day Doane had returned from the mapping reconnaissance to the mouth of the Musselshell River. He may have heard from others in the garrison about the three men, but there is no evidence that he expressed any interest at that time. When the trio returned from the Yellowstone region and gained such local celebrity for their achievement, however, Doane realized the national spotlight had yet to shine on the topic. By the summer of 1870, when it appeared that Washburn would follow up with a more comprehensive look at the country, Doane knew that his opportunity for gaining lasting fame had come. Major Baker promised Washburn a military escort if the surveyor general could get the headquarters of the Department of Dakota to order one from the diminutive garrison at Fort Ellis. Doane then began cultivating Washburn and Helena banker Samuel T. Hauser, letting them know how much he wanted to accompany their party. Desperate for this chance, Doane gave the two men complete instructions on how to telegraph Maj. Gen. Winfield S. Hancock, commander of the Department of Dakota, to make the

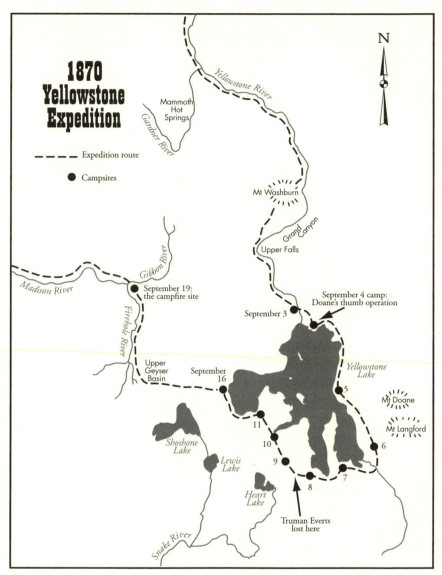

1870 Yellowstone Expedition.

request. "I will reimburse you the expenses of the messages," he wrote, "which should be paid both ways to insure prompt attention."[32] The money was well spent, because Hancock issued orders to the District of Montana on August 15, 1870, directing that "an escort be furnished, and that an officer be sent with it who could make a report of the trip, as well as a map of the country passed over."[33] Regardless of Doane's cartographic skills, Baker knew him to be the best officer he had for writing reports, as well as a steadfast ally in the continuing controversy over the Marias River incident, so he gave the choice assignment as promised.

Along with Washburn and Hauser, the civilians forming the party included some of the most prominent men in Montana Territory: Nathaniel P. Langford, former territorial collector of internal revenue; Truman C. Everts, former territorial assessor of internal revenue; Walter Trumbull, one of Evert's employees; Cornelius Hedges, a Yale-educated attorney; Warren C. Gillette, prominent Helena merchant; Benjamin F. Stickney, Jr., another Helena merchant and wholesaler. Frontier entrepreneur Jacob Smith also signed on for the trip. His subsequent antics so irritated Nathaniel Langford that he described Smith as little more than a pleasure-seeking tourist among a serious, sober group of Yellowstone explorers. Doane's command consisted of Sgt. William A. Baker and privates William Leipler, Charles Moore, George McConnell, and John Williamson, all of Company F. Two packers, Elwin Bean and Charles Reynolds, and two cooks, "Nute" and "Johnny," also accompanied the party, probably as paid employees.

The civilians arrived at Bozeman on August 20 and were entertained by the little town's leading citizens. After taking supper at the home of Lester S. Willson, the party retired to the Guy Hotel, where they were joined by Major Baker and Doane, who characteristically had left Amelia at home. The men imbibed champagne and listened to a banjo serenade performed by local barber Samuel Lewis before retiring for the evening. The next morning the party established a camp near Fort Ellis, and Doane arrived with a Sibley tent, rations, and other camping equipment. Jake Smith immediately challenged his colleagues to a game of blackjack, using coffee beans as poker chips, but Hauser bested him in no time. The men settled down after that in preparation for the morning's departure.

On August 22, 1870, the little party started out from the Gallatin Valley toward Trail Creek and over the divide to the Yellowstone Valley. The leisurely pace matched the high spirits of the adventurers, and the only thing marring an otherwise perfect beginning for Doane was a nagging pain in his right thumb caused by an infected abscess or "felon," as contemporary doctors described the malady. The pain had begun innocently, hurting just enough to cause Doane to dismiss it as a minor sprain; but as the day wore on and the throbbing increased, he realized that the source of his torment was more than just a pulled tendon. He kept the information to himself that evening as they set up their first camp along Trail Creek and probably forgot about it while observing the antics of Jake Smith. Smith wanted to recoup his blackjack losses and had devised a novel way of doing so. Observing dryly that he doubted any of the group could hit anything with the revolvers they carried, Smith offered his hat as a target to the group for twenty-five cents a shot. Several of the party took him up on the challenge, but at first it seemed Smith's assessment of their marksmanship was accurate. He gained quite a few quarters until Langford slipped away from the group, concealed himself in some bushes, and rapidly pumped four shots through Smith's chapeau with his repeating carbine. Smith immediately called a halt to the proceedings and then offered to host another game of blackjack, in which he promptly lost all his earnings. "He stood his loss and the jests of the party with the greatest good humor," according to Warren Gillette.[34]

The next day Doane discovered much to his disgust that the packers had turned his command's horses loose before breakfast, and the soldiers had to borrow mounts from the civilians to retrieve the animals before they walked all the way back to the fort. After this inauspicious start, Doane led his party down into the Yellowstone River valley, just a few miles downstream and opposite from the played out diggings at Emigrant Gulch. He knew he had to account carefully for the mileage of each day's travel as well as keep an accurate description of the country, so he continually scribbled notes on the topography in spite of the handicap of his painful thumb. The civilians maintained a great deal of vigilance too, but they were on the lookout for signs of Indians rather than the geographic features. Even though Langford and the others made no secret of their uneasiness on this matter, Doane rushed ahead with his men to Bottler's Ranch, the last outpost of civilization along the upper Yellowstone, leaving the civilians to follow along as best they could. The sight of some Crow warriors during this leg of the trip did little to allay the fears of the group, and Jake Smith earned the enmity of Nathaniel Langford that evening by loudly suggesting that it would be a waste of time to post guards at night even though they had spotted Indians that day. Doane disagreed, especially after he learned from Frederick Bottler that they could expect to meet additional Crows at a camp farther upriver, and welcomed Washburn's decision to keep watch for the security of the expedition's mounts. The loss of their horses, which had almost happened that very morning due to the packer's negligence, would result in the expedition's return to Fort Ellis on foot, a disaster from which Doane's career might never recover.

As Doane led his men out from Bottler's Ranch on the morning of August 24 the most suitable way seemed to lie along the course of the Yellowstone River itself, following the trail marked by the Indians that had gone before them; but by sticking to this route Doane bypassed the most significant feature to present-day tourists entering by way of the park's northern entrance: Mammoth Hot Springs. Influenced by previous travelers' accounts, which largely described the falls, lake, and the geysers beyond, and likely by his aching thumb as well, Doane did not indulge in the necessary detour. The party followed the river deeper into the mountains as Doane carefully noted the natural features of the area. Occasionally the utter grandeur of the country mocked his attempts at objectivity, as it did on August 26 when he first gazed into the Black Canyon of the Yellowstone. Peering down the sheer cliffs to the riverbed hundreds of feet below, he could only gasp in amazement. As he recalled the scene later he wrote, "It is grand, gloomy, and terrible; a solitude peopled with fantastic ideas, an empire of shadows and turmoil."[35]

Doane separated from the main party for his view of the Black Canyon and did not return to it until August 27. His time away from the others reminded Doane that his expedition certainly could not be engaged in "discovery" as much as it was in "exploration," for everywhere one could see evidence of other human travelers. Aside from the footprints and abandoned campsites of the Indians, Doane came upon many prospect holes left by miners who had recently tried to determine the mineral wealth of the land. He even met two white hunters making a trip through the mountains in search of elk and bear. The importance of his own journey would lie solely in his descriptive powers, Doane realized, and he dutifully recorded what he saw, between desperate attempts to lance the infection of his festering thumb.

As Doane led the Washburn party farther south along the river, his frustration mounted in proportion to the beauty they encountered. In the middle of the opportunity of his life, his thumb threatened to rob him of the ability to record his experiences. Traversing the most spectacular landscape in America, containing such wonders as the Grand Canyon of the Yellowstone, the Mud Volcano, and the Dragon's Cauldron, Doane steadily lost his ability to grasp a pencil or even get adequate rest due to the increasing agony of his infection. He could not sleep at all on the night of August 29 and spent the hours until dawn pacing around the campfire with his hand swathed in wet bandages. Doane could not bear to allow those bandages to dry either and all the next day galloped ahead of the expedition from one spring to the next in order to soak the dressing. Langford recalled years later how he watched Doane crawl gingerly from his blankets on the evening of August 30 only to plunge his hand into a bucket of partially frozen water to numb the aching appendage.[36] The ordeal began to have a serious effect on Doane's mental stability. After following a channel down to the base of the Grand Canyon of the Yellowstone with Private McConnell, Doane claimed he found the chasm so deep and dark that he could see stars in broad daylight.[37] He overcame his hallucinations through sheer nerve by climbing out of the canyon and getting back to the expedition's camp later that evening, but after the exertion and excitement wore off the pain again would not let him sleep.

Not all members of the party seemed as concerned about the lieutenant's health as Langford was. Jake Smith continued to encourage his fellows to indulge in games of chance at every stop, and his easy-going manner grated on Langford's nerves. "You can burn more and gather less firewood than any man I have ever camped with," Langford snapped at him one day. Smith responded by referring to him as the "Yellowstone Sharp" as a sarcastic reference to Langford's refusal to indulge in the card games.[38] Smith's relaxed attitude toward guard duty irritated not only Langford, however; even Walter Trumbull could not resist sketching in the pages of his own travel notes not the wonders of the landscape but rather the figure of a prostrate Smith snoozing his way through a stint at guard.[39]

Eventually even the ice-water plunges brought no relief for Doane's hand, and the lack of sleep that clouded his judgment began to sap his strength. By the time the party crossed the Yellowstone just below the lake on September 3, Langford could no longer watch the lieutenant's sufferings in silence. He told Doane that he felt the thumb would require emergency surgery and that if the lieutenant delayed he ran the risk of developing lockjaw. Unknowingly, Langford had used the most effective argument for treatment on Doane, whose memory of his father's slow death three years ago remained fresh. Langford also hinted he had some chloroform in his medical bag, holding out the prospect of a painless incision should Doane consent to the operation. All day as the party rode toward the northeast shore of the great lake, Doane considered the offer while Langford stropped his penknife on the pommel of his saddle. The next evening as they camped overlooking the lake, Doane's pain became completely intolerable, and he agreed to place himself in Langford's care. "I insisted that he submit to an operation and have the felon opened," Langford recalled, "and he consented provided that I would administer chloroform."[40]

Doane quietly ate his supper while Langford prepared a makeshift operating table out of a ammunition crate. Elwin Bean and

Cornelius Hedges then took Doane to the crate, where they firmly held the suffering man's arm down as Langford prepared his pen knife for the incision. At this point Doane balked and demanded the chloroform he had been promised, but Langford sheepishly admitted that he had never used the substance and feared its effects on the patient might be dangerous. Doane gritted his teeth and allowed his caretakers to proceed. Langford pressed the blade into the base of the lieutenant's thumb and quickly ripped a gash to its tip. Doane screamed as the released pus and blood spattered the men and then suddenly smiled. "That was elegant," he said with a sigh. Langford improvised a poultice of moistened bread, applied it to the incision, and bound the wound. Exhausted by the ordeal, and feeling the relief of having the pressure of the "felon" released, Doane fell into a deep sleep that lasted almost thirty-six hours.[41] The other members of the party stayed in camp all day on Sunday, September 4. When Walter Trumbull jokingly suggested that they not travel on the Sabbath anyway due to Jake Smith's deep religious sentiments, Smith cheerfully responded, "If we are going to remain in camp, let's have a game of draw!"[42]

By the time the expedition moved again on Monday, September 5, Doane had regained some of his strength and felt hardy enough to join Langford in climbing to the top of a peak just to the southeast of the lake. Contradicting the members of the expedition's previous resolution to avoid naming natural features after themselves, Doane suggested that the mountain be named for his wilderness surgeon. Langford later returned the compliment by pointing out another peak to the north and suggested it be named for Doane. The two mountains did not retain those names due to the mapping activities of subsequent Yellowstone surveys, and the peak that now bears Doane's name is not the same one that Langford suggested that day.[43]

Doane led the expedition around the south shores of the lake. With so many individuals taking side trips away from the group, the real tragedy of the expedition occurred on September 9, when Truman Everts lost his way and failed to return to camp. Although they remained in the area for six more days and made several attempts to find Everts, the lost man had wandered far beyond their reach and would eventually endure thirty-seven days of hunger, cold, and exhaustion while attempting to find his way back to civilization. The later rescue of Everts and his published account of his harrowing experience added dramatic aspect to the story of the expedition that attracted further national attention to the explorers. What strikes the modern reader in his tale, however, is the failure of the expedition leadership to admit culpability.[44] Also missing in any of the later published accounts of the expedition is concern about an incredible forest fire caused by Langford and Samuel Hauser on the evening of September 10. The two had climbed to a prominent height south of the lake and ignited a signal fire for Everts, which quickly burned out of control and scorched acres of virgin forest before being subdued by a heavy snowstorm on September 14. Doane described the destruction as "a vast conflagration before the devouring flames of which tall pines trees shrivel up and are consumed like grass,"[45] but not one of the expedition's chroniclers expressed any particular concern for having started the fire in the first place.

The main concern at the time, of course, was finding Everts. During the party's stay in the area around the West Thumb of the lake the men went out daily in pairs, firing guns and calling his name into the dense forest. Jake Smith took his turn in searching but not in standing guard at night. He also amused himself in camp by building a toy boat, which he launched onto the lake, watched disappear amid the waves, and miraculously saw returned the next day by the shifting winds.[46] When Smith made the motion to return to civilization without Everts on September 16 at a conference of the explorers, Doane reluctantly voted with the others to do just that. Warren Gillette protested the decision and the next morning claimed that he would stay and keep looking if anyone would join him. "That's a pretty good bluff," remarked Hauser, "since you know no one else is willing to stay." Doane intervened and ordered privates Moore and Williamson to join in a last-ditch attempt to locate the lost man.[47] This order demonstrated that Doane realized the gravity of losing a member of the party he had been assigned to protect, because Private Moore had been acting as his scribe while his thumb healed. Without Moore's help, Doane would have to take notes as best he could with his crippled hand.

The next part of the journey took Doane and the others northwest from the lake, crossing the Continental Divide to the upper reaches of the Firehole River. Along this leg of the trip both Doane and Washburn mistakenly believed that Shoshone Lake drained into the Firehole and so noted their conclusions on their respective maps. Their exhausting route, through miles of fallen timber interwoven with standing trees so close together at places that their packhorses got wedged, doubtless contributed to their confusion as to the exact location of the Continental Divide. This error was compounded by Doane's comments in his report, however, and would not be corrected until further surveys in the following years traced the true source of the Firehole.

The phenomenon that the expedition beheld in the Upper Geyser Basin overawed each member of the party, putting considerations such as accurate mapping of the area to the south completely out of their minds. They camped in the midst of the geysers, on the east bank of the Firehole south of Old Faithful on the night of September 18. Almost hypnotized by the incredible sight of Old Faithful in eruption, Doane could not help but depart from his clinical narrative style in his later report, remarking that "the beauty of the scene takes away one's breath. It is overpowering, transcending the visions of Moslem's Paradise; the earth affords not its equal, it is the most lovely inanimate object in existence."[48] Langford agreed: "We were convinced that there was not on the globe another region where within the same limits Nature had crowded so much grandeur and majesty with so much of novelty and wonder."[49]

After a brief survey of the geyser area, they followed the Firehole River to its junction with the Gibbon River. On the night of September 19, 1870, they made camp on the grassy meadow at what is now known as Madison Junction. Everyone had the feeling that the major objectives of the trip had been accomplished and that they were on their way home. After Langford published his account of the Yellowstone expedition in 1905, the nature of the discussion around the campfire that night became shrouded in myth. Langford claimed that the men talked about preempting sections of land around the most prominent features they had seen and prepared to reap the profits from future tourists but that they eventually all agreed with a proposition made by Cornelius Hedges that the region should be made into a national park so that all could enjoy for free the wonders they had beheld. This "great act of renunciation" grew in the retelling during the early twentieth century, becoming so convincing by 1929 that a writer for the *Saturday Evening Post* could unblushingly report of the famous campsite: "It is the Independence Hall of the National Park Service."[50] Even as late as 1972 a brass monument was placed at the campsite to commemorate the legendary conversation, and a nearby promontory has been named "National Park Mountain" to celebrate the location's importance.

The trouble with this national park creation myth goes far beyond its doubtful occurrence. The need for such a story in the culture of our present-day conservation movement can be understood when we recognize it as a vision of heroic self-abnegation for the sake of preserving nature; but even when viewed so romantically, the story falls short in considering Doane's input.[51] Even if the alleged discussion took place, Doane's participation should have been as an observer only. As the commander of a military escort on official army business, Doane could not have made a homestead claim on any of the property to begin with and had no personal interest to "renounce." Nevertheless, the patina of noble sacrifice adhered to Doane too as the particulars of this campfire council became entrenched in American folklore.[52]

Doane led the party down the Madison River the next day toward Virginia City. Here Doane, Sergeant Baker, and privates Leipler and McConnell left the civilians to return to Fort Ellis on September 24, 1870. Privates Williamson and Moore came back to the fort more than a week later after making their futile attempt to find Truman Everts with Warren Gillette. The rest of the civilians went on to Helena. When Jake Smith parted from the group he expressed his doubts to Langford that anyone would believe the latter's diary.[53] Langford and Washburn disagreed and upon their return to Helena published preliminary accounts of their journey in local newspapers. Langford announced his intentions to follow up with an article in a prominent magazine; as the preliminary writings appeared as fillers in other newspapers across the country the profile of the expedition's accomplishment began to rise nationally.

When Doane returned to Fort Ellis from the expedition he temporarily resumed command of Company F but became very ill, likely as a result of his infected thumb. For two months he languished in his quarters with Amelia, probably trying to write in spite of his handicap. Certainly he knew that the report he had to compose would be the most important of his life, a chance to write a story to rival anything that John C. Frémont had published. He labored slowly on the manuscript, calling into play all of his knowledge of geography, mineralogy, and botany, woven together in his very best rhetorical style. Doane intended to make his account the definitive scientific treatise on the Yellowstone country and clinch his reputation as the explorer who discovered it all. On November 17, while Doane continued to fight his fever, General Hancock (commander of the Department of Dakota) demanded to know when he could expect to see the report at his office.[54] Major Baker, feeling the pressure to produce some sort of report, finally assigned Pvt. Charles Moore to Doane to act as his clerk in writing out the final draft. Doane made sure that Moore did more than one copy, however. After sending the official copy to Hancock in January 1871, Doane also had Moore produce an additional copy to be sent to the Smithsonian Institution and another for his own records.[55]

The months of careful literary effort gained the results Doane had so earnestly hoped for. The treatise eventually made its way from the office of the secretary of war to the United States Senate Committee on Territories, where it was ordered into print on March 3, 1871. Doane had the satisfaction of knowing his account would be published, at least as a Senate document, simultaneously with the flurry of articles prepared for *Scribner's* and other national periodicals by Langford, Trumbull, and Everts. The fact that Everts had been found alive was another benefit in Doane's procrastination in preparing his report, for he could briefly describe the travails of Everts and still claim a complete success for the expedition.

Doane's report was a masterpiece of descriptive literary style, adding just enough subjective observations to accent the piece at critical passages. Aside from winning the admiration of the War Department and the Senate, the report so impressed a Department of the Interior geologist, Ferdinand V. Hayden, that he specifically called attention to the "remarkable report" created by a young officer with real talent. "The report is a modest pamphlet of 40 pages," Hayden wrote after seeing Yellowstone himself, "yet I venture to state as my opinion that for graphic description and thrilling interest it has not been surpassed by any official report made to our government since the times of Lewis and Clark."[56]

The accolades that Doane received on his report marked the high-water point of his life. Reflecting back on the crowning achievement of his career in 1875, Doane could not help comparing himself to his idol, John Charles Frémont:

> It is something to march under the guidance of the star of empire, and feel that a mighty nation follows on your trail. Frontier celebrity is cheap and lasting, as compared with other, and explorations furnish a source of reputation wherein the rewards are, and ever have been, more than commensurate with the efforts put forth. The fame of the pioneers of this country is as brilliant today as that of her statesmen and so will continue until the end of time. A single exploration by a junior officer in 1846 carried him afterward successively to a seat in the United States Senate, the possession of a princely estate, a candidature for the Presidency, and the command of the Western army at the commencement of a great war. The field is open still. This invasion does not require exalted rank. A poor subaltern, yet unknown, while traversing with weary steps the barren wilderness or scaling the mighty summits from which the waters part and flow, may stumble, under fortune's favor, upon

some new discovery, the merit of which will secure to him all that history vouchsafes to greatness—a paragraph in the encyclopedia of the human race.[57]

The quest for fame had finally borne fruit for Doane; he had at last become a "Pathfinder."

CHAPTER 5

"The existence of this lake Hayden denies, but it is there all the same"

The Hayden Expedition and

the Judith Basin Survey

S cholars who publish the fruits of their research have tradition-
ally withstood the scrutiny of their colleagues. Particularly strenuous peer review is the hallmark of scientific research: once a discovery has been announced by an individual scientist, the results of
an experiment are expected to be repeated by others and variant
outcomes duly reported. In other fields of academic inquiry a similar process occurs, and subsequent researchers routinely build
upon the foundations laid by an individual who first gave voice to a
particular idea or theory. Acceptance of this natural process of intellectual growth is a requirement for recognition in the community of
scholars, but that acceptance is exactly what Doane had difficulty in
grasping. His newfound celebrity as an explorer only whetted his
appetite for a more substantial "paragraph in the encyclopedia of
the human race" as the man who discovered Yellowstone National
Park. As Doane's hunger for recognition grew, so did his frustration
over the scientific community's need to build on his work. From
Doane's point of view these further investigations merely threat-

ened effectively to obscure his Yellowstone exploration fame in just one short year.

The *New York Times* recognized the importance of the scientific process of verification even if Doane could not accept it gracefully. "The accounts of the Yellowstone country hitherto received," reported the newspaper, "even when brought by authorities so respectable as Lieut. Doane, have been so extraordinary that confirmatory testimony has been anxiously looked for."[1] The *Times* specifically referred to a well-publicized reconnaissance of Yellowstone sponsored by the U.S. Department of the Interior launched in the summer of 1871 partially as a direct result of Doane's previous exploration. Ferdinand V. Hayden of the United States Geological Survey became interested in the Yellowstone country and announced his plans to examine the area for a more detailed report created by a team of scientists. Military commanders also wanted to confirm Doane's report on the geography of Yellowstone. At the same time Hayden had scheduled his trip, Gen. Philip H. Sheridan detailed two officers from the U.S. Army Corps of Engineers, captains John W. Barlow and David P. Heap, to make a thorough survey and produce a reliable map.

Doane's difficulty in sharing the limelight as Yellowstone's "discoverer" led him to fear that the publication of the Hayden and Barlow surveys would ignore his 1870 report. After all, Doane had done the same thing himself by omitting mention in his report of the 1869 Cook-Folsom-Peterson journey,[2] and he naturally suspected that others would do the same to his own. Even if Doane had taken a more professional view of the 1871 surveys and realized that they actually doubled his chances to connect his own name with Yellowstone, the army had other duties for the ambitious lieutenant that threatened to keep him from participating. One of Doane's colleagues, 1st Lt. John E. Batchelder, had begun siphoning off money from the post commissary funds during the summer of 1870 and deserted on December 27. Because Doane had signed some of the commissary vouchers, Major Baker had to come forward to protect his loyal subordinate and sent a plea for leniency in considering Doane's involvement to the Department of Dakota headquarters.[3] When Batchelder was later captured in California, Doane became the star witness in the army's case against the embezzler. In April 1871, just as the planning for the two Yellowstone expeditions began, Doane received the unwelcome orders that he would have to travel to department headquarters in St. Paul, Minnesota, for Batchelder's court-martial.

The agonizing banishment lasted for three months, and Doane fretted away his time in St. Paul while the new exploration parties prepared to "rediscover" Yellowstone. Hayden began assembling his team at a camp near Ogden, Utah, in May while waiting for the release of his congressionally funded appropriation due on July 1. The members of Hayden's team included a number of scientists, photographer William Henry Jackson, and artists Henry Elliott and Thomas Moran. The potential for all this talent to be the "last word" on Yellowstone exploration became obvious to Doane, who champed at the bit to return to Montana. Eager to join Hayden in early July, Doane left St. Paul in such haste that he lost custody of an enlisted man he had been ordered to escort back to Fort Ellis.[4] By the time Doane got back to Montana on July 28, the Hayden and Barlow surveys had left Fort Ellis and already penetrated deep into the Yellowstone country. Major Baker immediately assigned Doane the task of overtaking the Hayden party with orders for the military escort, commanded by Capt. George L. Tyler, to return to Fort Ellis for other duties.

As Doane rode up the Yellowstone Valley in pursuit of the explorers he must have noticed the changes a mere twelve months had brought to the countryside. Already entrepreneurs had moved into the area, planning toll roads and concessions for the pleasure-seeking tourists the future would bring. At Mammoth Hot Springs, which Doane had overlooked the previous year, he discovered that Henry Horr and James C. McCartney had already established a crude hotel and spa to cater to invalids attracted by the rumored curative powers of the waters. He also learned that frontiersman Jack Baronett had constructed a bridge spanning the Yellowstone River near its junction with the Lamar. When Doane caught up with the Hayden party on the shores of Yellowstone Lake on August 4, he learned that the explorers had launched a sailboat on the lake for a comprehensive mapping of its shoreline and had already named every geyser and spring they could find. Hayden duly recorded in his official report his first meeting with Doane at Yellowstone Lake, stating that "from that period to the time of our return to Fort Ellis we received the benefit of his experience the previous year."[5] In Hayden's private correspondence, however, he was less complimentary. "We [went] around the Tower Falls, upper and lower Falls of the Yellow Stone, Crater Hills, and Mud Springs," he wrote to his colleague Spencer Baird, "and found that all the descriptions given by Lt. Doane and others fell far short of the Truth."[6]

Doane may have had ample cause to feel threatened by Hayden. The potential publicity to be gained by the professor's superior reputation, bolstered by the photographs and paintings the expedition would produce, could easily eclipse Doane's more modest accomplishments. Doane tried to put his own stamp on the Hayden survey by vainly trying to lead the scientists to the fabled Two Ocean Pass, where the waters from a single stream branched over both sides of the Continental Divide. In his eagerness to recapture the limelight Doane actually led the party in a circle through six miles of dense timber,[7] and his subsequent disagreement with Hayden over the location of Bridger Lake underscored the rivalry he felt. Doane would later complain, "The existence of this lake Hayden denies, but it is there all the same, and more, he has seen it for I showed it to him."[8] Doane's jealousy of Hayden grew over the years, and he would eventually dismiss the geologist in a thinly veiled attack as one of the "engine-turned scientists whose published works are distributed by the ton through the franks of well intentioned congressmen and all expenses paid by the government."[9]

It is unknown if Doane had taken Amelia to St. Paul for the lengthy court-martial proceedings, but he certainly had left her alone at Fort Ellis for all his other field assignments. Almost immediately after returning home from the Hayden survey in September, Doane was sent with his company down the Yellowstone River to escort a survey party for the Northern Pacific Railroad, a task that would keep him away for another two months. How Amelia coped with the almost constant absence of her husband can only be guessed, but circumstantial evidence suggests that the isolation and loneliness of her life began to tell on her. 2nd Lt. Charles Brewster Schofield, a West Point graduate and brother of former secretary of war John M. Schofield, became one of Amelia's companions during this time; like any proper officer's wife she accepted the lieutenant's offer to escort her on those occasions when she wished to leave the post.

On October 26, while Doane shepherded the railroad surveyors in the lower Yellowstone Valley, Amelia and Schofield hitched up a carriage for a jaunt into Bozeman. During the short drive their horses suddenly bolted; and in spite of Schofield's attempts to reassert control over the team, the carriage completely overturned. The young officer escaped with only minor injuries, but Amelia had badly fractured her leg in the accident. Schofield got the injured woman to a nearby settler's cabin. Before he could return to the post himself to report the accident, Major Baker had sent out a patrol to search for the couple. The patrol found the couple after nightfall and brought them back to the post, where surgeons could tend to Amelia's injuries. By the time Doane returned from the survey escort on November 28, her leg had begun to heal, but the story of the incident appeared in Bozeman's newspaper.[10]

To Victorian sensibilities the misadventure hinted at impropriety: Amelia and an unmarried man had been together alone in a cabin long after dark, even if their situation had been the result of a serious accident. If the incident caused Doane any personal embarrassment he at least had the distraction of his promotion to first lieutenant in December. The vacancy provided by Batchelder's court-martial and subsequent resignation from the service opened the door for Doane's advancement, which nearly made up for the maddening delay that the trial in St. Paul had cost him. For the rest of the winter of 1871–72, Doane assumed the duties of company commander for G troop and kept the men busy performing various maintenance duties around Fort Ellis. One of Doane's troopers recalled how the lieutenant exceeded his orders to repair one building by completely tearing down the structure and rebuilding it.[11]

Doane quietly seethed over the supporting role he had been

forced to play on the Hayden Expedition, especially after the publicity of the geologist's journey culminated in the congressional act establishing Yellowstone National Park on March 1, 1872. Although Hayden had given Doane credit in his report for being the first to describe the country accurately, the lieutenant never tired of reminding the army and the public of the same thing for the rest of his life. While hoping for another opportunity to put his name forward as an explorer of note during the winter of 1871–72, Doane got word that the Fort Ellis cavalry battalion would accompany another Northern Pacific Railroad survey down the Yellowstone River valley that summer. The Department of Dakota headquarters assigned Capt. John W. Barlow as the chronicler of the expedition. Col. John Gibbon, commanding the District of Montana, received orders to contract a large supply wagon train for the use of the escort, which guaranteed the trip would be slow, tedious, and devoid of any opportunity for Doane to write a descriptive essay for his superiors.[12] Ironically, while Doane plodded along with his company escorting the cumbersome wagon train, Gibbon himself took a pleasure trip into the newly created Yellowstone National Park and managed to publish a well-received account of his adventures.[13]

Major Baker led the surveying party, consisting of about four hundred soldiers and civilians, from Fort Ellis on July 27, 1872. The expedition met with no Indian resistance during the first two weeks of the journey, even though the Lakota Sioux had made no secret of their opposition to the proposed railroad route; but when the surveyors reached a point just east of the present day city of Billings, Montana, the situation changed.[14] On August 12 a large camp of Sioux, Northern Cheyennes, and Arapahos just west of the junction of the Little Bighorn and Bighorn Rivers became aware of the large party, with its wagon train and beef herd, traveling slowly in their direction. Among the leaders of the tribesmen were Crazy Horse, Black Moon, and Sitting Bull.[15]

While the Indians prepared to move against the survey party on August 13, Major Baker led the command to a pleasant camping ground on the north bank of the Yellowstone River. The site, about four acres contained within a dry oxbow in the shape of an inverted

"U," looked out on a vast cactus and sagebrush covered flat extending to the northeast. The flat terminated in a long line of bluffs that stretched from a point a few dozen yards from the western portion of the oxbow to a rocky projection more than a mile to the east. Baker had chosen a good defensible location for the camp, because the banks of the oxbow provided natural breastworks. Along the eastern edge of the dry channel, however, a thick layer of underbrush grew between the cottonwoods on the riverbank and continued several hundred feet to the north, offering ample cover for the stealthy approach of any enemy. To provide complete security Baker would have been forced to concentrate a large number of guards in that sector. The major considered this precaution both extravagant and unnecessary. Even the presence of a few stray Indian dogs sighted during the afternoon could not shake Baker's confidence. After placing the wagons in an ellipse to serve as an emergency corral for the livestock, he ordered 1st Lt. William Logan of the Seventh Infantry to post a light guard of twenty-six men.[16] Then Baker invited Doane and some of the other officers to his tent for a few rounds of poker and to share the fellowship of a large whiskey jug. Not a drinker himself, Doane nevertheless played cards with the others long after sundown and watched while Baker drank more whiskey than he should have as the jug made its way around the table.[17]

While the soldiers quietly patrolled the dry channel in the valley, the Indians, nearly a thousand strong, watched from the bluffs overlooking the camp. No clear consensus had been reached among the tribesmen regarding the nature of the attack; but some of the younger warriors, when faced with such a tempting array of beef cattle, horses, and mules to steal, made up their minds to test the soldiers' vigilance that very night. Around 3 A.M. on August 14, after Doane and the other officers had left Major Baker's tent for their own bedrolls, Lieutenant Logan made his rounds among the sentinels and found all the sentries at their posts, with nothing to report. Some warriors had crept up into the brush along the perimeter's east side, however, and infiltrated the sleeping camp itself. Some of them actually entered tents and successfully pilfered firearms and horse tack, while several others positioned themselves to stampede the grazing livestock. One warrior had the misfortune to creep by a civilian teamster who was lying awake, and the man fired his pistol at the Indian's head. The shot alarmed the entire camp. While the warriors rushed to wave the frightened horses and mules away from the camp, Logan flew from his tent just as a bullet perforated the lantern-illuminated canvas.[18] The firing became general at this point, with the sentinels withdrawing into the camp while the teamsters desperately tried to corral the livestock within the wagon ellipse. Doane heard the firing and jumped out of his blankets, groggy from a lack of sleep but still lucid enough to assist in forming Company G for action. For a moment it seemed no one was in command, but Doane assembled his men in front of their tents on the company street and ordered them to lie down while awaiting further instructions.

Capt. Charles C. Rawn, commanding the infantry contingent, rushed to Major Baker's tent to report the attack and shook the officer from his stupor. Baker blinked awake in confusion and ordered Capt. Lewis Thompson, the officer of the day, to confirm the cause of the alarm. Disgusted by his commanding officer's delay, Rawn took matters into his own hands by assembling two companies to face the thick brush on the perimeter's east side. The infantrymen eventually fired several volleys into the dark foliage, and the screams of the wounded Indians amply demonstrated the wisdom of Rawn's unauthorized maneuver. Meanwhile Thompson ordered the rest of the command to face the dry oxbow channel and begin advancing to secure the protection of its sheltering banks. Doane's company took its position near the northernmost bend of the natural entrenchment and started firing at whatever targets could be seen in the darkness.[19]

Dawn began to lighten the eastern sky as the beleaguered soldiers fired at their attackers. Through the slowly disappearing gloom Doane could see most of the warriors retreating to the distant bluffs while a few stragglers galloped daringly around in front of the firing line. Bullets thudded all around Doane and his men as the warriors on the bluff tried their hand at long-range sniping in the growing light. Major Baker had composed himself enough to take personal command over the defense; but his befuddled, contradictory orders hardly inspired the men. He approved Capt. Edward Ball's proposal to advance Company H, positioned to Doane's left, to push the Indians away from the bluffs closest to the oxbow. The men only made it halfway before they realized the futility of the maneuver. Ball could easily see that there were too many warriors to engage effectively and recognized the prudence of returning to the command.[20]

As Doane watched the periodic "dare rides" of the hot-blooded young warriors across the front of his position, he noticed a peculiar event taking place far off to the northeast at the base of the bluffs. There, in a remarkable display of bravado, a lone Indian calmly dismounted from his pony, pulled out a tobacco pipe, and proceeded to sit down and light it. The Indian called to some of the younger men to cease their rides in front of the firing line to join him, and soon a small group had seated themselves around the smoker to display their courage. Doane ordered his men to fire at the knot of warriors; but in spite of their best efforts, Sitting Bull and his companions managed to finish their leisurely smoke unscathed while the ineffectively aimed bullets of the soldiers rained down all around them.[21]

By full daylight the Indians had withdrawn completely, but the attack had so rattled Major Baker that he waited until nearly noon before sending Captain Ball out to reconnoiter along the bluff line. The major initially announced his intention to pursue the enemy; but as one officer ungenerously remembered, "he soon forgot all about it or changed his mind."[22] Three soldiers had been wounded in the battle, and one killed, along with the loss of several cattle and a few mules. Aside from that, the soldiers had remained masters of the field and withstood the assault of a much larger force in spite of the confusion of their commanding officer. The survey continued the next day, following down the Yellowstone River. When they reached Pompey's Pillar on August 19, the engineers became too nervous to continue the work. Feeling the need for a much larger force for protection, the railroad men requested Major Baker to escort them back to the west via the Musselshell River, leaving the work of the survey incomplete that summer.

Although Baker could later claim to have repulsed a large force commanded by the legendary Sitting Bull and Crazy Horse, the major and his officers had to face the ugly rumors regarding their sobriety during the fight. This time even Doane's skill in crafting a report could not obscure the independent confirmation of Baker's drunken poker game. Peter Koch, a Bozeman store clerk who heard about the battle from one of the civilians who returned that summer, wrote his family that the survey expedition ended in failure because of "Col. Baker's drunkenness and incapacity, and unless the affair is hushed up, which I trust it will not be, he will doubtlessly be dismissed from the service."[23] After being informed about the battle on his return from Yellowstone National Park, Col. John Gibbon expressed himself at least as forcibly. Gibbon believed Baker's "condition" during the fight was such that Captain Rawn would have been justified in taking command and that Major Baker should have been placed under arrest.[24] For Doane the accusations proved a personal disaster. Baker would face a court of inquiry regarding the affair and was eventually transferred from command of Fort Ellis in February 1873. Baker had proven a valuable ally for Doane, but subsequent commanders would prove entirely different.

During the winter of 1872–73 Doane tried to attract the attention of his superiors with another well-crafted report, this time featuring an innovative idea. Since Captain Barlow had already filed the report on the battle at "Poker Flats," Doane had to find a unique topic to supplement the official dispatch that would allow him again to demonstrate his gifts as a writer. He chose to focus on an aspect of the railroad survey that had been entirely overlooked. All during the arduous journeys down the Yellowstone the previous two summers the supplies for the soldiers and railroad men had been hauled overland in clumsy freight wagons. Doane could not help but observe that the route they took paralleled the river so closely that the river afforded a much easier way to transport the tons of rations required by the expedition. His natural talents as an inventor also came into play; and in January 1873 Doane composed a detailed report on the problem and its solution. He suggested the construction of freight-hauling flatboats, forty feet long and twelve feet wide, with a depth of about three feet, estimating the cost of building the boats to the penny. He insisted that boats of his design could easily haul all of the forage required for a cavalry escort on shore and could maintain the same speed. Doane also compared the costs of his plan with that of the expeditions in 1871 and 1872, claiming that his plan would have saved the army $33,843.50 on the 1872 expedition alone. Departing from his usual verbose literary style, he tersely summarized the advantages: "no animals to be herded or lost. No roads to grade. Independence of grazing. Travel without fatigue. Security against surprise. Avoidance of the Bad Lands. Mobility."[25]

Capt. David P. Hancock, Major Baker's temporary replacement in command of Fort Ellis, forwarded the report to the headquarters of the Department of Dakota with his own endorsement. "Lt. Doane has given the subject a great deal of attention," he wrote, "and his opinions in regard to the matter should have great weight."[26] The report made its way to Gen. Philip H. Sheridan, commanding the Military Division of the Missouri. Although he praised Doane's inventiveness, Sheridan only returned a curt letter of thanks for the report, with no indication that any of the ideas the lieutenant had advanced would ever be implemented.[27]

A new commanding officer arrived at Fort Ellis shortly after Doane submitted his report to the vacuum of the army's bureaucracy. Maj. Nelson B. Sweitzer, an 1849 West Point graduate, had served the army with distinction his entire adult life. He enjoyed General Sheridan's personal confidence and a reputation as one of the army's most capable officers. Sweitzer established a cordial relationship with Doane, easily recognizing the lieutenant's literary skills, but it is doubtful the two officers enjoyed as close a bond as Doane had with Major Baker. Nevertheless, Sweitzer kept Doane busy with routine military duties during his first few months at Fort Ellis until another opportunity came up for an officer who could provide an accurate survey of a particular territory's resources.

By the summer of 1873 the pressure of gold seekers, settlers, railroad surveyors, and other Indian tribes on the boundaries of the Crow Reservation became a great problem for the commissioner of Indian affairs. A treaty with the Crows on May 7, 1868, stipulated that six million acres were to be granted the tribe as its reservation south of the Yellowstone River; but the proposed route of the Northern Pacific favored the south bank for part of the way, straight through the Crow lands. The location of the agency headquarters, established in 1869 at Mission Creek on the extreme western end of the reservation, also became problematical for the government. The Mission Creek location had been chosen partially to draw the Crows away from the Sioux who roamed the country to the east, but by 1872 white settlers had begun claiming land immediately opposite on the north side of the river.[28] Finally, the army wanted to establish two new posts along the Yellowstone: one near the mouth of the Powder River, and another near the mouth of the Bighorn, primarily to keep the Sioux out of the Crow country.[29]

In June 1872 the superintendent of Indian affairs for Montana, Jasper A. Viall, asked the Crow agent Fellows D. Pease to ascertain the feeling of the Crows toward changing their reservation. The commissioner of Indian affairs in Washington next dispatched Felix I. Brunot to all of the Indians residing along the proposed route of the Northern Pacific Railroad to advance the negotiations. On August 16, 1873, Brunot and his aides made an agreement with the Crows by which they were to give up their Yellowstone reserve of 6,272,000 acres in exchange for one of 3,625,000 in the Judith Basin.[30] After Brunot left, Dr. James M. Wright replaced Pease as the new Crow agent and immediately sent out a team to make a survey of the basin. His report, dated November 26, 1873, enthusiastically described the reservation site and the proposed location for an agency. Due to a bureaucratic mixup, however, the commissioner in Washington wrote to Pease on November 12 requesting that the former agent perform a survey of the Judith Basin, without realizing one had already been conducted by Wright. The request specifically mentioned Doane as the officer to accompany the survey, evidence that his 1871 Yellowstone report had established the lieutenant's reputation as a competent writer among officials beyond the War Department.[31] The assignment would allow Doane to produce an exploration report that would rival Hayden's in detail and would be submitted to the Department of the Interior, the very same agency that sponsored the professor's Yellowstone investigations. The fact that general features of the Judith Basin were already well known to military and civilian officials alike did little to dampen Doane's enthusiasm, and he resolved to put his descriptive talents to work as if the region had never before been seen by white men.

The expedition almost died in the planning due to Doane's overreaching ambition. The Bureau of Indian Affairs had warned Pease of the limited funds available for the survey; when Doane requested a junior officer, forty men, and five wagons for a fifty-day trip, the commissioner objected. After a series of telegram exchanges, Doane pared down his requirements to a sergeant, six men, and two wagons. The more realistic request had the desired results, and the expedition left Fort Ellis on December 16. Arriving at the Crow agency two days later, Doane asked Dr. Wright to send for the important chiefs of the tribe. He wanted a conference concerning the proposed reservation and to urge several chiefs to accompany the exploring party. In this and subsequent dealings with Indians, Doane demonstrated an appalling lack of understanding and lack of empathy for their culture. He complained about the delay of four days as the men waited for the Crow elders to assemble. Once the Indians arrived and the conference began, Doane grumbled that "its proceedings were farcical to the last degree."[32]

Doane seemed unable to understand Dr. Wright's practice of the diplomacy necessary to deal effectively with the Indians, allowing them to while away the hours in ceremonial smoking and lengthy speeches of greetings and complaints. Wright told the Crows that he could give no guarantee that the place Doane and Pease would select in the Judith Basin would be the final location of the new agency, an honest assessment of the situation but one Doane felt designed to discourage cooperation. Wright also implied that he would not issue annuities to the Indians unless some of the headmen remained to help with the distribution. To Doane's limited understanding the agent's comments seemed to be designed to convince none of the Indian dignitaries to accompany the party, because the "near approaching issue of the annuities was made ludicrously prominent."[33] Doane finally got a chance to harangue the Crow chiefs himself and bluntly demanded they hold the annuities for any volunteers who would agree to accompany the survey. "Of course the Indians all wished to stay," he remembered, "for to any Indian a present blanket counts for more than a future farm."[34] The Crows understandably reacted to Doane's requirements with indifference, because it made perfect sense that the government's largess in the form of blankets and rations at the agency was a more tangible reward than another vague promise of land allocation for their benefit. Unfortunately Doane could not fathom their logic. "The Indians consented that annuities might be issued to those going with us," he said, "but none of them appeared to care to go, nor did any of them seem to care about the matter whether their reservation and agency were moved at all."[35] With this inauspicious start Doane launched his career as the army's chief liaison with the Crow Nation, and time would show him to be a poor choice for the job.

The party left the agency on December 23 accompanied by only one Indian: Pretty Lodge, a chief of the River Crows. The expedition journeyed up the north bank of the Yellowstone to Hunter's Hot Springs, the new health spa constructed by Dr. Andrew Jackson Hunter. Hunter, a Missouri native who had been in the territory since 1864, established his claim at the landmark and began construction in early 1872. By the time of Doane's visit the complex boasted a bath house made of tightly fitted hewn timbers and some cabins for the Hunter family and the doctor's patients. At that time Hunter's family members, consisting of his wife and six children that the unreconstructed Southerner had named after Confederate generals, were all in residence at the hot springs, including the precocious fourteen-year-old Mary Lee Hunter. This could have been Doane's first meeting with Dr. Hunter, or perhaps they had encountered one another in 1870 when the doctor briefly served as a contract physician at Fort Ellis. In any case, the lieutenant obviously made a favorable impression on the family that would lead to closer relations in the future.

Doane guided the expedition up the Sweet Grass Creek drainage and then over the divide to the forks of the Musselshell River. Here they paused for a day due to a severe snowstorm before thoroughly scouting the area. Pease became favorably impressed with its resources, but he also realized that it stood in the crossroads of two established trading routes, which would further the discontent of the Crows should the agency be located there. On December 29 they pushed on through Judith Gap and entered the basin itself, carefully measuring distances and noting the resources for possible settlement. Near the intersection of Trout Creek with the Judith River, a trading post licensed by the Crow agency had recently been established by Bozeman businessman Nelson Story and his partners. Doane and his survey team arrived there on January 2, 1874, and took advantage of the hospitality offered them by the resident trader, Peter Koch. Koch, a Danish immigrant who had come to Montana in 1869, had been busy erecting buildings and a crude stockade to compete with other posts along the Missouri River for the lucrative Indian fur trade. James Stuart, another frontiersman with the trading post enterprise, told Doane how he had been sent by Dr. Wright to ask the Indians living in villages along the Missouri to come down to the Yellowstone agency for their annuities. At one of the villages, Stuart found W. H. Fanton, the Fort Belknap Indian agent, who refused to allow the Crows to return to their own agency. After Fanton threatened him with arrest, Stuart left the villages on the Missouri to tell Wright about the incident. Along the way he was attacked by Indians, his horse was shot, and he was forced to return to Koch's trading post on foot.[36]

If the army's bumbling efforts in Indian relations could be illustrated in its choice of Doane as emissary to the Crows, Stuart's adventures at least demonstrated a parallel confusion among the Indian Bureau employees in dealing with their charges. For his part, Doane did not hesitate to point out the mistakes of the agents in their conflicting claims for the management of the Crows. "A circumstance like this goes to show that however unanimous these gentlemen may be on the main issue," Doane wrote about the agent's argument over jurisdiction, "there appears to be some difficulty as to 'dividing the raiment.' "[37]

Doane and his command remained at the trading post for a week, scouting out a large warm water creek to the north and gathering information.[38] Peter Koch helped Doane draw a detailed map of the area, because Pease felt the location near the trading post would be the most practical for a new agency. During this time a group of Crows from the Missouri River camp drifted into the post, and Doane observed firsthand the evils that alcohol had brought to the Indians. The River Crows seemed to Doane "a ragged and dirty looking lot . . . very inferior to the Mountain Crows both physically and mentally," but he drew the comparison based on a chance meeting with only a few of the Indians.[39] The visiting River Crows substantiated Stuart's report on agent Fanton's hostility and confirmed the full-scale whiskey traffic taking place along the Missouri. In addition to Fanton's resistance to their movement to the Yellowstone to get their annuities, the Indians said the whiskey traders also used their influence, claiming they had supernatural powers to make it snow and starve all the Crow ponies if they went south. "It was easy to see that these Indians had been getting whiskey from their appearance," Doane remarked after describing their blotched noses, "and if Mr. Fanton failed to discover the fact and failed to report the same, he has certainly been neglectful of his duties."[40]

On January 15 Doane led his party back to the forks of the Musselshell and headed back for Fort Ellis, reaching the post at the end of the month after a grueling march through heavy snow. Once back at the post, he began the work on the report. After dispensing with a brief description of his command's geographic investigations with Pease, Doane critically evaluated the manuscript. He wanted the report to be published and realized the matter-of-fact description of a well-known area had little chance to duplicate the success of his Yellowstone journal. He set to work with a passion, adding no less than six appendices to the report, one a lengthy rehash of the geography of the Upper Yellowstone, as if Doane intended to remind his audience of his role in the "discovery" of the park. The other essays described the habits of the plains buffalo, meteorological conditions of Fort Ellis and the Judith Basin, and the effects of the whiskey and buffalo trade on the Indians. Editorializing on the last topic allowed Doane to present his views as an expert in military-Indian relations, an approach that most military officers of the time would have taken. The alleged advantages of transferring the management of western tribes to the War Department were never entirely abandoned by the army throughout the late nineteenth century.

In Doane's summary on the fur and liquor traffic he argued that independent traders, licensed for each tribe, allowed the Indians to travel from one agency to another, causing a great deal of competition for robes. Doane asserted that the Indians conceived an exaggerated idea of their own importance as manufacturers and producers, believing that the whites depended on Indians for articles of necessity and would grant them immunity for any depredations if they would only afterward consent to trade. He listed several incidents of annuities offered to tribesmen who had fought settlers, claiming without any substantiation that the examples were "only a few out of hundreds of instances where Indians have come home from raids with hands red with the blood of white men and have been supplied as if they had been continually at peace."[41] Doane also recognized the culpability of white frontiersmen in exacerbating tensions with the Indians and condemned the Missouri River whiskey trade in the strongest terms. "The larger traders do not trade whiskey," he reported, "but they sell it to emissaries of the vilest class, on credit, without asking questions; and afterwards buy robes and skins from these people at a previously stipulated price."[42] He even accused some agents of the Indian Bureau of collusion in the trade by either profiting directly or at the very least looking the other way when whiskey became the bartering item of choice. "If a man looking out in the morning sees the landscape covered with snow," Doane argued, "he does not need oral testimony to convince him that the snow fell from the clouds and would disbelieve any amount of evidence to the contrary."[43]

The report had none of the results Doane had hoped for. It did not become part of the published annual report by the commissioner of Indian affairs; nor did the government even carry through with its plans to move the Crow reservation agency to Trout Creek. An executive order of President Grant dated January 3, 1874, set aside the Judith Basin as a reserve; but with the threat of such a fertile region being reserved for the Indians, powerful civilian interests in Montana Territory became alarmed. Early in the spring of 1874, Brig. Gen. Alfred H. Terry, in charge of the Department of Dakota, received requests from frontier entrepreneurs for assistance in opening a road cutting through the heart of the Judith Basin. Well aware of the previous surveys that had explored the basin for purpose of establishing a new reservation, Terry gave the requested military guard anyway. Ironically enough, Doane himself received orders in May to lead a road-building crew cutting a path from Fort Ellis through to the mouth of the Musselshell, near where the new post of Carroll Landing had been established. Once constructed, the road proved very popular among white settlers, and they rushed into the basin in spite of the Executive Order setting it aside as a reserve. In the summer of 1875 the Indian Bureau again reversed its promises to the Crows and finally relocated the tribe in the valley of the Bighorn, even closer to their Sioux enemies than previously.

One unexpected benefit of his survey would return to Doane, a benefit of dubious value to his ambition. Even though the report had not been deemed worthy of publication and had done absolutely nothing toward changing the policy of handling the Indian trade or relocating the headquarters for the Crow reservation, the military came to the erroneous conclusion that Doane had a deep understanding of the tribe and its customs. As a result, Doane became the army's emissary of choice to the Crows, a position that would lead to some of the greatest disappointments of his life.

CHAPTER 6

"There is such an element in human affairs as fortune, good or bad"

The Snake River Expedition

D oane's frustration at the lack of recognition he craved only intensified after the Interior Department neglected to publish his massive Judith Basin report.[1] He most likely realized that unless he was given another choice assignment like the 1870 Yellowstone survey, his one claim to fame would be quietly forgotten, the very fate he was determined to avoid. Garrison duty at Fort Ellis, consisting of endless drilling, inspections, and building maintenance, took up the bulk of his waking hours in 1874, and even the chances for distinction as a combat officer appeared remote. Maj. Nelson B. Sweitzer reacted to sporadic horse-stealing raids by the Indians by posting a small contingent at Flathead Pass, an entryway into the Gallatin Valley through the Bridger Mountains about thirty miles northwest of Fort Ellis; but nothing really happened there. Although Doane took his turn in several troop rotations at the outpost during the summer of 1874, the only military action ever reported from Flathead Pass was the accidental shooting of several ranch horses one night when 2nd Lt. Lovell H. Jerome ordered his command to fire a volley in the direction of hoofbeats he heard in the darkness.[2] Jerome's "battle" underscored the lack of opportunity Doane felt; and as the months passed slowly his desperation for recognition would drive him to the brink of madness.

Doane's ambition caused him to suggest impossible assignments to his superiors, none more audacious than a plan to explore the Nile River in Africa. In the early 1870s the continent of Africa had engaged the imagination of American newspaper readers, especially after the famous expedition of *New York Herald* reporter Henry B. Stanley in search of Dr. David Livingstone. Stanley's alleged query "Dr. Livingstone, I presume?" became one of the most recognized quotations in the English-speaking world and rekindled the popular American image of the explorer as a daring hero. Doane craved the notice that Stanley earned and mistakenly thought he could interest the United States government in exploring Africa's interior by approaching the Smithsonian Institution rather than the army to sponsor an expedition. On September 1, 1874, Doane composed a lengthy letter conveying the breathless reach of his aspirations to the secretary of the Smithsonian, Professor Joseph Henry. He wrote that "under great embarrassment" he had to admit certain abilities that few other men possessed,[3] including an uncanny talent for finding his way in any region. "This faculty of travel I possess," he asserted, claiming never to have failed in accurately guiding troops since his first appointment with the regiment in 1868. Eager to describe his prowess as a pathfinder, Doane fell back on a particularly ironic stereotype when he bragged, "I always travel as an Indian does, without guide or compass, and do not know what it is to have the sensation of being lost."[4]

In his effort to impress the Smithsonian, Doane presented a detailed plan on how he intended to conduct his survey of the Nile, but his braggadocio obscured the technical points. Doane again made the error of attempting to advance his own stature by denigrating that of others. He summarily dismissed the announced intentions of Henry M. Stanley to return to Africa for the exploration of the Nile. "The [first] exploration of Stanley, its object being to hunt a man and not explore a country, was a success . . . ," he said, "but Stanley lacks calibre. He does well what he is sent to do, but does not rise to the Conception of Great Achievements."[5] Doane's aspirations interfered with judgment as to the possible effects of his tactless solicitation. When Professor Henry wrote back, he diplomatically observed, "It is to be regretted that the proprietor of the *New York Herald* was not cognizant of your qualifications and desires since . . . he has just sent Stanley out a second time to carry on African explorations."[6]

Instead of taking Professor Henry's subtle hint that sensational newspaper publishers would be the proper source for overseas expedition sponsors, Doane stubbornly continued to pursue government sanction for his idea and applied for leave to travel to Washington, D.C., himself. It is not clear whether Amelia accompanied him on this ill-advised journey, but he spent all of January 1875 at the nation's capital buttonholing every politician and high-ranking officer he could find to promote his African scheme. He even applied for a two-month extension to his leave when it briefly appeared that secretary of war William W. Belknap indicated a slight interest in the idea; but the only thing Doane accomplished during his time in Washington was making a favorable impression on Belknap before the secretary turned him down.

Doane's furious round of lobbying may not have convinced Belknap to support the Africa scheme, but the secretary of war recognized a good traveling companion when he saw one. Belknap planned a pleasure jaunt to Yellowstone for the summer of 1875 with several sportsmen friends, including the army's inspector general, Col. Randolph B. Marcy, Lt. Col. James W. Forsyth, and William E. Strong, a Chicago businessman and attorney. Doane would make the perfect guide for his well-heeled party, Belknap decided, and he told the lieutenant that the necessary arrangements would be made to give him the assignment. This golden opportunity to demonstrate his talents to the army's highest echelons buoyed Doane's sprits, and he returned to Fort Ellis at the beginning of May with the hope of continuing to advance his stature in spite of the Africa disappointment.

When Belknap led his distinguished party to Fort Ellis on July

26, Doane had already left for Mammoth Hot Springs with a mule train laden with camping equipment and luxuries such as fresh eggs, champagne, and camp furniture. Belknap and his party, accompanied by Major Sweitzer, departed the next day in two ambulances with an escort of twenty-four soldiers. Doane barely had time to get the camp prepared for the dignitaries before their arrival that evening because the pack mules had given him so much trouble. Nonetheless he managed to get the cooks to prepare a sumptuous dinner of ham, teal, and grouse for the enjoyment of the secretary and his friends. Pvt. William White, one of Doane's favorites who had been chosen to accompany the pack train, recalled that the lieutenant would often eat with the enlisted men during the trip, jesting in his coarse, rough manner about the "feather bed" dudes they had been assigned to shepherd through the wilderness.[7] When not trying to impress the enlisted men with his egalitarian manners, however, Doane devoted a fair amount of time trying to give Secretary Belknap and his friends the impression he was the epitome of the gentleman explorer. "Lieutenant Doane, who is the guide for our party . . . is a striking officer," wrote William Strong in his diary. "Tall, straight as an arrow, very dark complexion, with black hair and a long, sweeping, dark mustache, he would certainly attract attention in any company. This is his fourth trip into the park and he is perfectly familiar with it and knows more about the wonders it contains than anybody. In this country he is spoken of and pointed out as the man who 'invented Wonderland.' "[8]

Strong's admiration notwithstanding, Doane's perceived status as a Yellowstone Park expert suffered while he led the party through the country. Belknap's friends had come to hunt big game in the park, and after several days of spotting none they turned to Doane for an answer. He claimed that the shortage of elk could be explained by the fact the ungulates preferred higher elevations during the summer, causing even the admiring Strong to grumble: "We have seen no elk as yet, and I am sure we were high enough today."[9] In addition to his questionable explanations on the wildlife, Doane had trouble with topography as well. After taking the men to the rim of the Grand Canyon of the Yellowstone for a brief peek, Doane lost the trail completely; if not actually experiencing the "sensation of being lost," he certainly gave that impression to Secretary Belknap. Doane spent hours in the woods reconnoitering while the party members waited with their horses tethered, growing more impatient as the sunlight began to fade. "The Secretary and General Forsyth were annoyed and disgusted at the way Doane led us," Strong admitted. "Doane seems to have the most magnificent contempt for a trail."[10]

At least one incident occurred to help Doane's reputation before the trip concluded. Colonel Marcy, during an enthusiastic fishing excursion, managed to drench himself in the Yellowstone River; and as the days passed he developed a serious illness. By the time the party camped in the Upper Geyser Basin on August 5, Marcy's condition had deteriorated to the point of threatening his life. Doane rose to the occasion with his inventive talent and devised a special litter, consisting of two poles strapped to the pack saddles of a pair of mules positioned one behind the other. With a lacing of rawhide to connect the poles, the contraption provided support for a comfortable bed padded with blankets and robes. Doane chose the most gentle mules for the purpose and took the precaution of assigning an enlisted man to ride each one as they loaded up the sick man and prepared to get him back to Mammoth Hot Springs. Marcy eventually recovered enough to ride again before the trip was over, but Doane had succeeded somewhat in regaining Belknap's good graces by demonstrating his inventiveness, if not his woodsmanship.

Doane had tried his best to impress Belknap and to reestablish his fading reputation as the man who "discovered" Yellowstone National Park. Evidence that he partially succeeded came after the secretary and his friends left Montana. Belknap gave the lieutenant an expensive set of binoculars as a thank-you present.[11] On his return to Chicago, William Strong published a limited edition of his travel diary, complete with photographs of Doane and all the other participants. "Doane saw it first, wrote the first report, and brought it all to the attention of the world," Strong wrote of the lieutenant's Yellowstone accomplishments. "Give him the credit."[12]

Even with a favorable notice in an obscure publication, along with a tangible expression of gratitude from the secretary of war, Doane did not gain the favoritism he needed to pursue his exploration schemes. After Belknap returned to Washington, D.C., accusations by government investigators of corruption within the War Department grew more and more strident. On March 7, 1876, the secretary of war was impeached by a unanimous vote of the House of Representatives. Whatever assistance Doane thought he could count on for Africa or any other exploration proposals ended along with Belknap's career. Another serious blow to Doane's ambition came in spring 1876 when a new commanding officer was assigned to Fort Ellis.

Maj. James Sanks Brisbin arrived at the frontier post on February 9, 1876, as a replacement for Major Sweitzer. Thirty-nine years old and a brevet major general, Brisbin had enjoyed every success in his military career that Doane had been denied. Like Doane, Brisbin had come from a modest family and obtained a classical education at a private college. Also like his ambitious subordinate, the new commanding officer had entered the Civil War as a private soldier in a volunteer regiment and risen from the ranks. But while Doane's dismal experiences in the war kept him from advancing beyond the rank of lieutenant, Brisbin seemed to gain distinction and promotion by consistently being in the right place at the right time. By war's end he had achieved the rank of colonel in the volunteer army. After mustering out of the volunteer service in 1866 he joined the Second Cavalry with the rank of major. An able orator who had gained fame as an abolitionist speaker, Brisbin also had some talents as a writer, completing the list of categories in which he had bested Doane.[13] Friction between the two seemed unavoidable, but it was delayed by a season of unusually intense activity.

Major Brisbin took command of Fort Ellis just as the opening events of the Great Sioux War transpired. The interference of the Sioux with the railroad surveys along the lower Yellowstone, along with their understandable rage over the 1875 invasion by gold miners of their sacred lands in the Black Hills, led to the military campaign of 1876. Demanded by the Interior Department to report to assigned reservations by January 31 or be considered "hostile," the

Sioux who insisted on their 1868 treaty rights were thus automatically deemed at war with the United States. Massive operations by the War Department got underway in March to crush the Indians with a three-pronged attack designed to encircle and destroy them. The plan, formulated by Gen. Philip Sheridan, called for one force to be led north from Wyoming into southeast Montana by Brig. Gen. George Crook while troops simultaneously moving west from Dakota, led by Gen. Alfred Terry and his subordinate, Lt. Col. George Armstrong Custer, marched into the same area. A third force, informally called the "Montana Column," would be led east from Forts Shaw and Ellis by District of Montana commander Col. John Gibbon, with the cavalry battalions under the direct supervision of Major Brisbin.

Colonel Gibbon led his infantry troops south from Fort Shaw to Fort Ellis, arriving at the latter post on March 28, where they received a hearty welcome. Dinner parties (presumably without drink for the teetotaling Gibbon) were mixed with arduous preparations on the part of the cavalry battalion to join the expedition. Doane had met Gibbon before on the general's previous visits to Fort Ellis and probably had listened to the colonel's temperance lectures at the post's Good Templar lodge with interest,[14] but circumstances suggest that the lieutenant had yet to gain Gibbon's complete confidence. The expedition got underway on April 1: Gibbon pushed the command down the Yellowstone valley to the confluence of the Stillwater River and on to the new Crow Agency at Rosebud Creek to enlist scouts for the command. Instead of Doane, Gibbon chose 1st Lt. James H. Bradley of the Seventh Infantry to accompany him to the agency. After successfully enlisting twenty-five warriors, the colonel placed them under Bradley's command. Blackfoot, one of the chiefs who met with Gibbon in council, told the colonel that his warriors would "want white men with them who can speak their language,"[15] but Bradley could not fulfill this requirement any more than Doane could. The selection of Bradley to lead the scouts suggests that Gibbon did not share the army's perception of Doane's strong familiarity with the tribe.[16]

If Doane felt snubbed by the Gibbon's choice he kept it to him-

self and instead used what contact he had with the colonel to interest him in a new tent design that summer. Ever since his days with
the California Hundred, Doane had been familiar with the Sibley
tent, a conical design that tautly staked out the canvas sides supported by a single center pole. Like the tipi of the Plains Indians, the
Sibley tent withstood fierce wind very well, but the shelter sacrificed
headroom for the occupants by the sharp angle of the shelter's
anchored bottom edge with the apex of the pole. Doane's solution
to the problem was to allow a short wall to descend from the bottom
edge and to stake down the edge by lead ropes, rather than directly
attaching the edge to the ground. This simple innovation increased
the headroom space dramatically and allowed the suspended wall to
be raised in hot weather to permit ventilation. Doane had several
handmade examples of his invention sewn at Fort Ellis, and a few
traveled with his company that summer. By the time the Montana
Column reached Fort Pease on April 20, Gibbon had become thoroughly fascinated with Doane's tents and the lieutenant's suggestion that they could both profit from it should army officials adopt
the innovation.[17]

At Fort Pease, an abandoned trading post near the mouth of the
Bighorn River, the campaign had stalled long enough to allow such
speculative daydreams by Doane's commanding officer. Once Gibbon had reached the fort he learned the other two wings of the
planned troop movements would not be underway for several
weeks. Aside from sending out a scouting party up the valley of the
Bighorn River, the soldiers at Fort Pease had little to do. Doane may
have privately gloated when the cumbersome supply trains sent
back to Fort Ellis periodically bogged down while some of Bozeman's private merchants easily managed to float luxuries such fresh
vegetables and kegs of beer down the Yellowstone on flatboats to the
soldiers' camp.[18] Had the army heeded his report on river transportation, all of the expedition's supplies could have come the same
way. Doane could also feel quiet vindication over Lieutenant Bradley's misfortunes. The Crow scouts lost every horse they had one
night to some stealthy Sioux raiders, setting them temporarily afoot
and completely neutralizing their effectiveness for the army.[19]

Bradley eventually got replacement mounts for his scouts, but Doane could be thankful the loss did not happen on his watch.

Colonel Gibbon eventually led his little army farther down the Yellowstone. When Bradley's scouts reported a large village in the Rosebud River valley, Gibbon briefly considered attacking it. Major Brisbin tried to cross to the south bank of the Yellowstone with his cavalry, but the process proved slow and dangerous. After four horses drowned and only one company partially crossed in the course of an entire afternoon's labor, Gibbon called off the attack and thereby likely saved his own command from the fate that would befall Custer's men a few short weeks later. By attacking a village of unknown strength, without the option of calling on additional supporting troops, Gibbon's proposed foray would have stood a very small chance of success.

Gen. Alfred Terry, commanding the force sent out from Fort Abraham Lincoln in Dakota Territory, finally rendezvoused with the Montana Column on June 9 when the steamboat *Far West* came churning up the Yellowstone River toward Gibbon's camp near the mouth of the Powder. Doane accompanied Brisbin and Gibbon on board for the initial conference. There they learned that Custer, with the rest of the Seventh Cavalry, was approaching their position from the south bank of the Yellowstone. Terry's plan, outlined to the officers present, called for the Montana Column to backtrack to Fort Pease and cross the Yellowstone with the assistance of the steamboat, while Custer would sweep south and west from the Powder toward the valley of the Little Bighorn. With Gibbon's force moving south along the Bighorn valley and Custer moving north, Terry felt sure the Indians would be trapped between them.

General Terry accompanied the Montana Column and allowed Custer to lead the Seventh Cavalry himself, without the addition of Brisbin's battalion or either of the two Gatling gun batteries that had been offered. Custer refused the offered assistance on the grounds that it would impede his progress and by so doing for a second time that summer spared Doane and the rest of Brisbin's battalion possible annihilation. Custer left the rendezvous point and led his command to their spectacular defeat at the Little Bighorn on June 25, while Terry led the Montana Column south from the Yellowstone River paralleling the Bighorn. After days of hard marching, the soldiers reached the battlefield on June 27 and discovered the bodies of Custer's command scattered across the barren hillsides across the river from the abandoned site of a huge Indian village. They also found the survivors of the battle, commanded by Maj. Marcus A. Reno, on another hill several miles to the south, who had held off the victorious warriors in two days of desperate fighting.

For once during the disastrous campaign Doane got an opportunity to distinguish himself. Many wounded soldiers among the survivors required speedy evacuation to the *Far West,* but the steamboat could get no closer to the battlefield than the mouth of the Little Bighorn River, about fifteen miles away over fairly rough terrain. Carrying the wounded by hand-held litters over such a distance proved to be agonizingly slow for all concerned, and Doane quickly saw the solution in the dozens of dead horses and abandoned tipi poles that littered the site of the former Indian village. He ordered his men to skin the horses, cut the hide into strips, and begin weaving the material to connect the tipi poles. By manufacturing copies of the same two-mule litter he had used to get Colonel Marcy out of Yellowstone the previous year, Doane got the wounded men quickly off the field and back to the boat with a minimum of discomfort. The whole operation so impressed Terry that he asked Doane to write a report describing the invention, which he did a week later, in his usual meticulous style.[20]

The campaign against the Sioux continued until September. Doane stayed in the field with his company for the duration but saw no action. He used his newly won favor with General Terry to lobby for another exploration scheme that summer and even worked out a preliminary business arrangement with Colonel Gibbon for the marketing of the "Centennial Tent." When Col. Nelson A. Miles arrived in Montana with his Fifth Infantry command in August, Doane managed to curry favor with him as well, probably as a natural result of his warm relationship with Terry and Gibbon. By the time the Second Cavalry returned to Fort Ellis on September 3,

Doane's service over the summer had earned him praise in all these officers' official reports, and he was singled out for special mention in Gibbon's published version of the Montana Column's summer operations as an officer of "energy, skill, and confidence."[21] The public notice of his services gave Doane the impression that he had at last cultivated the friendship of the correct men in a position to help him. Had he been more perceptive, however, he would have realized that he had overlooked a critical player whose name did not get mentioned for special praise in any of the same reports. Doane soon learned the consequences of failing to add Major Brisbin to the list of officers he wanted to cultivate.

Doane's reunion with Amelia at Fort Ellis in September 1876 was brief. She had only seen him for a few weeks during the entire year, enduring lengthy absences during which she felt his life to be in imminent peril, yet Doane had no plans to linger with her during a quiet winter at the Gallatin Valley garrison. No sooner had he returned to the fort than he began preparations to leave again, this time on the most ambitious project he had undertaken to date. The Snake River, with its headwaters in Yellowstone National Park and its 700-mile length unevenly charted, presented an opportunity that Doane convinced General Terry to endorse during the summer campaign. Like the Colorado River prior to Maj. John Wesley Powell's 1868 reconnaissance, the Snake River's central portion had never been completely explored, although it was vaguely known to traverse a massive canyon in a torrent of white-water rapids. Just as Powell had become famous for unlocking the secrets of the Grand Canyon, Doane hoped to make his own name by daring to descend the Snake in exactly the same way. He planned the trip down to the last detail, with the exception of one rather important point. Doane worked so hard to get Terry to authorize the expedition that he went completely over the head of his commanding officer, Major Brisbin.

Doane already had ordered the Fort Ellis carpenter shop to construct a special boat he had designed when Brisbin first heard about the proposed expedition. One can easily imagine the commander's reaction when he received a telegram from General Ter-

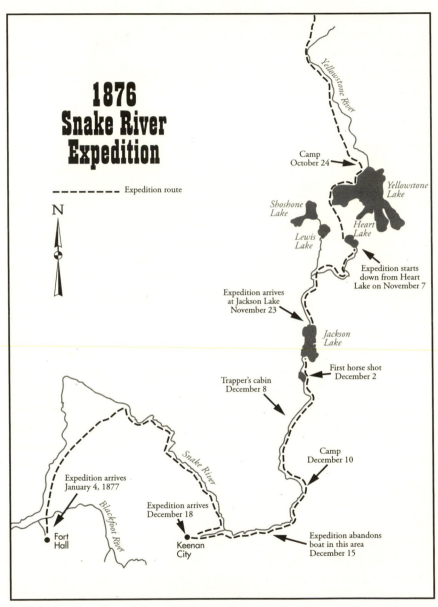

1876 Snake River Expedition

- - - - - - Expedition route

N

Camp
October 24

Yellowstone River

Yellowstone
Lake

Shoshone
Lake

Heart
Lake

Lewis
Lake

Expedition starts
down from Heart
Lake on November 7

Expedition arrives
at Jackson Lake
November 23

Jackson
Lake

First horse shot
December 2

Trapper's cabin
December 8

Camp
December 10

Snake River

Expedition arrives
January 4, 1877

Blackfoot River

Expedition arrives
December 18

Fort
Hall

Keenan
City

Expedition abandons
boat in this area
December 15

1876 Snake River Expedition.

ry's adjutant on October 4 ordering the post to provide Doane with the men and supplies he needed. If Doane's burning ambition had blinded him to the folly of starting such a journey so late in the year, Brisbin suffered no such illusion. He wrote angrily to Colonel Gibbon at Fort Shaw, complaining that he did not have enough officers at the post; but Gibbon had his own reasons for protecting Doane. The lieutenant's tent design had convinced the colonel that he could personally profit from a business partnership, and he directed Brisbin to comply with Terry's order.

While Major Brisbin fumed, Doane picked the men he wanted for the expedition. Sgt. Frederick E. Server and privates William H. White, C. B. Davis, Daniel Starr, John B. Warren, Fowler R. Applegate, Morgan Osborne, and John L. Ward were detailed to accompany Doane. Osborne had helped construct the boat from Doane's specifications, a large wooden craft with upturned bow and stern that could be disassembled, packed on mules, and rebuilt by means of wood screws and pitch caulking. Doane intended to launch the boat on Heart Lake in the southern portion of Yellowstone Park and ride it down the Snake River while some of the men paralleled the stream with the command's horses and mules, keeping the animals available to repack the boat for any difficult portage.

Doane wanted to start the journey by going through the entire length of Yellowstone Park for two reasons. The expedition could have started with much more efficiency at Fort Hall in southeastern Idaho Territory, the start of the unknown portion of the Snake, but that section flowed entirely through the boundaries of the Military Department of the Columbia. General Terry could only authorize the journey if it started in Yellowstone within the boundaries of his own geographic command, the Department of Dakota. A more important factor for Doane in planning the route, however, was his established habit of disparaging the accomplishments of others. By 1876 the headwaters of the Snake had been thoroughly mapped by the investigations of Ferdinand V. Hayden and other explorers. Subsequent events suggest that Doane believed he would get the opportunity to point out any geographic errors committed by his rivals and that the resulting report might help reestablish his claim to be the man who "discovered" Yellowstone. The proposed route would have presented no problem had the men started out in the beginning of the summer, but the lieutenant's insistence that they start just as winter descended on the Northern Rockies led to disaster.

Doane prepared his command by packing the boat, overcoats, rubber boots, map-making equipment, and sixty days' rations in a wagon pulled by eight pack mules. The party, all mounted on good horses, left Fort Ellis on October 11 and headed up the Yellowstone Valley toward Mammoth Hot Springs. Unfortunately, the wagon overturned once they got beyond Bottler's Ranch, dumping all of the equipment in the midst of Yankee Jim Canyon and "reducing the body to something resembling kindling wood."[22] This omen of the disasters to come forced the men to repack all of the supplies and the heavy boat on the mules, subjecting the animals to far more strain at this early part of the journey than Doane had anticipated. Other dangerous delays plagued the expedition, such as a fierce snowstorm that caught them at the base of Mount Washburn, which prevented them from reaching the shores of Lake Yellowstone until October 23. To spare the mules the continuing burden of packing all of the expedition supplies around the lake, Doane decided to assemble his boat, load all of the packs into it, and tow the craft along the shoreline. The men lost more time as they carefully assembled the boat. As Private White recalled, they carefully finished the job, and "there was no leak in that boat when we launched it."[23]

On October 27 Doane tied a team of mules to the boat and drove them along the shoreline as White tried to steer the craft from running into the beach. After fifteen miles of progress heavy waves completely swamped the vessel and soaked all of the supplies. The men spent the night in front of a roaring fire to dry out their belongings, and the next day Doane decided to split up the party. "I was very uneasy on account of the snow in sight on the continental Divide in front of us," he recalled, "and [I] decided to leave Starr, Applegate and Ward to recaulk the boat while the rest of us, with all the property on the packs, should push on, cross the divide, break a trail, and return with the mules and horses to the lake shore and meet the party with the boat."[24] Private White, who stayed with the

boat party along with Private Osborne, carefully packed all the expedition's flour, sugar, and salt in the boat with them as Doane
hurried away with the livestock, hoping that they could save the
mules' strength by repacking them once the men had rowed across
the West Thumb estuary of the lake.

While Doane picked out the trail over the divide to Heart Lake,
the boat detail worked feverishly to get the vessel seaworthy again,
fighting dropping temperatures and periodic snowstorms. They
waited until October 30 for a break in the weather before attempting the crossing and got halfway across the lake before another
fierce squall came up and mercilessly pounded the boat. "The boat
did not leak on the bottom nor at the sides," Private White wryly
recalled, "but there was a big leak in the air that was our only
covering from above!"[25] The icy water from the storm-tossed waves
threatened to sink the vessel and drown all on board, but fortunately Applegate and Starr had some sailing experience and knew
how to handle the emergency. They turned the bow into the wind
while everyone desperately bailed and alternated prayers with
curses. All day the fight for survival continued; aside from thoroughly soaking the men, the waves reduced the expedition's flour,
salt, and sugar to an inedible paste that pooled in the bottom of
the boat.

As the cavalrymen-turned-sailors fought for their lives, Doane
and Server waited on the south shore with "great apprehension."[26]
They had been to Heart Lake and back, expecting their comrades
already to be at the beach and prepared to continue, but all they
could see in the gloom of advancing nightfall was the churning of
the incredible waves on the lake's surface. Suddenly from out of the
darkness Doane and Server heard the roar of "double jointed profanity" above the storm as Private Starr pulled the boat to shore.
"We ran to meet them and helped them beach and unload the few
articles the boat contained," Doane recalled. "The oars were coated
an inch thick and the boat was half full of solid ice. When the three
men came in front of the campfire they were a sight to behold.
Their hair and beards were frozen to their caps and overcoats and
they were sheeted with glistening ice from head to foot."[27]

The party spent the night before a roaring fire to thaw out the frozen men, and the next morning Doane turned his attention to the boat itself. The flour-sugar-salt paste had frozen solid in the bottom of the boat, and the men used axes carefully to hack out chunks before placing burning embers on the remainder to thaw the ice and dry the wood. The next morning Doane decided to put runners on the boat to drag it over the snow with his rapidly weakening mules. Once they wrestled the boat over the divide and down to Heart Lake, Doane ordered privates Osborne and Ward to return to Fort Ellis with their horses and three of the weakest mules. The two thankfully took their leave of the expedition as the weather continued to worsen. Their arrival at Fort Ellis a week later would be the last word from the expedition for nearly two months.

Another round of caulking repairs took place on the shores of Heart Lake, conducted as the snow continued to fall and the temperature dropped. When the repairs were completed, Doane ordered the boat launched on November 6. Even then the danger of delay did not affect the lieutenant's behavior, for he insisted on periodically stopping as they rowed the boat across the lake to take meticulous measurements and scribble in his notebooks. Oblivious to the subzero temperatures and the rigors of Sergeant Server in getting the remaining mules to the outlet of the Snake on Heart Lake's southern shore, Doane wanted to make sure he recorded every measurement to check against Hayden's data and to point out any discrepancies to the world. By the time they reached the southern part of the lake, the men in the boat found it frozen over with a covering blanket of snow, effectively blockading their progress to the river's outlet. After leading two mules out onto the lake and dragging the boat over the frozen surface, they reached the start of the Snake River and found it a mere trickle of water within a rock-strewn streambed. They would have to haul the boat farther down the river until they met with sufficient water to float it, and again they had to repack their mules with all the expedition's supplies.

Day followed monotonous day as Doane and his men struggled to push their cumbersome boat down the stream while it steadily froze up for the winter. Agonizing delays plagued the party as they would periodically transfer loads from the boat to the pack mules and then, when the river's flow seemed sufficient, shift the loads back from the mules to the boat. Several days they made only two miles' progress. While the temperature continued to drop, they lost more of the starving draft animals. Doane began abandoning horses and mules on November 9; by November 26, two days after they ate the last of their flour, they had lost three mules and three horses, including the lieutenant's own mount.

Once the expedition reached Jackson Lake, the incredible cold and scant food began to tell on the men's strength too. Private Warren proved himself to be a capable fisherman, and Doane managed to down a blacktail deer on the lake's shore, but for the most part the countryside provided few additions to their swiftly depleting larder. Even these ominous developments could not shake Doane from his purpose, because he insisted on taking the time to measure and describe every natural feature in the area as if he was the first white man ever to have seen it. His obsession with besting Hayden had taken a very dangerous turn, which risked the lives of all his men. "At Jackson Lake we stayed in camp a week or longer while Doane made a survey of it," recalled Private White. "He made a map of it and jotted down many notes of the natural conditions around it."[28] If White or any of his comrades began to doubt the wisdom of lingering to survey a lake already well mapped, they kept it to themselves.

Toward the end of their stay at Jackson Lake the men suffered a debilitating attack of diarrhea, which weakened Sergeant Server so much that Doane had to detail Private Warren to lead the pack animals to the lower end of the lake while Server lay in the boat. When they finally reached the outlet of the Snake River on December 1, they had exhausted all of their food; even the fish that Warren caught that day could not relieve their fierce hunger. The next day, after a fruitless pursuit of elk, Doane ordered Warren's horse shot and butchered. The men ate the revolting boiled flesh by desperately attempting to season it with gunpowder instead of salt. "The meat cooked to a watery, spongy texture," Doane recalled, "the flesh tasted exactly as the perspiration of the animal smells."[29] In the cheerless cold of the Teton wilderness that night, the men gnawed at the meat until their jaws ached, rested a while, and then resumed the grim task of delaying their starvation.

The channel of the river widened enough to float the expedition's boat once they left Jackson Lake, but now the flow of water became so violent that handling the craft required constant vigilance. Unfortunately, the men struck a submerged rock on December 4, which punched a hole in the bottom of the boat, forcing them to lay over a day to fix it while trying to subsist on Private Warren's trout catch. No sooner had they launched it again than the boat hit another rock. This time the men had to spend the night of December 6 on a cold and barren island in the middle of the river, drying out before a huge fire and chewing desperately on the remaining horsemeat.

On December 7 the expedition had its only good luck when, following a game trail near a bend in the river, Sergeant Server stumbled on to an isolated trapper's cabin. John Pierce, "a gigantic, rawboned and grizzled old volunteer soldier,"[30] gasped incredulously as the two cavalrymen approached his mountain hideaway and begged for food. Pierce could not believe that anyone would be crazy enough to attempt a boat journey down the Snake in the middle of winter, but he fed the two a good meal and even gave them some salt out of his limited winter's supply. The old trapper appeared at Doane's camp the next day, carrying an elk quarter and some flour, for which the lieutenant gratefully traded extra clothing and ammunition. Doane also pumped Pierce for information on any settlements that might lie ahead along the Snake, because he realized his command would run out of food long before they ever reached Fort Hall.

When the men continued their downstream plunge the next day they faced the roughest water they had yet encountered as the river twisted through a defile they called the "Mad River Cañon." Sergeant Server had to lead the remaining livestock far from the river to ride along the hills overlooking the canyon while Doane and the others struggled to keep the boat upright, dashing here and there over rapids too severe to navigate. They had to walk along the icy shoreline of the river, holding the supply-laden boat by a tow rope, playing out the line until its end before moving forward to coil up the length for another start. For two days the men struggled across a nightmarish combination of frozen water and angry rapids, unable to ride in the boat. When their horsemeat ran out on December 11, they shot Private White's horse for more.

"It was evident that we were not going to run the cañon with the boat but must tug away slowly," Doane recalled, "[but] I desired to get the boat through if we had to risk everything to do so."[31] The risk of starvation stared the men in the face at this point, and even then Doane did not hesitate to gamble his own life as well as his command. He ordered all of them to pool what little money they had brought along and delegated Sergeant Server and Private Warren to ride the two remaining horses to Keenan City, one of the mining settlements Pierce had told them about. There they could buy food, Doane hoped, and the expedition would then be able to continue to Fort Hall, where they could draw government rations. The two men left the camp the next morning, leading the last emaciated pack mule, while Doane and the others again tried to walk the boat on the tow line down the rushing current like an unruly dog on a leash. In spite of the men's best efforts, disaster struck with stunning finality that afternoon.

The boat hit an unusually rough spot in the river, and a large chunk of floating ice hit the floundering vessel in just the right place. The boat jerked the tow line violently and, out of control, suddenly overturned in mid-current, spilling all of the expedition's equipment into the icy water. Doane and the others desperately tried to salvage the flotsam from the wreck, managing to snag some of the clothing and blankets; but all of the maps, notebooks, guns, and camping equipment went to the bottom of the Snake. Some matches, their sheath knives, and a miserable slab of stringy, tough horsemeat remained to carry the expedition through to Fort Hall. The situation changed from desperation to immediate peril. The men had no shelter and no idea if or when Server and Warren would be successful in their quest to find food. After two more days of slowly moving downstream, the men consumed the last of their horsemeat. Doane made the reluctant decision temporarily to abandon the expedition in order to save them all from starving to death.

On December 15 Doane, Applegate, Davis, Starr, and White stashed the boat as far from the edge of the river they could drag it. After also abandoning their blankets to save weight, they began the arduous climb out of the canyon up along its south wall. Once they had gained the canyon's rim, they looked out on a seemingly endless frozen wilderness with snow a yard deep at its shallowest and in some places piled up to the men's armpits. Slowly they followed the river along the edge of the canyon, having to descend deep crevices formed by tributaries that flowed into the Snake from the south. The up and down climbs sapped the men's fading strength, and in their weakened state each new challenge seemed insurmountable. At one such point on that terrible afternoon the strain finally proved too much for Doane.

While attempting to climb across the ice ledge of one tributary gulch, Doane became dizzy and had to crawl on his hands and knees to reach safety. Once there, he began shrieking uncontrollably, cursing and pounding the ground in impotent fury at the fates, which he felt had robbed him of the glory he craved. "Doane nearly went crazy," remembered Private Davis.[32] The others who gathered nervously around the ranting officer agreed. "That was the only time in all my association with Lieutenant Doane, past, present, and future, that I ever saw him show any sign of weakening," recalled Private White.[33] The enlisted men began to talk among themselves in order to calm Doane, and they purposely turned their conversation to a sarcastic nostalgic refection on how easy their lives had been back at Fort Ellis. This topic apparently touched a nerve in Doane and brought him out of his hysteria. "Brass buttons polished, boots shining, salute your superiors, starve to death on the prairie," he muttered ruefully. Getting to his feet and cursing, he turned to them and said, "Come on boys, let's be going."[34] Thoroughly embarrassed about his breakdown in front of the men, Doane vainly hoped that the incident would be forgotten and resumed leading the group on in their desperate race for food and shelter.

The expedition spent another freezing evening in front of a

blazing fire, completely chilled on one side and scorched on the other as they fitfully turned over and over during the long night. The cold dawn found them pushing on again, their steps becoming steadily shorter and their stops for rest steadily longer. Private Davis in particular felt the starvation affecting his reason, and Doane had to keep an eye on the delirious soldier to keep him from wandering away from his comrades. The biting cold tortured the struggling men and forced them to build a fire each time they stopped to rest, because they lacked the strength to resist the subzero temperature. Again they stopped for the night, and again they slept very little, spending all their time trying to keep warm while babbling incoherently about food. When they started out the next day, Private Applegate swore he could smell the fire from a cookstove. By mid-afternoon Doane and his men, looking like human scarecrows, staggered up to a miner's cabin tucked away in a clump of trees. The bewildered occupant admitted the frozen soldiers and began cooking what food he had on hand for them while hearing their incredible story. As Doane and the others drank tea and waited in agony for the food to cook, they heard voices outside the cabin. On investigation they found Sergeant Server and Private Warren leading their staggering animals and, like themselves, starving and cold. The pair had wandered through the wilderness for days searching for Keenan City and only that very morning providentially discovered the Doane party's footprints in the snow. Now the cabin's owner had two more mouths to feed, and he soon exhausted his supplies trying to satisfy the men's hunger.

The next day, December 18, Doane and his reunited command set out for Keenan City, led by their host, who now had to restock his own larder at the town's mercantile. The mining town lay only five miles from the cabin, and they covered the ground without incident to arrive at the place by noon. Keenan City, in the heart of the Cariboo mining district, was an isolated collection of log cabins and dugout huts where two hundred men sat idle, waiting to resume their mining operations in the spring when the ground thawed. No draft animals were kept in the town, since the forage to keep them had to be hauled miles through the mountains, and the only contact with the outside world was a private mail carrier who used snowshoes once a week to reach the distant post office at Eagle Rock Bridge. The only store in Keenan City, owned by Hezekiah D. Moore, had to maintain an entire winter's inventory when the first snow came, and this tenuous supply depot was where Doane headed first. After introducing himself to the clerk, Doane presented a list of supplies he needed and proposed to pay for the items on the credit of the government. The clerk tried to explain that he only worked for the absent Mr. Moore and that such a payment would have to be approved by him. Doane drew himself up with righteous indignation and assumed a totally new character with the clerk.

"I am an officer in the United States Army," Doane declared in formal and decisive tones. "These six men with me are United States soldiers under my command. We are in distress. We need food. You will supply us or I'll put you under arrest, take charge of the place, and we'll help ourselves."[35] The audacious demand worked: the men got their supplies, although rumors of the incident greatly exaggerated the details of the transaction. By the time the mail carrier left on his weekly trudge he conveyed along with letters from Doane, White, and Davis a story that the soldiers had actually robbed Moore's store.

Doane settled the men into an abandoned cabin and hired a Chinese laborer to keep them in stovewood. For five days after sending their letters they ate and rested, trying to regain their strength and hoping that their messages home would let everyone know they had not died in the mountains. Back at Fort Ellis at least two people had been spending anxious weeks waiting to hear from Doane. Amelia's anxiety over her husband's disappearance must have been extreme, and Major Brisbin began sending nervous inquiries regarding Doane as early as December 17. "Can you give any information about Lt. Doane and his party exploring Snake River?" he wrote to the adjutant at Fort Hall. "They were to get rations at your post. Inquire of hunters and answer as soon as possible."[36] Capt. Augustus H. Bainbridge, the commanding officer of Fort Hall, Idaho Territory, could only reply in the negative to Brisbin's initial inquiries and seemed to have difficulty believing that anyone could be so foolish as to attempt a passage down the Snake River in the middle of winter.

Doane's wife and commanding officer were not the only ones concerned over his whereabouts. Col. John Gibbon had also written to Doane, but his concerns centered on their proposed business partnership in developing the Doane Centennial Tent. Gibbon sent his letter to Eagle Rock Bridge, enclosing a legal contract and urging Doane to have the design patented before they went any further in the business. The letter must have raised a bitter smile from Doane once he got his hands on it. "I shall be glad to hear from you now and then," Gibbon wrote in closing, "and hope you will have a pleasant and prosperous trip down the Snake River."[37]

On December 27 Captain Bainbridge received the letters that Doane and the others had written from Keenan City, along with the rumors from the letter carrier that the soldiers had been terrorizing the community. Bainbridge hurriedly telegraphed Brisbin the news and then sent his adjutant, 1st Lt. Joseph Hall, with a detail of four men to find out exactly what was going on at the mining town. While the soldiers hurried toward Keenan City, Doane had decided to lead his men back to the abandoned boat in order to continue the journey down the river to Fort Hall. Still weak after five days of recuperation, the men made slow progress, pulling extra supplies on some homemade sleds until they were intercepted by Hall. Although he had come expecting to arrest a band of outlaws, Hall quickly learned from Doane about his interrupted journey down the river and the true nature of his business transaction in Keenan City. Doane then convinced Hall to assign a couple of his soldiers to accompany Sergeant Server as he backtracked toward the boat. The plan called for Server to recover the boat and bring it down to Fort Hall while Doane and the others went overland to the post with Lieutenant Hall, but circumstances prevented the operation from succeeding.

The morale of all the men Doane commanded could not have been at its best after they had nearly frozen and starved to death, and his announced intentions to continue the expedition may not have been as enthusiastically received by Sergeant Server as Doane chose to recall. Pvt. Emil Wolff, one of Hall's soldiers who accompanied Server back to the boat that afternoon, remembered decades later that the sergeant told him that Doane had gone mad and that he would kill them all if they continued their insane journey down the river. When they reached the place where the boat had been cached, Server merely noted in his diary "arrived there at 2 P.M. and found it [the boat] a total wreck. Ice piled up for 20 feet all around."[38] But Wolff claimed that Server actually helped wreck the boat himself, borrowing an ax to complete whatever destruction the ice had left undone.[39] Regardless of what caused the wreck of the boat, it is doubtful the enlisted men received the news of its destruction with any great sorrow.

Doane arrived at Fort Hall on January 4, insisting on taking the time to measure the Snake River along the route they had traveled. At the post they learned that Captain Bainbridge had forwarded all their messages to Fort Ellis; but as yet, no word had come back. Doane read the letter that Colonel Gibbon had sent and immediately set two of the men to work sewing a prototype of the Centennial Tent, ostensibly for Bainbridge's use but more likely as a sample to accompany the patent application. Doane also started drawing up plans for a new boat, announcing to his incredulous followers his intentions not only to resume the journey downriver but actually to retrace their steps to Jackson Lake so he could redo all the measurements that had been lost when the first boat capsized. The lunacy of the proposal spoke for itself; but in his determination to outdo Hayden and establish himself as the premier explorer of all Yellowstone's environs, Doane could not face reality. "In exploring as in hunting there is an element of chance which cannot be provided against," as Doane explained his obsessive determination at this point; "no foresight will avail, no calculations will detect, no energy will overcome. Caution may prevent, but with caution no results will be obtained. Risks must be taken, and there is such an element in human affairs as fortune, good or bad."[40] Doane had clearly allowed his ambition to obscure any sense of reality regarding the expedition, and the enlisted men would be the ones to pay the price of the lieutenant's lust for fame unless something happened to prevent them from going on.

Fortunately for the anxious soldiers, Major Brisbin had not been idle at Fort Ellis after receiving the first news of Doane's disastrous journey. "I hear Doane lost all his horses—seven—and mules—three—his boat and camp equipage, even to blankets; lived three weeks on horse meat straight," he telegraphed to General Terry on January 2. "I recommend that he be ordered to this post for duty with his company."[41] The appeal achieved the desired result; on January 8 a telegram arrived at Fort Hall, ordering Doane and his command to return to Fort Ellis at once.

Although they affected deep disappointment when the order came, the soldiers' actions spoke loudly to the contrary. "Lt. Doane was very mad in consequence of his having to return and so were all the men," wrote Sergeant Server in his diary, "but we tried to make the best of it. Applegate got a gallon of whiskey to have a good time with. Had quite a time at night."[42] While the men celebrated with Doane's indulgent approval, Captain Bainbridge questioned the wisdom of allowing such latitude. Doane, purposely within earshot of his men, replied, "Oh, hell, let 'em have a good time."[43] Now that he had been forced to face the inevitable, Doane's fraternization with the enlisted men became more important, especially since all would return home to tell their own versions of the debacle they had endured.

A stagecoach conveyed Doane and four of the others back to Fort Ellis, while Sergeant Server and Private White followed with the only survivors of the expedition's livestock. By February 2 all of the men had arrived safely at the Gallatin Valley post. Doane received Major Brisbin's explanation of how he had actively worked to have the expedition canceled because he had never sanctioned it in the first place. Doane never completed a report on the expedition that winter, although he had to file the proper vouchers and related paperwork to account for the lost government property and to get payment for Hezekiah D. Moore, the store owner in Keenan City. Being reunited with an understandably upset Amelia added to

Doane's headaches, along with the whispered rumors of his mental breakdown passed on by Private Davis. The winter of 1876–77 would be one of the lowest points of Doane's career, with his marriage in jeopardy and his best chance for fame turned to ashes by his own foolhardiness and a recalcitrant commanding officer.

CHAPTER 7

"Doane begged him with tears in his eyes to go forward"

The Nez Perce Campaign

In 1892, when Doane was preparing to take an extended sick leave in Montana, word reached him at Fort Bowie, Arizona, that Maj. James S. Brisbin had passed away in Philadelphia. The years had not softened the loathing Doane felt for his old commander. In the middle of a letter home he paused to report Brisbin's death and added, "Good Riddance!"[1] The hatred that still consumed Doane at the end of his life had its origins in Brisbin's cancellation of the 1876 Snake River expedition, but that incident was really only the opening salvo in a continuing feud between the two officers. Brisbin simply wanted Doane to perform his duty as a company officer and insisted on obedience, while Doane demanded independence and preferential treatment. In the pursuit of his goals during the summer of 1877 the lieutenant would test the limits of the major's forbearance; and as Doane continued to chafe under Brisbin's control his resentment grew. Doane's attempts to circumvent authority would lead him to use his unwarranted reputation as an expert with the Crow tribe to receive the accolades that he craved.

Following Custer's defeat in the summer of 1876, Sitting Bull had led a large band of the Sioux and their allies into Canada. While scattered bands remained on the high plains of eastern Montana Territory, they proved difficult to locate and engage in battle. Col. Nelson A. Miles, commanding the army's forces along the lower Yellowstone, conducted a successful winter campaign against some of the tribesmen who remained in eastern Montana, and he anticipated completing the job during the spring and summer of 1877. From his base on the Yellowstone River at the Tongue River Cantonment, Miles carried out plans to make the military presence on the Yellowstone River permanent and to prevent the Indians on the north side of the stream from rejoining those who remained on the south side. Along with the garrison at the Tongue, Miles would be charged with constructing another at the confluence of the Bighorn and Little Bighorn Rivers and continuing his relentless pursuit of the enemy to force their capitulation. In partial preparation for this offensive, Miles sent orders to Major Brisbin in late February, ordering him to prepare his cavalry battalion to march to the Tongue River Cantonment. Brisbin ordered two companies out at the beginning of March.[2]

As Doane readied for the march he may also have been dealing with Amelia's growing unhappiness. His constant absences had provoked alienation, but there is no direct evidence that she confronted him with an ultimatum. From subsequent events it seems that she had finally found the courage to leave her husband; but when the time came for Doane to say good-bye to her on March 30 it is not clear if he realized it was the last time he would ever see her. If the couple did discuss divorce at the time, Doane's actions later that summer suggest that any such conversation could not have weighed heavily on his mind.

Companies F and G marched over the Bozeman Pass and slowly made their way down the Yellowstone River toward its junction with the Stillwater. At the Crow Agency twelve miles up the Stillwater River, the two companies went into a temporary camp on March 12, where they waited for the balance of the Fort Ellis contingent to join them. Major Brisbin arrived with the remaining two companies of the Second Cavalry battalion on April 4, and the combined force renewed its march down the Yellowstone to join Colonel Miles at the Tongue River Cantonment. On April 12, just as Brisbin led the battalion past the confluence of Porcupine Creek, a courier from Miles arrived with special orders for the major. "I sent La Forge for some Crow Scouts and Allies (Indians)," wrote Miles. "I wish all that can be brought down to move in concert with your command. You had better send an officer — Lieut. Doane — let him enlist seventy (70) with La Forge and take as many others as will go as allies."[3]

If Major Brisbin suspected that Doane had gone over his head to request an independent assignment he could not have confirmed it at that time. Still more than a week away from meeting Colonel Miles face to face, Brisbin had no choice but to obey a written order. He allowed Doane to pick out four men to take along to the Crow Agency and issued an order authorizing the lieutenant to draw on any army rations to convince the Crows to cooperate.[4] Doane sought out Sergeant Server and privates Applegate, Long, and White as the soldiers he wished to go on the mission. The lieutenant reacted negatively when someone suggested taking Pvt. Daniel Starr along, though. "No, I don't want him," growled Doane. "He tattles too much." White explained, "I knew that my regular companion [Starr] had enjoyed himself in telling our Fort Ellis people about the leader's temporary breakdown at the time we were on our way out of the Snake River Canyon."[5]

Colonel Miles hoped that Doane's self-touted influence with the tribe could move the Crows speedily to any particular strategic point, but that is not what happened. Doane and his squad left the battalion on the Yellowstone River and backtracked to the Crow Agency on April 16. Once they established their camp at the agency they did little more than make themselves comfortable. Doane parleyed with the Crows shortly after his arrival, but he did not officially enlist any scouts as his orders suggested. Instead he promised all of the Crows a generous allotment of rations and ammunition in return for their cooperation and then found it impossible to deliver the goods. Sergeant Server carried Doane's requisition for 12,000 rations back to Fort Ellis on April 18, but severe snowstorms delayed the shipment until May 16. During the month's wait privates White, Applegate, and Long simply idled away their time and consorted with the Indians they had been charged to keep within the government's influence.

Although Doane had been sent to the agency to practice his diplomatic skills with the Crow tribe, he ended up spending far more effort ingratiating himself with the family of Dr. Andrew J. Hunter. While the enlisted men applied their time with the Crows to learn a bit about their customs and language, Doane made his way to the agency headquarters, where Hunter and his family made their temporary home. That spring Hunter had moved his wife and children from their hot springs claim along the Yellowstone River to the Crow Agency, where he worked to get a permanent appointment as the government physician with the Indian Bureau. Doane convinced the doctor to let him board at the house, a circumstance that allowed the lieutenant to make a closer acquaintance with Hunter's daughter, Mary Lee. Although Mary, just three months shy of her eighteenth birthday, captivated Doane's affections, he needed to pay more attention to her parents than to their daughter. Despite the glaring handicap of being twenty years her senior as well as a married man, Doane successfully managed to charm the girl's unreconstructed parents. Hunter had been forced out of Missouri in 1864 by Union-sympathizing guerrillas who burned his home, so he had no particular reason to welcome the sight of a blue uniform, but Doane overcame that obstacle. "Your pa is well pleased with the choice you have made," Mrs. Hunter would write to Mary after she announced her engagement to Doane two years later. "You know he always fancied him long before he even thought of marrying you."[6] Busy practicing whatever diplomatic skills he possessed on the Hunters, Doane sent no dispatches to Colonel Miles explaining the delay in executing his orders and gave little indication to his squad that the postponement caused him much distress. "The Crow were not in a hurry to go for their summer hunting," recalled Private White, "and we were content to wait for them; to wait all summer if necessary."[7]

When the supplies from Fort Ellis finally arrived, Doane made a dramatic presentation of the distribution and got assurances from the Crow leaders that all the Indians camped at the agency would accompany the soldiers on a march toward the scene of Colonel Miles's operations against the Sioux and Cheyennes. None of the warriors expressed any desire to enlist as official scouts, but they did agree to scour the country south of the Yellowstone with small war parties. Doane put forth the best possible explanation of his failure to enlist the scouts that Miles had requested by reporting that "this will be an advantage in saving expense and preventing jealousy [among the Crows]."[8] The entire village of men, women, children, and livestock began its slow migration east on May 22, well over a month behind schedule and far too late to be of any direct military assistance to Miles.

The prolonged delay also caused further deterioration in Doane's relationship with Major Brisbin. During the long wait at the Crow Agency Doane receive a dispatch from Brisbin's adjutant dated April 3, the day Brisbin had left Fort Ellis with the remaining two companies of his battalion. The message, written on Brisbin's direct order, took the lieutenant to task for his delay in settling the account of Hezekiah D. Moore, the Keenan City, Idaho, storekeeper. Moore had been waiting since the previous December for payment on the groceries Doane had commandeered at the end of the disastrous Snake River trip and had complained to Brisbin about the matter. When Doane read the dun notice, his temper flared. He lashed out at the major with an angry reply on the day he led the Crows away from the agency. "I have no report to make, not being accustomed to be settling my business under the surveillance of any post commander," he wrote heatedly. "I do not need any urging to be induced to pay my debts, nor shall I tolerate for an instant any imputation on my honesty, expressed or implied (as in this note) from anyone, however it may please or affect any citizen to hear an officer disparage his juniors."[9] No matter how justified Doane may have felt in writing his tirade, he unknowingly picked the very worst time to send it. Brisbin had returned to Fort Ellis early in May due to illness and also to be with his wife in the final days of her pregnancy. The couple's baby girl had been stillborn on May 18. Just a few days later, about the same time Doane's petulant reply arrived, Brisbin got word that $2,500 of his personal savings had been lost in a Boulder, Colorado, bank failure.[10]

Blissfully unaware of his letter's bad timing, Doane moved the Crow tribe toward the Bighorn River valley as the month of June began. Their progress was maddeningly slow, and Doane found it impossible to maintain the Crows' cooperation without making promises of more rations and ammunition from the army's supply steamboats. Attempts to have the warriors perform accurate reconnaissance scouting or courier service met with mixed results, and Doane's inability to speak their language did little to help matters. When a party of couriers he had sent with dispatches to the Tongue River Cantonment came back in a panic without delivering them, Doane said he "made them ridiculous in camp" and attributed their frightened stampede to a bad dream.[11] He could not understand the concept of a religious divination causing the Indians' return, and an interpreter's attempt to explain it as a "dream" gave Doane license to mock them as cowards. His distrust of the interpreted information he got from the Crows also caused delays in his dispatches to Miles. When other hunting or war parties would return to the main camp, he always waited for the corroboration of two groups before believing their reports.[12]

Doane's inability to empathize with Indians, both those who allied with the army and those who opposed it, did not mark him as radically different from other frontier officers. Lt. James Bradley, who commanded the Crow scouts during the 1876 campaign, also distrusted the intelligence his warriors brought back to camp; but, unlike Doane, Bradley did not accuse the Indians of cowardice.[13] Doane's refusal to familiarize himself with the Crows' language and customs was also shared by many other officers who were detailed to work with Indian scouts, regardless of the particular tribe. However, few soldiers who shared his dismal view of Indian character would have taken the assignment to begin with.[14] The real difference between Doane and his military contemporaries was his consideration of the "little children" he had been assigned to shepherd as primarily a means to achieve an independent command. He made a halfhearted attempt to foster good relations with the Crows, but his contempt for all Indians was difficult to conceal. He dismissed the concerns of Iron Bull, one of the principal chiefs who requested better treatment in exchange for his tribe's cooperation with the military campaign, as "claptrap" and described the headman as "an old humbug, as are all the council chiefs."[15] Doane's unfavorable assessment of the scouts compared them to their incompetent tribal elders. "The warriors are not much better," he complained. "What they need is a backbone of soldiers to fall back on and enforce authority, then they can be managed."[16]

Doane's disgust with the Crows grew as he realized how accurately they gauged his effectiveness in delivering on his promises. "The stupid Indians will believe nothing they do not see," he reported after the Crows refused to leave a camp on the Bighorn where they had expected to receive rations. "I could make them move but do not think it advisable as they would take it as an indication that I did not think a boat would come. It draws terribly on one's patience to deal with these people."[17] After one violent argument with the Crow elders, Doane described their attempt to appease his anger by offering him a hefty cache of fifty-eight buffalo robes. He accepted the gift on behalf of the government but announced his intention to sell the robes at the first opportunity to buy matches and sugar for the tribe, which he would distribute equitably. "The Indians were quite amazed at such an idea," he wrote Miles when reporting his intended generosity. "If pecuniary interest were my object I could have made a thousand dollars a month while I have been out and without any apparent injury to the cause."[18] Apparently Doane wanted to convince Miles of his financial probity, especially since Major Brisbin had formally announced his concern over the late payment to Hezekiah D. Moore.

The several orders that Colonel Miles sent to Doane that summer alternated between approval for his efforts to keep the Crows allied with the army and demands for small forces of warriors to rendezvous with his troops at specified points. The commander had sent an order on May 23, telling Doane to move as speedily as possible to join Capt. Edward Ball, Company F, Second Cavalry, at the headwaters of the Tongue River; but Doane failed to convince any of the warriors to leave the main camp and comply with Miles's request. Once it became obvious that the Crows would stay together to exploit the vast buffalo herd they had found in the Bighorn Valley, Miles sent another dispatch, confirming that their driving the beasts across to the Yellowstone's north bank would at least help deplete the sustenance of any Indians allied with the Sioux still lingering in the countryside south of the river. "If the country is clear south of the Yellowstone I wish to transfer my force and operations to the North side and wish to know at once if your force of allies can be moved North of the Yellowstone," Miles wrote: "If we move in that direction we will go in strong force, possibly as far as the British line."[19]

Even after reducing his expectations of the Crows, Colonel Miles still had to wait for Doane to gain their compliance with his request. Doane could not get the Indians to move for almost a month after getting them as far as the Bighorn River; and after following that stream down to the Yellowstone they waited stubbornly on the south bank for the rations Doane had promised them and a steamboat to assist them in crossing. On July 2 Doane, tired of waiting for the steamboat, managed to get his hands on a large mackinaw boat. He demanded that the Crows use it and some makeshift rafts to cross to the north side of the Yellowstone, but forty-five lodges of the tribe refused to go unless they got the promised rations and ammunition. When the tribesmen who balked announced their intention to return to the agency, Doane sent a courier to the agent requesting that all foodstuffs be withheld from the dissenters once they arrived, hoping to force them to return. The tactic eventually backfired on Doane by establishing a vocal group of Crow critics at the agency who later called into question his effectiveness with the tribe that summer.

After the departure of the Crows who wanted to go back to the agency, Doane turned his attention to hustling his remaining charges across the Yellowstone. The colorful scene of the village crossing the river impressed Private White, who admiringly remembered the "marvelous achievement." White described the colorful gathering of three thousand men, women, and children, "from infancy to senility," who along with all their stock successfully crossed the river. What amazed him the most was the speedy reassembly of their village in exactly the same array as it had been when on the south bank of the Yellowstone. "Less than an hour later every lodge in camp had all of its interior furnishings in their proper places," he reported, "the women had the pots boiling, and the Crow Indian tribe was at home again."[20]

The Yellowstone crossing completed, Doane next moved the Crows down the north bank of the river toward the Big Porcupine Creek so he could rendezvous with a shipment of supplies he had requested from the Tongue River Cantonment. After so many weeks of delay and vexations, Doane had finally managed to get the Crows where they would do Colonel Miles the most good. However, a natural disaster no one could have foreseen occurred. On July 6, while halting the Indians near the mouth of Froze-to-Death Creek, Doane surveyed the mass of humanity that surrounded him. "There were about two thousand people in the camp," he reported, "men, women, and children and about ten thousand animals." The normal routine of setting up the lodges and herding the ponies took place as Doane watched, noting with impatience that "everybody [was] busy excepting the warriors, who smoked calmly throughout it all in dignified stupidity, too lazy even to unsaddle their own riding horses."[21] The intense heat of the day made the scene shimmer before the lieutenant's eyes, and without a breath of wind the other soldiers sought the shade of the cottonwood trees to escape the oppressive atmosphere of their tents.

Around noon the weather changed abruptly. The air cooled, and to the southwest roiling masses of clouds darkened the sky. The stillness that precedes an intense storm became uncomfortably apparent, and even the Crows who had been assigned the important duty of watching over the horse herd on the bluffs overlooking the river came drifting back into camp with a wary eye on the darkening atmosphere. Doane watched in fascination as the black clouds drew nearer and began to spiral: "The whole heavens flashed with electricity now, the mighty clouds blazed, sheets of flame passed through and through, continually, with the quickness of thought they passed to be renewed again. The darkness became an ocean of vivid flashes, a panorama of electric splendor."[22] A blast of intensely cold air rushed by him, and a panic-stricken Crow warrior came galloping into the camp screaming that ice was falling from the sky and all were doomed.

"What's the matter with that Indian?" Doane asked Jirah Allen, one of his interpreters. At that moment a chunk of ice the size of a grapefruit hit the ground at his feet. "The matter with the Indian?" yelled Allen incredulously. "He's running a race with a hailstorm! Do you not hear it coming nearer every moment?"[23] The two white men broke and ran for cover, glancing up at the bombardment of ice chunks that struck the pony herd on the bluff beyond and seemed to melt the sagebrush under its merciless pounding. Diving into Iron Bull's buffalo hide tipi, Doane had enough time to see the old chief chanting his death song before burying himself under a pile of buffalo robes. The hail smashed through the tough hide lodge covering as if it were paper. All over the camp the screams of women and children mixed with the thunderous downpour that sounded like the beating of a thousand drums at once, and the ominous thunder of the pony herd stampeding in terror added to the deafening roar. Jirah Allen had taken refuge in the enlisted men's tipi, standing with Doane's soldiers under the cover of a buffalo robe in the center of the lodge, but the incredible bombardment shredded the tough hide covering and even broke the supporting poles.[24] Private White remembered that the ice chunks tore through the tipi with such force that they broke the inch and a half thick pine boards on top of an ammunition box.[25] Allen, White, and the others evacuated the destroyed lodge and dove for the cover of a nearby cottonwood tree. There they saw one warrior, a member of the Crow Fool Dog Society, standing out in the downpour in an ill-advised attempt to demonstrate his bravery. Knocked senseless by the hail, the man would have died had not some other warriors dashed out into the storm and dragged him to safety.[26]

Doane had the presence of mind to pull out his pocket watch while huddling under his buffalo robe and timed the onslaught. After six and a half seemingly endless minutes the storm passed, and Doane crawled out from under the buffalo robes to see what

Gustavus C. Doane, 1866.

29064

©HAYNES

Photographer J. E. Haynes's staged reenactment photo of the fictitious campfire discussion at the junction of the Gibbon and Firehole Rivers, September 19, 1870. Courtesy Montana Historical Society, Helena, Montana.

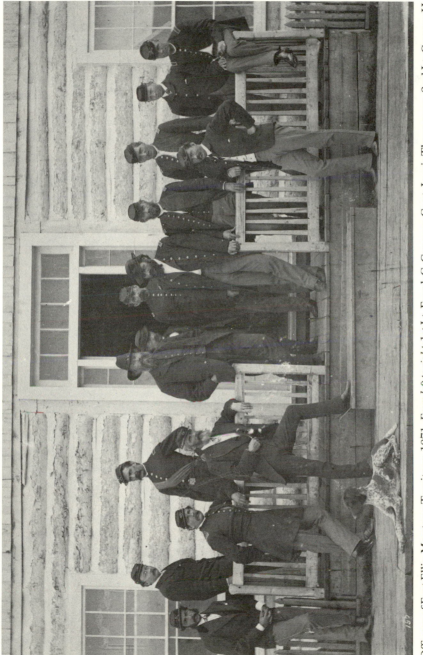

Officers of Fort Ellis, Montana Territory, 1871. *From left to right:* 1st Lt. Frank C. Grugan, Capt. Lewis Thompson, 2nd Lt. George H. Wright, 2nd Lt. Gustavus C. Doane, Capt. Lewis C. Forsyth, Assistant Surgeon Archibald B. Campbell, Dr. Robert M. Whitefoot (contract surgeon), 1st Lt. Samuel T. Hamilton, Maj. Eugene M. Baker, Capt. Edward Ball, 2nd Lt. Lovell H. Jerome, Capt. George L. Tyler, 2nd Lt. Edward J. McClernand, 2nd Lt. Charles B. Schofield. Courtesy Museum of the Rockies, Bozeman, Montana.

Gustavus C. Doane, 1875.

Mary Lee Hunter, ca. 1877.

Susan C. Hunter, ca. 1890.

Headquarters, Fort Assinniboine, Montana Territory, 1881. Doane is the officer standing in profile third from the right side of the porch.

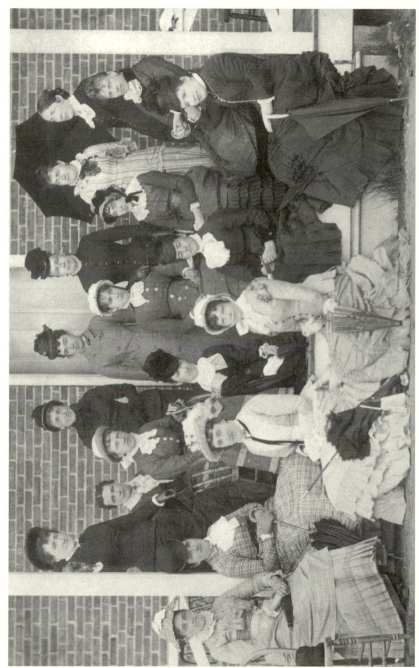

Officers' wives and friends, Fort Assinniboine, Montana Territory, 1881. *Back row, standing and seated, from left to right:* Mrs. Miller, Mrs. Lloyd (*seated*), Mrs. Potter, Mrs. Broadwater, Mrs. Baldwin, Mrs. Anderson, Mrs. Curtis. *Middle row, sitting in chairs and on porch:* Mrs. Bates, Mary Wheeler (kneeling on porch), Susie Gill, unidentified, Mrs. Kellogg. *Front row, sitting on porch and on steps:* Mrs. Cabaniss, Mrs. Morris, Mrs. Warwick, Miss Gene Gill, Mrs. Mary Doane, Miss Hinton. Not pictured in this group is Mary Doane's nemesis, Mrs. Norwood.

Gustavus C. Doane, ca. 1882.

Mary Doane, San Francisco, ca. 1885.

Gustavus C. Doane, San Francisco, ca. 1889.

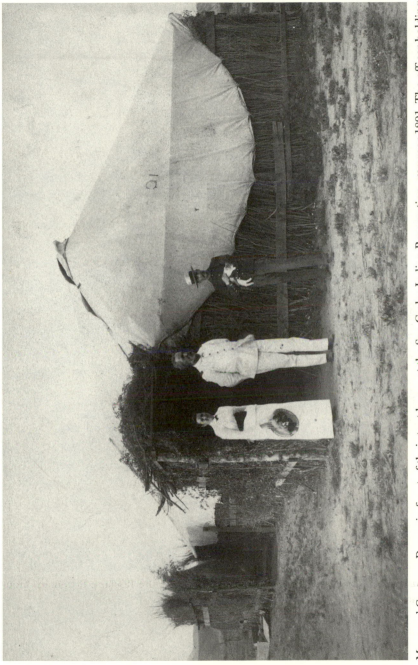

Mary and Gustavus Doane in front of their tent home at the San Carlos Indian Reservation, summer 1891. The officer holding the cat is unidentified. Courtesy Museum of the Rockies, Bozeman, Montana.

Gustavus C. Doane, ca. 1891. Courtesy Museum of the Rockies, Bozeman, Montana.

Mary Doane, ca. 1892.

Mary Doane at the National Park Service monument commemorating the September 19, 1870, camp at the junction of the Firehole and Gibbon Rivers.

Merrill G. Burlingame, C. Max Bauer, Isabelle Haynes, Lida Haynes, William H. Jackson, and Mary Doane at the Jack E. Haynes home, Yellowstone National Park, summer 1939.

Tombstone of Gustavus Doane, Sunset Hills Cemetery, Bozeman, Montana.

had happened. "Such a scene of destruction I never witnessed," he said. "In the whole camp there were not twenty lodges standing. The rest were cut to pieces and flattened upon their contents. Hundreds of lodge poles were shattered, not simply bent and broken, but cut in two as if by cannon shot."[27] All around Doane could see the Indians begin to crawl out from under the cover of their ruined lodges and then scatter in search of ponies, dogs, and children. Howls of rage, fear, and sorrow soon replaced the roar of the storm, especially from those parents who thought their children had been killed. As it turned out, no humans had died; but hundreds of horses had stampeded over the bluff and into the river to drown or had been trampled to death in the muddy sloughs leading to the banks of the Yellowstone.

Doane needed no interpreter to understand the furious warriors who soon gathered around him, gesturing angrily at the sky, the floating pony corpses in the river, and then at the soldiers. "There was no time to argue the matter on scientific principles," said Doane, "so I cursed them with a fluency which they seemed to regard with wonder, and called them a set of cowards and old women."[28] Doane's tactless bluster at the Crows threatened to escalate their outrage, but fortunately Jirah Allen defused the situation by pointing out that the soldiers had also lost their horses and tents in the storm. Another attempt to fix the blame for the disaster almost ended in murder. As soon as the storm was over Iron Bull went down to the place where the River Crow faction of the tribe had been camped and told them he had conjured up the storm to punish them for refusing to submit to his authority. The ruse worked too well, for the frightened warriors drew their rifles and forced the chief hastily to withdraw to his ruined lodge. He eventually reappeared to assure everyone that the storm had been sent by God and that no one was responsible.[29]

For two days the villagers repaired their lodges and tended their bruises. The dead horses that floated downstream alarmed steamboat crews and the garrison at the Tongue River Cantonment, who thought such a massacre could only be the result of a fierce battle. Doane managed to get a dispatch to Colonel Miles to report the storm and explain yet another delay in the progress of his march.

Miles had transferred some of his soldiers to a camp opposite the Tongue River Cantonment, several miles up Sunday Creek, and he wanted Doane to try to get the tribe to move in that direction. The Crows wanted to follow the buffalo herd into the Judith Basin, however, and Doane could not persuade them otherwise. He reported to Miles that the Crows intended to move northwest up the Big Porcupine Creek and cross the divide into the Musselshell River drainage. Hoping that they would continue to follow the buffalo through the Judith Basin toward the Missouri River, Doane asked Miles to approve their projected movement and to have supplies sent by wagons to the Crow camp on the Porcupine. "I made them all swear on receiving ammunition this time to obey orders, and to go where sent, and to tell the truth on returning," he reported, adding as a qualifying afterthought: "Please do not expect too much from them, for they are the greatest of cowards, excepting only all other Indians."[30]

On July 17 Colonel Miles asked Doane for fifty to seventy-five Crow warriors to go with a company after some Cheyennes below Powder River. He also requested Doane to come to the Tongue River Cantonment with a few of the Crow chiefs for a conference. This time Doane succeeded in having some warriors leave the village and come south with him. The villagers continued their movement up the Big Porcupine and over to the Musselshell, where the vast buffalo herd had moved to graze. When Doane reached Miles's headquarters on July 19, his arrival coincided with a visit from commanding general William T. Sherman, who was on his way to Yellowstone National Park. Miles proudly introduced the lieutenant as the officer responsible for keeping the Crow allies within the army's control as well as the explorer of the region Sherman intended to visit.[31] While at the post Doane got his first word that his wife had left the territory. When Maj. John Ewing Blaine, the army paymaster, completed his tour of Montana posts at Fort Ellis on July 7, he offered his services to escort Amelia to the "states." Amelia left the post with the major and his civilian clerk, Blaine Walker, the next day and eventually made her way to Chicago, where she would stay with some relatives.[32]

Doane had little time to reflect on Amelia's leaving because Colonel Miles had brought him to headquarters for discussions on further uses for the Crow Indian allies. Even though the Sioux war appeared to be ending with the submission of all the scattered bands south of the Yellowstone River, Miles still worried that those Indians under Sitting Bull's influence in Canada might try to reenter the United States and renew hostilities. Miles wanted the Crows to remain in the Musselshell River drainage and wanted Doane to dispatch scouting parties all along its length to the Missouri. This desire did not take into consideration that the Crows, aside from their discontent with Doane's leadership, had an understandable reluctance to continue acting as a buffer between the army and its enemies. Doane pointed out the need for more soldiers to keep the Indians under control and also stressed the requirement for more supplies to keep the Crows contented. Miles agreed to address both concerns, but before he could act the army in Montana would have an entirely different tribe of Indians than the Sioux to worry about. The entire focus of the army in eastern Montana changed dramatically in late August 1877. Instead of focusing on mopping up isolated bands of Sioux and Cheyennes in the country south of the Missouri River, the soldiers shifted their attention to the pursuit and capture of the Nez Perces, with the goal of preventing their rendezvous with Sitting Bull's band in Canada.

The Nez Perces had left their reservation in northeast Oregon in June after their rejection of a government treaty allowing further settler encroachment on their homelands. Killings committed by young hotheads among the nontreaty bands precipitated a full-scale evacuation of nearly seven hundred men, women, and children on a flight to the buffalo plains east of the Rocky Mountains. Brig. Gen. Oliver Otis Howard, commander of the Department of the Columbia, had ordered troops to halt the fleeing tribe; but in each encounter that summer the Nez Perces had bested the soldiers and escaped. The fugitive Indians crossed the Bitterroot Range at Lolo Pass at the beginning of August and thereby became the concern of other military subdivisions, the District of Montana, commanded by Col. John Gibbon, and the newly designated District of the Yellowstone command of Col. Nelson A. Miles. Both command-ers would claim jurisdiction over Doane's independent assignment with the Crow Indians that summer, and he quickly realized that he could play one off the other to maintain his autonomy.

Doane's opportunity came after Colonel Miles responded to his pleas for more soldiers by assigning Company E of the Seventh Cavalry to the lieutenant's command. Along with the sixty enlisted men, Doane received the services of two subordinate officers, lieu-tenants Charles C. De Rudio and Hugh L. Scott. First Lieutenant De Rudio, a veteran of the battle of the Little Bighorn, made an inter-esting contrast to Second Lieutenant Scott, who had graduated from West Point just a week prior to that epic encounter. De Rudio was born in 1832 to an Italian count and countess; after attending an Austrian military academy he served briefly with Giuseppe Gar-ibaldi in the 1848 Italian War of Liberation. The record of De Rudio's early life read like a dime novel, including military service in Algeria, imprisonment on Devil's Island, and even a failed as-sassination attempt on the life of Napoleon III. Since his arrival in the United States during the Civil War and subsequent enlistment in the army, however, De Rudio's career had been singularly lacklus-ter. Derisively dubbed "Count No Account" by his brother officers in the Seventh Cavalry, De Rudio had the reputation of being a gifted storyteller but a soldier who practiced caution more than courage.[33]

Twenty-five years De Rudio's junior, Hugh Lennox Scott had desired to serve in the cavalry ever since his graduation from West Point and took advantage of the vacancies in the Seventh Cavalry caused by Custer's defeat to achieve his goal. In contrast to Doane, Scott spent his first year in uniform learning as much as he could about the people the army had been sent to subjugate and taught himself how to sign and speak several different Indian dialects (an interest that would result in an authoritative text on the subject years later). He had never heard a shot fired in anger, however, and was so anxious to see some action in the summer of 1877 that he actually traded places with 2nd Lt. Edwin P. Brewer of Company E for the chance to follow Doane.[34]

To the novice Scott, Doane appeared the epitome of a frontiersman, able to assume the airs of a polished officer at times while at
others performing with ease the mundane tasks of a muleskinner.
Unkempt, loud, awkward, and profane, Doane provided an field
example for the green second lieutenant that he strove mightily to
imitate. "I modeled myself on him as a soldier," said Scott, "watched
him carefully and learned from him how to set up an aparejo and to
throw the diamond so that, if the packing should be delayed, we two
would pitch in to help pack ourselves and get the command out of
camp in a hurry."[35] But Scott found one omission in his new commanding officer's talents completely bewildering: Doane had been
living with the Crows since April and still had learned nothing of
their language. "He could do anything anybody else could do on
the prairie save interpret," he recalled. "He never seemed to realize
what power a knowledge of their language would give him among
those wild tribes."[36]

Scott may not have been impressed with his new commander's
language skills, but Doane's ability to interpret orders liberally
should have made a lasting impression. Colonel Miles had intended
to send Doane back to the Crows to scout for any Sioux south of the
Missouri River (all the way from the Judith Basin to the mouth of the
Big Dry) and also authorized the official enlistment of twenty-one
Crows as paid army scouts.[37] News from the western border of Montana Territory had arrived before Doane could leave the Tongue
River Cantonment on August 3, however, and Miles amended his
first instructions: "You will use every effort to intercept, capture, or
destroy the Nez Perce band of hostile Indians that have been recently
engaging US troops in Idaho and who will doubtless, if defeated,
endeavor to retreat and take refuge in the Judith Basin, or vicinity."[38]
Doane could certainly spot ambiguity in official orders when he saw
it and realized the leeway to head in whatever direction looked the
most promising for action. After ordering 30,000 rounds of ammunition to be dropped off at Carroll Landing on the Missouri River,
Doane replied to Miles that "owing to the uncertainty of all Indian
movements I am unable to exactly state what minor movements can
be carried into effect" and thereby kept his options open.[39]

Doane led De Rudio, Scott, and the rest of Company E back to the Crow village at the big bend of the Musselshell River on August 6. Once there, Doane tried using the ammunition waiting at Carroll Landing as a bribe to again win the Crows' cooperation. Many of the warriors had grown weary of his unfulfilled promises, however, and found the prospect of continuing to act as the army's buffer against Sitting Bull less than attractive. Some of the dissatisfied tribesmen refused to follow Doane's proposed route through the Judith Basin to the supply dump at Carroll and announced their intention to return to the Crow Agency for their annuities. Doane could do little more than send a note to the agency to report their departure, demanding that the defectors be punished by withholding their rations. He had done the same thing in July, when some families left before he led the tribe across the Yellowstone; but since that time a new agent had been assigned at Crow Agency: George W. Frost. He refused to deny rations to any of the returning tribesmen: "I cannot quite see how the Crows 'in the eyes of the law' can be in the military service of the U.S. unless they are duly enlisted and properly paid." When the Crows arrived, he gave them not only rations for their hunger but also his sympathetic ear for their complaints.[40] Based on their grievances and those of the earlier returnees, Frost correctly concluded that Doane had alienated the very Indians he had been entrusted to keep loyal to the government.

Crow loyalty certainly occupied much of Colonel Miles's attention on August 11, when it became obvious the Nez Perces could possibly move north through the Judith Basin and collide with the Crows that Doane was leading there. On that day Miles ordered Col. Samuel D. Sturgis, commander of the Seventh Cavalry, to march as rapidly as possible from the Tongue River Cantonment to Judith Gap. There Sturgis could absorb Doane's command and wait for the Nez Perces to make their move.[41] Miles only asked Doane to "communicate" with Sturgis in the effort to capture the Nez Perces, again allowing the lieutenant the leeway to operate independently.[42] By the time Doane received the next order making cooperation with Sturgis more explicit, he had already moved the Crow village far west up the Musselshell River and prepared to take up his position at Judith Gap.

The Seventh Cavalry moved steadily closer to Judith Gap by way of the Yellowstone River, and Sturgis sent ahead what scant information he received by courier. In that manner Doane first learned of the battle at the Big Hole and the present location of his business partner, Col. John Gibbon. Gibbon, with a force of four hundred regular army troops and volunteers, had attacked a sleeping village of Nez Perces camped on the Big Hole River of western Montana Territory on August 9, but the Indians quickly rallied and put the soldiers on the defensive. After routing their attackers, the Nez Perces turned east and headed toward Yellowstone while the soldiers made their way back to the settlements. Gibbon himself had been wounded in the leg during the battle and was recovering in Helena by the time Doane got the message. Along with this news Sturgis included orders for Doane's detachment to rendezvous with the Seventh Cavalry at Judith Gap on August 21.[43]

Fortunately for Doane, Colonel Sturgis specifically instructed him to intercept any messages coming from Fort Ellis or Camp Baker and read them prior to forwarding in order to learn more about the Nez Perce movements. This left Doane in a perfect position to have the first intelligence of any tidings from the west and to react without waiting for approval from Sturgis. Orders from Colonel Gibbon telling Sturgis to abandon his Judith Gap objective and resupply his regiment at Fort Ellis came into Doane's hands on August 21, the day Sturgis should have arrived at the Crow camp. Gibbon theorized that a quick march up the Yellowstone into the National Park might put a force in front the Nez Perces, and he wanted the Seventh Cavalry to be in a position to do so. Meanwhile Sturgis, reacting to earlier orders from Colonel Miles, had turned back from his march to Judith Gap to the Yellowstone River valley to gain a more central position to chase the Nez Perces should they turn south into Wyoming Territory. Before Sturgis could request Doane to join him there, the lieutenant had already moved out with Company E and about forty Crow scouts to march to Fort Ellis as

ordered by Gibbon. Before leaving the Crow village, Doane suddenly announced to the Indians that they should return to the
agency, where they would receive their annuities ahead of schedule.
This complete reversal of the entire summer's effort in keeping the
Crows where Miles wanted them did not seem to bother Doane in
his haste to keep a few days ahead of Sturgis.

Doane realized if he could not get to the National Park in time,
Colonel Sturgis might actually be in a better position to catch the
Nez Perces, providing they left Yellowstone by way of the Clark's
Fork or Stinking Water Rivers. As he started his strenuous ride to
Fort Ellis, Doane sent ahead a reply to Colonel Gibbon. "[I] do not
understand why we go to Ellis?" he queried. "This spring rations
and forage were ordered to the Crow Agency and there is the natural point to watch from! The Nez Perce may come down on the
Boulder, Clarks Fork, Pryor Fork, Big Horn, or up No Wood Creek,
barely possible — down the Yellowstone — but not probably."[44] All
the same, Doane chose to bet everything on the remote possibility
that he could head off the Nez Perces should they emerge from the
National Park by way of the Upper Yellowstone River, a gamble that
even the inexperienced Lieutenant Scott had to question. "I admired his knowledge more than his discretion," admitted Scott,
"for one troop of cavalry would not have been a mouthful for that
band that had already defeated Howard and Gibbon a short time
before."[45] With the opportunity to lead troops against the Indians
while they emerged from the National Park, Doane could not be
deterred from a chance to link his name forever with Yellowstone as
a soldier as well as an explorer. Everything depended on his staying
ahead of Sturgis to reach Fort Ellis first.

While they pushed on to the fort, the numbers of Crows accompanying his force continued to dwindle. Aside from a natural sympathy for the Nez Perces, the warriors realized that Doane was leading them toward a confrontation with a much superior force, and
they dropped behind periodically to seek a chance to return to their
people. Interpreter Jirah Allen worried about the number of Crows
who continued to fall out of the column, thinking they might actually be leaving to join up with the Nez Perces or, at the very least,

warn the renegade tribe of the army's plans. In anticipation of such treachery, Doane had at first posted Allen to the rear of the column to arrest all defectors; but in the race to reach Fort Ellis the lieutenant decided that security would have to be sacrificed for speed. "Let them go," he told Allen when the interpreter asked about a father and a son who wanted to leave. "We have enough anyway."[46] With an entire company of white soldiers at his command, Doane felt more than ever that the unreliable Crow warriors casually accompanying them were expendable.

Doane's troop arrived at Fort Ellis on August 26, about the same time that news came from Capt. Randolph Norwood and Company L, Second Cavalry, on service with General Howard's column and en route to Fort Ellis. Doane learned that Howard's force had continued to trail the Nez Perces following the Big Hole fight but had failed again to capture the tribe after a sharp engagement at Camas Meadow, Idaho Territory, on August 20. The fight and subsequent march had so exhausted Howard's soldiers that they had paused to rest at Henry's Lake while the general himself went to Virginia City to telegraph the news that the Nez Perces were heading into the park. Doane ostensibly prepared his command to return back down the Yellowstone River and rejoin Sturgis's force, but he hoped for a way to get to the National Park himself and try to stop the Nez Perces. While he was impatiently supervising the loading of supply wagons and waiting for his scouts' ponies to be reshod, Doane's luck took a fortunate turn. A telegram arrived on August 27 from Colonel Gibbon, who had recovered from his wound enough to resume command of the District of Montana from Fort Shaw. The telegram, marvelously brief and ambiguous, provided Doane with exactly the authorization he needed:

> Your letter of twenty first sent me from [Camp] Baker shows you know exactly what is required to be done. Proceed to do it using your force to obtain early information of the hostiles movements. I do not fear the loyalty of the Crow Nation, but individuals may prove traitorous hence in using them as scouts let them know the penalty for treason and do not

hesitate to shoot on the spot any Crow who betrays your movements to the Nez Perce. I believe these hostiles can yet be caught. Let us do our part towards it. These will supersede all other orders you have unless given by some superior on the spot. Get scouts on the trail leading to Clarks Fork as soon as possible.[47]

The order had been written in response to Doane's earlier suggestion that the army wait at Crow Agency for the Nez Perces to emerge from the park. It is likely that Gibbon wanted Doane to get back to Sturgis immediately to make sure the Seventh Cavalry remained at the agency in a position to send scouts to watch the headwaters of Clark's Fork as a possible Nez Perce escape route. With such vague language, however, Doane realized the order could also be used to authorize his desire to lead his troops directly into the park from Mammoth Hot Springs and try to bag the game himself.[48] He sent a message to Sturgis informing him of his plan and on August 29 hustled his tiny force down the Trail Creek path to the upper Yellowstone Valley. Along with the soldiers marched several civilian scouts, including Jack Baronett, the builder of the first bridge across the Yellowstone River in 1871, and William White, whose enlistment in the Second Cavalry had expired. The supply wagons delayed the march, as did the presence of settlers who volunteered to join the troops as they made their way toward Mammoth Hot Springs. Doane feverishly issued government arms and ammunition to the volunteers and pushed everyone hard along the road to Henderson's Ranch, an outpost on the Yellowstone near the mouth of the Gardiner River.

While Doane raced to his objective, Colonel Sturgis impatiently awaited Doane's arrival at Crow Agency. Sturgis had moved the Seventh Cavalry to that point when he learned that supplies and forage could be had for his hungry regiment, and he continued to send Doane messages asking for the return of Company E. "I fail to see what good can possibly be accomplished by your proposed scouting round the Yellowstone Lake with Company E, 7th Cavalry, marching up the east fork of the Yellowstone," he fumed in a letter written

August 29. "I desire that you remain with your cavalry and such Crows as may not be retained for scouting, at the lower canyon of the Yellowstone."[49] Fearing that his courier would not get through, Sturgis copied his letter and sent it again that same day with another note: "you will please . . . hasten to join this command as rapidly as possible, the moment you are satisfied that it is no longer necessary to guard the Yellowstone route."[50] Obviously Sturgis needed the intelligence Doane's scouts could bring from the park, but he also needed the strength Doane's troops could bring once the Nez Perces emerged from Yellowstone. As it turned out, he would receive neither.

The wagon road led through Yankee Jim Canyon toward Henderson's Ranch. All along the way Doane used the guns, ammunition, and rations he hauled to recruit settlers for his tiny army. On the morning of August 31, as they rounded the bend below the Devil's Slide, Doane (riding in the rear of the column) saw smoke curling up ahead in the distance. He sent Jirah Allen, Jack Baronett, and William White ahead to investigate, and soon they returned reporting that a war party of Nez Perces had attacked the ranch house. Lieutenant De Rudio, leading the column at that point, decided against sending a squad forward, which would have weakened his company. White interpreted the Italian's caution as cold-blooded cowardice. Emboldened by excitement as well as his recent discharge from the army, White cursed De Rudio and Scott with such vehemence that he galvanized the junior officer into action. Without knowing if the raiders had acted alone or represented the vanguard of the entire Nez Perce force, Scott rushed back to Doane to ask his permission to ride back alone with the scouts. Doane insisted the young hotspur take ten troopers along, but Scott complained they would just slow him down. "You can't go without them," said Doane. Scott replied: "Get them out then, in a hurry!" and exchanged his horse for a fresh mount.[51] Doane ordered a detail forward, and in ten minutes Scott galloped ahead toward the plume of black smoke.

Fortunately for Scott, the attack on Henderson's Ranch had indeed been a small raid separate from the main body of Nez Perces.

About eighteen warriors had appeared at the ranch earlier that afternoon, and the occupants had fled the house to shoot at the Indians from rocks along the riverbed. The warriors returned fire for two hours but did not advance on the white men. Instead they contented themselves with stealing all of the horses they found in a nearby corral, setting fire to the ranch house, and then driving their plunder back toward Mammoth Hot Springs. By the time Scott and his detail arrived on the scene, the badly shaken civilians had emerged from their cover and pointed out the direction of the withdrawing warriors. Without hesitation, Scott pushed on after the Nez Perces, chasing them as far as McCartney's hotel at Mammoth Hot Springs. There they found the body of Richard Dietrich, a tourist who had encountered the Nez Perces a few days earlier in the park and had unfortunately taken refuge at the hotel, thinking it safe. One of the warriors shot Dietrich in the heart as they passed by with the stolen horses from Henderson's Ranch heading for Baronett's Bridge. Scott ordered his men to continue the chase; but as they passed by the Liberty Cap formation, Baronett convinced him that they could possibly be riding into an ambush. Scott heeded the frontiersman's prudent advice, and they returned to Henderson's Ranch.

Doane kept his command together that night, receiving into the camp more refugees from other tourist parties that had been attacked by the Nez Perces in the park's interior. Ben Stone, a cook who had escaped not only from the Indians but also from an encounter with a bear, arrived at the camp long after dark and loudly praised the Lord for his deliverance, much to the annoyance of soldiers, who wanted to sleep. Another unwelcome addition to the camp was a courier from Fort Ellis, who brought Doane a dispatch from Lt. Col. Charles C. Gilbert of the Seventh Infantry. "General Sherman and General Gibbon had a conference in my presence in Helena day before yesterday the issue of which amounts to this," wrote Gilbert, "that I am to overtake you, assume the command of you and your party, and then communicate with General Howard, whose presence General Sherman much needs in the Department of the Columbia, and should Howard go at once, I am to take the command of his column."[52] Sherman, apparently frustrated with the lack of progress shown by the pursuing forces, had picked Gilbert as the highest-ranking officer he could find to replace Howard. A fifty-five-year-old West Point graduate of dubious military talent, Gilbert had actually been in Helena to negotiate a flour contract when Sherman tapped him for command, and he eagerly accepted. If Gibbon had reservations about the command choice he did not voice them, but he had to admit that Doane, camped at the northern entrance to the National Park, was in the best position for guiding Gilbert through the wilderness to find Howard.

After reading the note, Doane could feel his chances for glory evaporating. Still, he knew better than to leave his post now that Sherman's decision had effectively rescinded Gibbon's carte blanche instructions of August 27. The next morning, September 1, Doane sent Scott out with twenty men to examine the trail to Baronett's Bridge. None of the Crow scouts would accompany the reconnaissance, except for one that Scott bribed to ride along with him, but the young lieutenant eagerly took the assignment and moved out as ordered. Doane had instructed Scott to burn all of the grass between Baronett's Bridge and Mammoth to deny the Nez Perces forage for their livestock.

After Scott left on his perilous mission, Doane sat down to write a letter to General Howard, intending to forward Gilbert's letter with it. After all, Gilbert's missive spelled just as much bad news for Howard as it had for Doane, and perhaps he hoped a timely response from the general would allow him to preserve his independence. Doane also realized his ideal geographic position should the Nez Perces actually attempt to exit the National Park by way of the Yellowstone River and wanted Howard to know he was there. "[I] have sent forward today to find the Nez Perce main camp," he wrote, "am of the opinion that it is in the Valley of the East Fork of the Yellowstone."[53] With the hope that the Seventh Cavalry had effectively sealed off the eastern route out of the park by taking up positions watching the Clark's Fork and Stinking Water Rivers, Doane gambled that his small force could provide the same function from their location at the northern exit. He sent Sergeant Server out with the letter shortly after noon and then devoted his

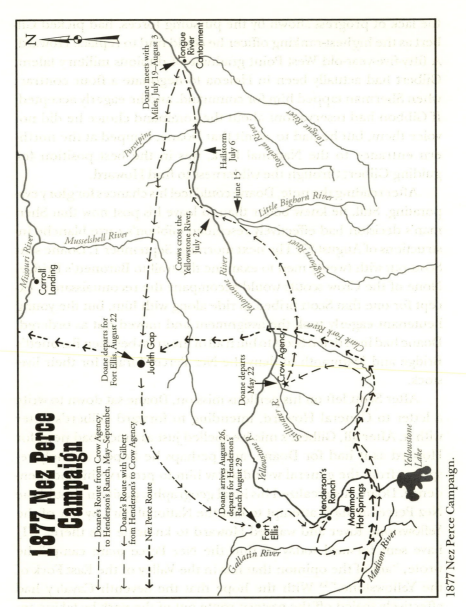

1877 Nez Perce Campaign.

energy to fortifying his position at the ranch. The soldiers improved an irrigation ditch to serve as an entrenchment, and all extra guns and ammunition were distributed to the civilians. Should the Nez Perces be forced to attempt a passage, Doane felt confident his contingent would stall them long enough for Gilbert's reinforcements to join them. Now all they had to do was wait.

After a fatiguing day of cautiously reconnoitering the country from Mammoth Hot Springs to Baronett's Bridge and seeing no sign of the enemy, Lieutenant Scott and his detail turned back. They attempted to comply with Doane's orders and set a grass fire, but a passing rain shower stalled its progress only an hour later. Scott refused to follow the trail directly back to the camp at Henderson's and kept his command moving slowly through whatever cover they could find, all the while imagining that a host of Nez Perces watched their every move. His apprehension turned out to be justified, for three civilian scouts sent out by Colonel Sturgis at Crow Agency had come to grief that same afternoon by keeping to the main trail. The scouts had gone up the Clark's Fork and over the divide into the valley of the east fork of the Yellowstone, looking for any sign of the Nez Perces' advance. Along the trail to Mammoth they had been fired on by concealed warriors, who killed one and wounded another, and they were badly shaken when Scott's patrol found them. They all returned to the fortified camp at Henderson's ranch before nightfall.

An uneasy night followed, with the soldiers maintaining extra vigilance to meet the attack Doane felt likely to come. But when dawn arrived on September 2 with no Indians in sight, Doane had every reason to believe the Nez Perces had abandoned any intention of coming down the Yellowstone River and instead had turned east, crossing the river somewhere north of Yellowstone Lake and south of the Grand Canyon of the Yellowstone. Doane received further support for this hypothesis when Sergeant Server came dashing back to the ranch an hour or two after sunrise. Server had been unable to deliver Doane's message to General Howard. He had ridden south on September 1 trying to reach the Lower Geyser Basin on the Firehole River, where Doane correctly estimated Howard's column would be, but too many Nez Perces still lingered in the woods. Familiar with the country from his previous trips with Doane, Server had tried several paths and found them all too dangerous to travel.

The confirmed presence of Nez Perces still in the country convinced Doane that the exodus of the tribe to the east had not yet been completed. The return that morning of another scout sent to Baronett's Bridge confirmed that the hostiles had burned the structure but left no sign of having crossed there in large numbers. Doane then realized that by pushing forward toward the lake with a reinforced column he could put pressure on the fleeing tribe's left flank while Howard's men prodded them from the rear. Getting information to Howard became all the more critical in the face of such a maneuver, though, and Doane decided to send his message to the general again, but this time by a safer route. Server could take the trail back down the Yellowstone toward Fort Ellis for a few miles, meet Colonel Gilbert's company to give them the news, and then turn to cross the mountains over a rough trail of forty miles to the Gallatin River canyon. Once he gained that drainage it would be necessary to continue over another divide to the Madison River and follow it upstream about sixty miles back into the National Park and the rear of Howard's force. Before sending Server on such a roundabout mission, Doane scribbled a quick note to Gilbert on the back of the envelope containing his letter to Howard:

> The bearer started with this to General Howard yesterday but was driven back. He will give you particulars. If you can mount him he will take a dispatch through by lower trail. I think Gen. Howard must have met the hostiles on the divide, on the trail to East Fork of Firehole River and lower basin. Hostiles are not in East Fork valley but are feeding on an elk herd there. Baronett's Bridge burned this morning.[54]

After Server had cantered out of sight Doane prepared to move forward in anticipation of Gilbert's arrival. He ordered his men to pack some mules with rations and ammunition and then told the civilians he would leave all of the extra supplies with them if they would hold their position until more help arrived. De Rudio and Scott prepared Company E to march, and all waited impatiently for Gilbert to arrive.

Late in the afternoon troops could be seen coming upriver from the north, and within a few moments 2nd Lt. Charles B. Schofield, leading Company L, Second Cavalry, arrived at the camp. But Doane could not share in the joy that everyone else felt in greeting the reinforcements. Colonel Gilbert came forward on his tired mount, and along with him was Sergeant Server. Gilbert had quizzed Server on his mission and proposed route and then refused to provide the sergeant a fresh horse. He told Doane that he saw no need to send the messages ahead to General Howard; instead he would lead the entire command by the same circuitous route to overtake the general himself. Gilbert's justification for such a ridiculous undertaking was based on his belief that Howard's command was still at Henry's Lake, Idaho Territory, the last place anyone at Fort Ellis had heard from him. However faulty his rationale, the colonel was fully prepared to throw away the chance of a lifetime for Doane. The lieutenant could do nothing but rail against the idea. "Doane begged him with tears in his eyes to go forward," as Scott wrote of the confrontation with Gilbert, "but he refused, saying that he was only trying to reach Howard and did not want to be delayed by a fight and miss him."[55]

The combined force of Company E, Seventh Cavalry, and Company L, Second Cavalry, left the camp at Henderson's Ranch that evening and made for the trail to the Gallatin Valley. Disgusted and utterly defeated, Doane suggested the civilians evacuate the ranch and accompany the supply wagons back to Fort Ellis. Although he would eventually be held accountable for all the supplies, Doane was past caring. He knew that they were headed in the opposite direction from any further participation in the campaign and that if only they had gone forward as he asked they would have linked up with Howard and been in the very epicenter of the chase. Even an officer as inexperienced as Lieutenant Scott could tell that Gilbert's plan was ridiculous and his capacity to command questionable. "He had no idea of marching cavalry," Scott wrote of Gilbert, "and fearing to separate his command, although away from the zone of operations, he camped two troops and two pack trains without grain in a mountain pocket where there was grass for only half the number."[56] Gilbert led the men by brutal forced marches up the Madison River and struck Howard's trail more than two days behind him. "The Grey horses from the Company . . . began to give out," Jirah Allen remembered, "and as no extra horses could be secured the soldiers had to foot it."[57]

While Colonel Gilbert led Doane's command on its pointless and exhausting march, General Howard's column pushed on east after the Nez Perces, trailing the fleeing tribe out of the National Park and down the Clark's Fork. Howard never received Doane's letter of September 1 and had no idea that a company of soldiers had even been in the Mammoth Hot Springs area until September 6, when his soldiers paused to rebuild Baronett's Bridge. Some scouts sent downriver brought back the news of the Indian raid encountered by Doane's command from the civilians remaining at Henderson's Ranch. On September 7, after crossing the river with his men, Howard finally got a message from Sturgis, confirming the location of the Seventh Cavalry — a critical piece of information that Doane's message could have told him nearly a week earlier.[58] The general did not know exactly what Gilbert's mission had been when he diverted Doane's company, but he certainly realized that Colonel Gibbon's "very unmilitary and inconsiderate conduct" had prevented Company L, Second Cavalry, from proceeding to the Clark's Fork by ordering the troopers to accompany Gilbert.[59]

If General Howard had been irritated at the District of Montana's meddling in his campaign, Colonel Sturgis became positively livid. He called Gibbon's authorization allowing Doane such leniency "cruel interference with my orders and plans" and blamed both officers for nothing less than the escape of the Nez Perce band and the prolongation of the war.[60] On September 9 the Seventh Cavalry had been lured from an excellent position in the Clark's Fork Valley to turn their attention to the Stinking Water drainage. Sturgis tried to monitor both possible escape routes from a camp at Heart Mountain. On September 10, when scouts mistakenly reported that the fleeing tribe had chosen the Stinking Water trail, Sturgis committed his whole force to stop them. Unfortunately for the soldiers, the Nez Perces had instead neatly sidestepped their sentinels and managed to pass through the Clark's Fork route to make their way to the Yellowstone valley and the buffalo plains beyond. Sturgis bitterly denounced Doane's lack of cooperation. "I was deprived of the information which I expected and which I ought to have received from his large body of Indian scouts," Sturgis complained in his official report. He gave a backhanded compliment to Doane by admitting that his knowledge of the country was "superior to that of any other individual in that country"; but he pointed out that if the lieutenant had joined the main body of the Seventh Cavalry as ordered Sturgis would have had enough manpower to monitor both the Stinking River and Clark's Fork passes at the same time.[61]

While the Seventh Cavalry waited for the Nez Perces and General Howard pursued them through the park, Colonel Gilbert doggedly pushed his men on in pursuit of Howard's column, paying no attention to their exhaustion or attrition. One by one the soldiers dropped out, forced to abandon equipment and walk alongside their dangerously weakened mounts. Lieutenant Scott had to give up when the soldiers reached the Yellowstone River just north of the lake and, with his orderly, walked the fifty miles back to Mammoth Hot Springs while pushing and pulling their starved horses up every hill they encountered.[62] Only Doane, De Rudio, and twenty troopers managed to finish Gilbert's fruitless march on September 15. On that day they staggered into the Crow Agency, where they received news that two days earlier Sturgis and the Seventh Cavalry had tried to head off the Nez Perces at Canyon Creek, north of the Yellowstone River, and had again failed to stop the Indians. By that time, too, Gilbert realized he would never catch up with Howard to assume command and allowed the survivors of his roundabout march to rest a few days before returning to Fort Ellis. They arrived there on September 21, having traveled almost 300 miles and accomplishing absolutely nothing.

On his arrival back at Fort Ellis, Doane had the added humiliation of having to report to Major Brisbin, who knew that his subordinate's latest attempt to circumvent authority had ended in a fiasco. Brisbin wanted to place the lieutenant back on duty at the post immediately. Doane stubbornly insisted that, since he had complied with Colonel Gibbon's directive and had been subsequently released from his obligation to report to Colonel Gilbert, his obedience automatically reverted back to Colonel Miles and the District of the Yellowstone. Even if he had been able to prevail in his creative argument, Doane quickly found himself with no troops to command anyway.

Orders arrived at Fort Ellis from Colonel Miles's headquarters, discharging all of Doane's officially enrolled Crow scouts, and Colonel Gibbon's office ordered Lieutenant De Rudio's troopers to Fort Shaw.[63] This left Doane with a force of a dozen pack animals, four mule skinners, scout Jack Baronett, and no clear assignment for any of them. "I do not know what to do exactly," he wrote to Miles on September 28, "as I had been taken very far in the rear when I had gotten pretty well to the front at Henderson's Ranch, which has been a great disappointment."[64] Major Brisbin had no desire to allow Doane to wait for a reply from Miles. When a call came the next day from General Howard for supplies to be sent to a battalion of the First Cavalry marching toward Fort Ellis, Brisbin ordered Doane to take the rations on his pack train.

The rest of Fort Ellis's cavalry battalion participated in the last desperate pursuit of the Nez Perces and were there for the final capture of the tribe at the Battle of the Bear's Paw Mountains, October 5, 1877. Ironically, had Doane remained with his company back in April rather than seeking the independent assignment with the Crow tribe, he would have been in the thick of the fight too. To make matters worse, Doane's responsibility for thousands of dollars worth of supplies weighed heavily on his mind. Not only would he be required to account for them with reams of paperwork, but he may also have realized that his extravagant requisitions had almost contributed to a successful escape of the Nez Perces. The ammunition that Doane had asked to be left at Carroll Landing at the beginning of August had never been picked up, and the officer in charge had it moved to another supply dump at Cow Island a few miles up the Missouri River. The Nez Perces had attacked Cow Island on September 23 and nearly made off with the ammunition, in addition to the other supplies they had successfully appropriated. Fortunately for Doane, a fire destroyed most of the supplies at the dump and the Nez Perces moved on, sparing the lieutenant at least one more embarrassment during the disastrous campaign of 1877.[65]

While Doane completed the supply mission, more trouble for his career began to come from Crow agent George W. Frost. Frost had listened to disgruntled tribesmen complaining about Doane ever since midsummer and had been irritated when Doane sent the Crows back to the agency at the end of August, far in advance of their annuity shipment. He wrote first to Colonel Miles to report on the Crows' refusal to join Doane's command at Henderson's Ranch. "Doane asked me to threaten them and compel them to go by taking away their rations," he stated, "but I did not think that there was any law that allowed me to give such an order. They claim to have had bad treatment from him and they are very bitter in their denunciations, and while they will not follow him they express great willingness to follow any other commander and to fight the Nez Perces or any enemy of the whites."[66] Frost went even further, writing to the headquarters of the Department of Dakota to point out that none of the scouts Doane had recruited had been paid and that the army could expect no further cooperation from the tribe, "at least while this very bitter feeling against Lt. Doane exists."[67]

When Doane returned to Fort Ellis from his mission to drop off the supplies for the First Cavalry, he stubbornly refused to place himself under Major Brisbin's command and insisted that he still answered to Colonel Miles now that his obligation to follow Colonel Gilbert had ended. While the lieutenant made preparations to return to Crow Agency and enlist a new force of Crow scouts for service in the District of the Yellowstone, Brisbin wrote directly to Colonel Gibbon and requested that he, as commander of the District of Montana, order Doane to report for duty at Fort Ellis.[68] To get Doane away from the protection of Miles required more effort on Brisbin's part, but he found a willing ally in George Frost.

Frost wrote to Brisbin on October 10 after being informed that Doane intended to return to his agency on the Stillwater. Becoming much more strident in his accusations against Doane's malfeasance among the Crows, Frost asserted, "I do not think he could raise a company by any possibility and besides, from common rumor and many positive statements that have come to me, I am inclined to the opinion that he has not only attempted to usurp the authority that was not delegated to him and did not belong to him, but his influence over the tribe and at the agency has been anything but what should have been exercised by an officer entrusted with the care and control of Indians."[69]

Armed with Frost's letter, Major Brisbin acted quickly. He stopped Doane from leaving the post and presented him with a formal letter, demanding that the lieutenant produce a copy of the orders from Colonel Miles that he claimed to be operating under. When Doane failed to come up with anything more current than his general instructions from the previous summer, Brisbin issued three orders in rapid succession, demanding that Sergeant Server and privates Long and Applegate return to their companies, the mule skinners be discharged, and the pack train be returned to the Tongue River Cantonment. Doane wrote to Miles after getting Brisbin's orders, begging to be allowed to return to the Crow Agency with scout Jack Baronett, not to recruit new scouts as earlier planned, but ostensibly to make arrangements to pay those who had already served that summer. Brisbin again moved quickly, forwarding to Miles agent Frost's accusatory letter on October 10. In his written endorsement to Miles, Brisbin insisted that Doane's actions with the Indians had done the army a great injury and added that he had reliable information that the lieutenant had "consorted with squaws" while otherwise demoralizing the Crow camp. "I do not think it best, General, that such a man be allowed to run around lose," Brisbin told Miles. "I think most decidedly the best place for him is with his company. He seems to have an abhorrence of Company duty and is all the time trying to get away. This of course is wrong and if you had known him well I do not think you would have detailed him with Indians."[70]

Brisbin knew better than to be as frank with Colonel Gibbon, whose fondness for Doane as an officer and business partner would likely shield the rebellious lieutenant. Just four days after sending his message to Miles, Brisbin filed an official report of his battalion's campaign activities to the Department of Dakota through Gibbon's office. In the report Brisbin praised Doane's work with the Crows, asserting that the lieutenant's actions had prevented the Nez Perces from obtaining fresh horses from the Crows.[71]

Major Brisbin's duplicity in reporting Doane's activities achieved the desired results on November 1, when Colonel Miles's headquarters issued notice to Doane that his services with the District of the Yellowstone were no longer needed. The lieutenant sadly gave up his ambition to lead into the field another independent command of Crow scouts and white troopers for service against a possible return of Sitting Bull's Sioux across the Canadian border and reluctantly placed himself under Brisbin's authority. The major lost no time in finding a suitable assignment for his prodigal subordinate. On November 7, 1877, Special Orders Number 216 decreed that Doane, along with Sergeant Server and four enlisted men, "would start down the Yellowstone River on the 10th of November and bury all potatoes worth saving left behind by the Big Horn and Tongue River potato boats."[72]

CHAPTER 8

"You do not realize how tenderly I love you"
Divorce and Remarriage

Mary Lee Hunter grew up on the frontier, and her early life had interesting parallels to Doane's own background. Like him, Mary was the oldest in a family of six children and at the age of six crossed the Great Plains in a covered wagon. Also like Doane, Mary early displayed indications of intelligence and keen powers of observation. At a noonday stop during her family's overland journey along the Bozeman Trail in Wyoming, Mary possibly saved her little brother's life when she noticed the infant's foot poking out from beneath a blanket that some parleying Indians were about to spirit away and shouted the warning to her parents.[1] Just as the lure of gold seduced Solomon Doane to abandon his Oregon homestead and force his family to relocate in the squalid mining camps of northern California, Dr. Andrew Jackson Hunter led his family from their comfortable Missouri home to the various boomtowns of Montana Territory.

As Doane's father had discovered, the western mining camps offered no opportunities for quick riches. After a brief residence in

Virginia City, Hunter hustled Mary and her siblings off to other promising El Dorados such as Helena, Confederate Gulch, York, and Canyon Ferry. At each of these towns the doctor's wife, Susan, made as much money gardening as the family realized on the mining investments her husband made. By the time Dr. Hunter moved his family to Bozeman during the summer of 1869 he had resigned himself to abandon the search of gold to resume the practice of medicine. The garrison command at Fort Ellis three miles east of the infant town helped convince Hunter again to take up his profession, by offering him a job as a contract physician for the army. While the doctor extended his practice and served as a probate judge for Gallatin County, Susan took care of the growing family and continued to supplement their income by selling cabbages and other garden truck. The Hunters were well on their way to becoming a Bozeman fixture by 1871, when the doctor secured his second appointment as the Gallatin County hospital physician for the indigent.[2]

Dr. Hunter again uprooted his family in 1872 when he became enamored with a new money-making project. The hot springs along the Yellowstone River about thirty miles to the east of Bozeman had long been a landmark for travelers along the Bozeman Trail, and Hunter himself had carefully examined them in 1864 with a vague thought of someday exploiting their alleged curative powers. During that time gold seekers routinely bypassed the springs in their hurry to reach the diggings; subsequently the thermal pools were ignored after the Bozeman Trail was closed by Red Cloud's successful campaign, forcing the army to forsake the route. Undeterred by the potential danger of Indian resentment, Hunter claimed the springs in 1871 under the provisions of the Homestead Act and began to make the required improvements to the property, establishing first a bath house and vegetable garden and in the following year a permanent residence for his family. During the interim the Crow Agency had been located on the south bank of the Yellowstone River at Mission Creek, not far from Hunter's Hot Springs. This resulted in a ready market for the vegetables and watermelons that the doctor and his family grew with the aid of the heated water. Soon other settlers began to file claims on the adjoining sections of land.

Mary began the life of a pioneer commuter once her father had committed the family to developing the springs. Periodically the family would come back to Bozeman for prolonged visits, but they always returned to establish their residency for the claim. Even periodic Indian troubles failed to keep them away for long, and Susan Hunter and her children became hardened by the rough environment the doctor had chosen for their home. Susan once bested a Sioux who had cornered her naked and alone in the bath house, whipping him with his own riding quirt until he fled in terror. On another occasion she armed her daughters to help defend the cabin when Indians approached during her husband's absence.[3]

As the oldest child, Mary had been the object of special concern to her parents, who made sure she had periodic opportunities to remain in Bozeman to continue her lessons when the rest of the family returned to the springs. In 1875 the Gallatin Female Seminary, a Presbyterian girls' school in Bozeman, relocated to the nearby community of Hamilton. The remaining limited public school facilities gave Mary no further local options to continue her education. In 1876 the Hunters sent Mary to St. Vincent's Academy, a Catholic school for girls in Helena. Established in 1869 by the Sisters of Charity, St. Vincent's had become an established institution in the territorial capital, and Mary attended classes at the boarding school in 1876 and 1877. Her sister, Lizzie Kate, joined her at the school in 1878. Although not a Catholic himself, Dr. Hunter knew that the school offered the best opportunity for his daughters to refine their social education in such a raw frontier environment and had no compunction about sending them to a "nunnery school."[4] There Mary put the finishing touches to her education as a lady of refinement, tempered by the exigencies of frontier life, resulting in a combination of qualities that would make her an ideal choice as a wife for Doane.

Doane already had a wife, of course, a fact that he handled with considerable tact when visiting at Hunter's Hot Springs during 1877. Everyone in the tightly knit communities of Fort Ellis and Bozeman knew that Amelia Doane had left Fort Ellis for Chicago on

July 7. Doane could safely play the role of a guiltless abandoned husband while hoping that Amelia could secure a divorce decree quietly in distant Chicago, and he sent her money to retain an attorney. For a while it seemed that the strategy would work and that his rumored dalliance with the Crow women during the summer, and his continuing pursuit of Mary Hunter, would not become fuel for further gossip. Amelia wrote at the beginning of December to report on her progress. "I have grounded the application on the plea of 'incompatibility' in order to avoid publicity," she informed her husband. "The life led by us during the past years causes me to think that no opposition to the granting of the decree will be made by you but that you are as anxious as I am to be released from bonds hateful to us both." Amelia also threatened Doane by telling him that if he would not cooperate and sign the papers she would be forced to "give other causes than that of incompatibility upon which a divorce will certainly be granted me."[5] Doane promptly complied, but as it turned out Illinois law would not allow the dissolution to be handled discreetly in distant Chicago. The divorce would drag on well into the next year before it could be settled in a Montana territorial court.

On November 10, 1877, when Doane finished the humiliating potato reconnaissance along the Yellowstone River, he chose to return to Hunter's Hot Springs to write his report rather than proceed to the new Crow Agency on the Stillwater River as his orders had specified. During his visit Mary, temporarily home from school, remained aloof from him, as befitted an eighteen-year-old Victorian female in the presence of a married army officer nearly twice her age. But her coldness did not prevent Doane from subtly courting her.[6] He spent at least as much effort on her parents too, and he relied on a legitimate reason for lingering at the springs. Responsible for thousands of dollars in government property issued under his authority during the Nez Perce campaign, Doane had an excuse to write to Major Brisbin for an extension of his current detached assignment. He reported on November 18 that all the potatoes had been stolen and asked for the reassignment of his favorite, Sgt. Fred

Server, and an enlisted man to assist in visiting the Crow camps to gather equipment and get the paperwork signed for the previous summer's scouts to receive their pay.[7]

Major Brisbin did not receive Doane's latest request with good humor. The lieutenant had once again violated the spirit, if not the letter, of his orders. Although Brisbin had to recognize the legitimacy of Doane's request to settle the property and payroll issues, the major had no intention of making it easy on his subordinate. "In view of the long campaign this summer and the hard service performed by the men of the battalion, the commanding officer does not feel justified in ordering soldiers out in winter unless to pursue or repel an attack," Brisbin directed his adjutant to reply. "Lt. Doane, if he desires it, can have one man from G Company as an orderly and to take charge of his stuff."[8] Doane had already prepared himself for Brisbin's resistance. In addition to flirting with Mary and charming her parents that November, he had taken the time to contact Colonel Miles at Fort Keogh to request assignment within the District of the Yellowstone, based on the same justification of settling the Crow scout payrolls. As a result of Doane's skillful manipulation of the army's command structure, Brisbin once again found his authority usurped and on November 28 was forced to reverse his earlier decision. Under the direction of the Department of Dakota headquarters, Brisbin authorized two enlisted men, mules, and a cart to be placed at Doane's disposal and directed him to report to Miles at Fort Keogh.[9] In a final face-saving gesture, however, Brisbin still refused to allow Sergeant Server to be assigned to Doane and demanded that he report back to Fort Ellis no later than February 10, 1878.

Doane had used the delay caused by the exchange of orders to good purpose, and by the time he left Hunter's Hot Springs at the beginning of December he had made sufficient progress with Mary to give him hope for the future. In his discussions with her parents, Doane made sure the Hunters understood his potential as a suitor included a possibility of wealth for their daughter. His intentions to pursue that wealth became obvious after he made his way down the Yellowstone Valley to arrive at Fort Keogh. Instead of working immediately on the payroll claims of the Crow scouts as his orders called for, Doane used his time with Colonel Miles to interest him in the Centennial Tent design scheme. Miles found the idea of Doane's new invention fascinating, and the lieutenant convinced him to put the Fort Keogh garrison to work during the idle winter months ripping apart the surplus "A" frame and wall tents on hand and use the canvas to sew models of the Centennial Tent.[10]

While Doane worked on his future financial security, the present financial paucity of the unpaid Crow scouts continued to cause problems. Scouts reporting on the disposition of the Crows in various winter camps along the Yellowstone described their disappointment with the delay of their promised payment. Crow agent George Frost added his voice to the complaints, including in his annual report a repetition of his charges that Doane's handling of the Indians during the summer left them embittered against the government.[11] Nevertheless, Colonel Miles helped Doane with his task by officially appointing him acting assistant quartermaster to date from his first assignment to the Crow tribes in April 1877, an action that would assist the lieutenant in completing his official property returns. Then Miles sent Doane to Fort Custer, a post closer to the various wintering camps of the Crows, so that the correct scouts could be located to sign their discharge papers for eventual payment. Miles may have been aware of Doane's tendency to procrastinate in order to prolong his independent status, because the colonel sent a telegram to Fort Custer at the end of January reiterating that "it is of the first importance to have the money long due the Crow Scouts paid them without further delay and there will be a Paymaster at Fort Custer in the early part of March."[12] Doane welcomed the order because it would keep him from having to return to Major Brisbin's authority on February 10, but circumstances came into play that would allow an even more tardy return to Fort Ellis.

On February 9 Miles again heard rumors of Sitting Bull's intentions to cross the border from Canada and return to the United States. Doane would already be among the Crows, so Miles authorized him to represent the army's wishes and convince them to again scout for Sioux, but this time without any pay at all. Miles's confidence in Doane to execute this delicate matter of diplomacy was certainly not shared by agent Frost, who continued to be baffled as to why anyone would place reliance on the lieutenant. "While I am willing to use all my official and personal influence with the Crows to have them follow wherever you desire, I am not willing to cooperate with Lt. Doane," he wrote to Miles on February 12. "I think he would have less influence with the Crows than any officer that could be sent. Some of them absolutely refusing to follow him at all, and among these are some of the best scouts and warriors."[13]

Regardless of agent Frost's dismal opinion of Doane's influence on the tribe, the lieutenant did manage to get a handful of Crows to follow him. His relationship with the Crows during the previous summer may have been tempestuous, but he obviously befriended at least a few of the warriors during his time with the tribe. Doane and the warriors performed scouting duties for Maj. Eugene Baker's battalion around the headwaters of the Little and Big Porcupine Rivers during the latter part of February. While serving under his old commanding officer, Doane increased the wrath of his present one, and Major Brisbin reacted angrily to his subordinate's successful evasion of his authority. He had Doane officially listed as absent without leave to date from February 10 and reported the action to Colonel Gibbon's headquarters. A few days later he went over Gibbon's head to write directly to the headquarters of the Department of Dakota to vent his frustration. "Ample time was given Lt. Doane to settle any accounts he might have outstanding," Brisbin complained; and he asked specifically that Doane be ordered by the department commander to return to Fort Ellis. Word had reached Brisbin indirectly that Colonel Miles had authorized the continued absence of Doane; but no official letter confirming the fact had been sent, and the major expressed disbelief that Miles would retain Doane's services without providing formal notice.[14]

Ironically, Major Brisbin's anger and agent Frost's hostility both worked to prolong, rather than shorten, Doane's independent assignment. The major demanded that the Crow scouts be paid at Fort Ellis, thinking that the requirement would force Doane to return to the post. Agent Frost cooperated by sending the final pay statements for the scouts from Crow Agency directly to Brisbin. As a result, when Doane returned to Fort Custer on March 1 as required, the paymaster could not be authorized to release the money to the scouts. Doane wrote to Brisbin, informing him that the scouts could not be paid without combining the paperwork at Fort Ellis with the final discharge papers, which Doane held at Fort Custer. While waiting for that bureaucratic complication to be solved, Doane wrote another letter, an angry rebuke to agent Frost for his part in the mixup. The "arrangement" that Frost had made with Brisbin had done nothing more than delay a simple payment that could have been made at Fort Custer, Doane accused, adding a personal rebuke to the agent: "If you will be kind enough to lay aside all feeling and act *with* me instead of endeavoring to balk me the result will be better for the Indians."[15]

The severe weather that spring allowed the pay issue to drag on for weeks as the slow-moving messages of Doane, Brisbin, and Frost made their respective journeys up and down the Yellowstone Valley. In the meantime Doane could linger at Fort Custer with no clear assignment or duties, only sure that he would not have to report back to Brisbin until Miles said so. While Doane spent his time writing to Mary and trying to look busy, Brisbin's anger grew, and he looked for ways to succeed in reprimanding the errant lieutenant.

Unaware of or uncaring about the danger of further irritating his commander, Doane tried to extend his absence even further. He volunteered on April 21 to lead a squad of men to rescue a snowbound detachment stranded along the old Bozeman Trail and received a commendation from the Fort Custer commander for successfully completing the mission.[16] His procrastination also paid off when the headquarters of the Department of Dakota finally forced Major Brisbin to abandon his demands to have the scouts paid at Fort Ellis and send all the paperwork back to Doane at Fort Custer for final payment in May. Again, Doane had trumped the major, and Brisbin's anger grew accordingly. He renewed his requests for the lieutenant's immediate return to Fort Ellis, stressing his need for officers at the post due to renewed Indian troubles.

In the spring of 1878 the Bannock tribe of Idaho Territory had reacted angrily to settler encroachments on their lands at Camas Prairie. As in the case of the Nez Perces the previous year, the anger of the Bannocks led to attacks on white settlers by some factions of the tribe, while others remained on their reservation determined to avoid trouble. As Generals Howard and Crook sent troops to meet the outbreak in southern Idaho, Major Brisbin was ordered by Colonel Gibbon's headquarters of the District of Montana to establish an outpost at Horse Prairie near the Idaho border in case any of the reservation Bannocks attempted to join their more rebellious kinsmen. Capt. Edward Ball of Company H established Camp Mulkey in April and began the routine duty of monitoring the Bannocks at the nearby Lemhi Agency. Tendoy, a tribal leader anxious to avoid trouble, requested a military escort at the end of May for his band to travel safely to a buffalo hunt in the lower Yellowstone valley. Brisbin gave the assignment to Ball's command after pointedly writing to Gibbon that he would send either Doane or Lt. Lovell H. Jerome to command the escort "as soon as either of these officers arrive."[17]

Doane's excuses for lingering at Fort Custer had all but run out as the month of June began; but still he procrastinated, spending his time writing letters to the Hunters and playing poker with the other garrison officers. Major Brisbin fumed over the lieutenant's absence; while waiting for someone who outranked Colonel Gibbon to take action in the matter, the major did what he could to express his growing frustration with Doane. He wrote to the headquarters of the Department of Dakota on June 4 to bring up the matter of the Snake River exploration again. Disparaging Doane's earlier attempt and recounting its near-fatal results, Brisbin hastened to add: "I do not wish the General Commanding to believe that because Lieutenant Doane's and a previous expedition failed to make the exploration of Snake River that it cannot be done, for the sole cause of failure was the selection of an improper season for starting out."[18] Obviously intending to snub Doane in the request, Brisbin finished the letter by pointedly suggesting that two other officers make the survey.

Major Brisbin's exasperation with Doane was also hinted in his next letter to the Department of Dakota headquarters. The protection of Yellowstone National Park from poachers and vandals had long been of major concern to many individuals, civilian and military alike. Congress had responded to these concerns by appointing first Nathaniel P. Langford and next Philetus W. Norris as superintendents of the park and charged them to protect the place without providing much financial support to do so. Langford had hardly set foot inside the park during his term, and even though Norris pledged to be more involved after his 1875 appointment he had a reputation among some army officers as a self-promoting braggart who could not be counted on. On the day after Brisbin wrote his Snake River letter, an incident occurred that reminded him of Yellowstone's need for proper oversight. Hearing that a party of hunters had stopped by the Fort Ellis sutlers store to purchase provisions for their proposed elk shoot in the park, the major again took up his pen. "I have long intended writing the Department Commander on this subject, but we have been so much engaged with Indian trouble during the past two years I have put it off," he began. "There are now in the Park thousands of Elk, so tame a person can ride or walk about among them. I am reliably informed that one hunter has slaughtered as many as seventy-five of these animals in a single day."[19] Brisbin also bemoaned the wanton destruction by tourists of rock formations at the park's basin, claiming the silicate deposits "have been hundreds of years in forming and a man can destroy in a day what cannot be reproduced in three times the span of his life."[20] To answer the destructive onslaught of thoughtless tourists, Brisbin proposed setting a military guard over the park by posting squads of men reporting to sergeants at the two major entrances of the park to register tourists and monitor their activities. Conspicuously absent from the request was a provision for any commissioned officer in the proposed Yellowstone detail, keeping direct command over the guard the purview of the post commander at Fort Ellis.

Unaware of Brisbin's correspondence regarding the Snake River and Yellowstone, Doane continued to dally at Fort Custer until June 12, 1878. Capt. James Egan of Company F, Second Cavalry, prepared to march from the post to Fort Ellis and ordered Doane to accompany him. At first Doane told the captain that he still reported to Colonel Miles of the District of the Yellowstone and refused to obey. Egan reacted angrily to the lieutenant's insubordination and threatened Doane with arrest. If Doane felt inclined to continue resisting, he quickly changed his mind when Egan produced a copy of the order from the headquarters of the Department of Dakota specifically mandating that Doane return.[21] While Egan and his reluctant subordinate rode back to Fort Ellis, Major Brisbin got a curt reply to his request for the Yellowstone detail. General Terry, commander of the Department of Dakota, had forwarded the suggestion to Commanding General Sherman, whose no-nonsense view of the army's role was summarized in a terse response. "Congress has charge of the Yellowstone Park and has appointed a keeper," he growled in reply. "The troops have enough to do without guarding it. The public cannot carry away the Geysers — the only real objects of great natural curiosity. New incrustations form each year and are of no real value."[22]

Brisbin's genuine concern for the park's welfare overcame his anger at Doane after receiving Sherman's brusque rejection. Regardless of his personal feelings regarding the lieutenant's continued resistance to authority, Brisbin had to admit that Doane spoke with some authority when it came to Yellowstone National Park. On Doane's arrival at Fort Ellis, the major formally requested in writing that Doane report to him on the state of the park, paying particular attention to the matter of tourist vandalism to the geyser formations so that he could effectively rebut Sherman's contention that the rock formations rejuvenated themselves annually.

Since his arrival at Fort Ellis, Doane had been dealing with the emotional and social fallout from Amelia's departure, along with settling long overdue financial claims for which he had been responsible. The combination of these vexations, along with Doane's wounded pride regarding anything having to do with his acknowledged role as an expert on Yellowstone National Park, resulted in a report clearly expressing all his bottled-up rage and showed how truly reckless of his career he had become. "In answer to your letter of inquiry of present date herewith returned, I have the honor to reply that the National Park has had no care taken of it in any way whatever up to the present date by any official as far as I have been able to learn," he began haughtily. The primitive improvements, such as Baronett's bridge over the Yellowstone River and the wagon road that General Howard had constructed, were entirely inadequate, Doane charged. Before launching into a multipage essay on tourist vandalism and poaching, the lieutenant paused to express his frustration with the lack of recognition he had received for his explorations. "As might be expected there is not a line on any of the engineer maps showing that I was ever in the park," he complained, "though my report has been published in extracts and references all over the world." Doane went on to denounce Montana territorial officials "desiring a cheap reputation as public guardians or in the hope of public plunder from expected appropriations."[23]

By using an altruistic argument to advance a personal agenda, Doane's essay committed the same offense that he accused others of committing. He insisted that the park could only be protected and improved by posting a permanent military guard commanded by an officer to supervise construction and prevent vandalism. Doane mocked the idea that the same goals could be accomplished by civilians, charging that their own self-interest "would be about as ornamental or useful as would be the statue of the Plantation Bitters Man if painted on the dome of the Capitol at Washington." Not satisfied with criticizing civilians in the abstract, Doane turned his scorn directly toward Philetus Norris and the ten thousand dollars that Congress had authorized the new superintendent to spend on the park's maintenance and protection. "The result will be simply ridiculous and disgusting," he charged, describing Norris as "exceedingly loud mouthed" when the superintendent had questioned the propriety of using military transportation for the 1875 trip of Secretary of War Belknap through the park. "The airs and ignorant assumptions of such people as this fellow Norris disgust well-disposed and honest men, citizens of the frontier," he concluded.[24]

Dismayed by the vehemence of Doane's reply, Major Brisbin called the lieutenant to his office and angrily confronted him over his insubordination to Captain Egan. Doane realized too late that his intemperate remarks had brought him to the brink of disaster when Brisbin threatened him with arrest and court-martial. Insisting that Egan had overreacted, Doane quickly explained that his initial refusal to leave Fort Custer was based on his misunderstanding of Colonel Miles's orders. Doane also accused Egan of attempting to use Brisbin's authority to settle a personal grudge. After insisting that he was more than willing to join Captain Ball at Camp Mulkey as ordered, Doane breathed easier to see Brisbin throw the arrest order into his desk drawer, lock it up, and gruffly wave the lieutenant out of his office.

The next day after he had time to cool off, the major wrote a letter to Doane that attempted to give the lieutenant some badly needed advice. After reminding Doane he had narrowly escaped court-martial, Brisbin offered paternal counsel. "You are a useful officer but you seem to have got some queer fancies into your head," he observed. "One is that you need not serve with your company. My dear fellow, the right place for every officer is with his proper command. . . . If you don't want to be a first lieutenant of cavalry then try and get some other place under the government, but while you are a Lieutenant stick to your company." Doane's obvious disappointments with the various setbacks of his career had adversely affected his ability to perform his duties, Brisbin asserted, and he correctly observed that the lieutenant's overbearing pride contributed significantly to this problem. "I am afraid you have allowed yourself to fall into the habit of grumbling and become embittered against your fellow man," he continued. "We must all live and let live and for any one to imagine for a moment that he is all wise or perfect is folly."

The major pointed out to Doane that his continued success in the regiment depended on his ability to comprehend his proper station as a junior officer, without entitlement for special privileges or recognition. "All I shall ever require of you is very simple," the major counseled. "First that you will stay with your company a reasonable time and when you want detached service apply for it through the regular channels. Second, that you will promptly obey my orders while you are under my command. Third that you will refrain from making disrespectful speeches and committing disrespectful actions toward myself or my officers."[25] Doane should have paid particular attention to Brisbin's first requirement, which would have dire consequences for his career ambitions when he disregarded it.

Doane's career ambitions centered on Yellowstone National Park, and both he and Major Brisbin had correctly forecast the military's future role in its management. Brisbin's advancement of that role, however, had been stymied by Doane's bombastic reply. "I wanted to use your report on the Park ever so much but I cannot," the major informed the lieutenant. "The first part is about yourself and the last part contains a bitter attack on Col. Norris. I do not think any more of the Colonel than you do, but what is the use of attacking him in an official report? We have nobody we want made Superintendent of the Park, and as long as we have not it is no matter to us who is the Superintendent."[26] Brisbin returned the original report and said he regretted that he would be unable to use it, but he had not been entirely honest. The full text of Doane's essay had been transcribed verbatim into the post records, and Brisbin had his clerk edit out the offending portions on a second draft. He then mailed the amended version forward as an authoritative source for his rejoinder to General Sherman. Although Doane would bitterly denounce Brisbin's forgery once he discovered it, the report did advance the notion of setting a military guard over Yellowstone National Park, and it also linked Doane's name with the idea. Brisbin may have felt that it was "no matter" who became the superintendent, but Doane had a definite idea of the perfect man for the job: himself.

When Doane arrived at Camp Mulkey that summer his thoughts turned far adrift from his Yellowstone ambitions or the possible consequences of his intemperate report to Major Brisbin. The post had little to do with mopping up any of the scattered bands of Bannocks still resisting the army's authority, and Doane had the leisure time to dream of both his future happiness with Mary Hunter and his present problem of getting a divorce settlement with Amelia. As mentioned, the strategy of finalizing their arrangements in Chicago had fallen through, so Amelia had to retain a

Montana lawyer to press the suit in a Virginia City court. Under Montana territorial law, a divorce could not be granted for "incompatibility" as they had hoped, and Amelia had to allege "abandonment and extreme mental cruelty" as cause, charges to which Doane had to agree even though she had been the one to leave. The court at Virginia City would not convene until fall, so Doane spent his time at Camp Mulkey anxiously, writing love letters to Mary and fishing for trout to pass the time. "After the September Court Term I hope to feel less restless, and to have more settled plans," he wrote to Mary in early August. "Now I am utterly in deep water, can depend on nothing, only live and hope. . . . Dear, noble Mary, you do not realize how tenderly I love you."[27]

Doane thought about things financial as well as romantic while idling on Horse Prairie. He had invested some of his money in Dr. Hunter's spa at the Hot Springs, and the court fees in Virginia City, along with the money he had sent to Amelia, strained his finances. Were he to be successful in his suit for Mary's hand, he would need money to establish their household. A possible answer to the problem would be the successful marketing of the Centennial Tent, but Doane had not yet patented his design; nor could he expect to convince the War Department to adopt the invention without personally going to Washington, D.C., and lobbying for it. After his unpleasant exchange with Major Brisbin earlier that summer, Doane knew his chances of getting permission to travel to the nation's capital were quite slim. An interesting turn of events in Doane's favor resulted in his securing the leave of absence he needed, however. Colonel Gibbon, who had all but given up on the tent business partnership, had temporarily replaced Gen. Alfred Terry as commander of the Department of Dakota in the summer of 1878. Doane realized he could follow standard military procedure by first applying for leave to Captain Ball as his battalion commander and then having the request forwarded directly to Gibbon at his St. Paul, Minnesota, headquarters.

As Doane's leave application wove its way through the various layers of army bureaucracy, Mary and her sister, Lizzie Kate, arrived in Helena to begin the school year at St. Vincent's. Mary particularly enjoyed the school in her third year, applying herself to the lessons in needlework, voice, and harp from the sisters, who also allowed her to answer her suitor's letters every Saturday afternoon. The school did not place much emphasis on religion for the students, although they could choose to attend an optional daily mass. Still, the nuns strictly supervised the girls even while remaining friendly enough to enjoy romping and roughhousing with them. Doane had to be very careful with the content of the letters he wrote to his "dear little lady friend" now that she was no longer at Hunter's Hot Springs.[28] Mary also refrained from saying too much in her replies to the lieutenant, although probably more from a sense of propriety than from concern about potential censorship from the St. Vincent's faculty. "Today Dear Sister Clotilda kindly gave me permission to answer your kind letter," she wrote one week after receiving two lengthy letters from Doane. "You of course do not expect much news from a schoolgirl, if you do you will be disappointed. All the news I can give you will be in reference to our school."[29] Such empty replies to his heartfelt missives drove Doane to distraction.

After receiving the welcome news that the divorce had been finalized in Virginia City, he became bolder in his messages to Mary, writing with more direct purpose than he had ever dared before and sometimes revealing quite frankly the crushing weight of disappointments he had endured. "The waste of my life has a rose root within it," he wrote in a poem. "And thy fondness alone to sunlight can win it."[30] When the Camp Mulkey garrison returned to Fort Ellis at the end of October, Doane took advantage of the first opportunity to get to Mary at Helena by escorting the army paymaster, Maj. John E. Blaine, the same officer who had taken Amelia to Chicago. Having secured the permission of Dr. and Mrs. Hunter formally to request Mary's hand, Doane now pressed his suit in person and received the reply he had long hoped for. The only obstacle that stood between the engaged couple and their embarkation on life's journey together was Major Brisbin.

When Doane's leave application had been returned from Washington, D.C., as Special Orders 237 from the War Department, he informed Major Brisbin that he had been granted five months' furlough, to commence on December 15. Enraged, Brisbin realized that Doane had done exactly as he was specifically told not to do. The major angrily sent a telegram to Washington on November 18. "The leave of absence granted First Lt. G.C. Doane . . . was obtained without the knowledge or consent of his company or his post commander," Brisbin fumed. "He can not be spared now and I request that the leave be suspended until such time as in the opinion of his company and post commander his service can be spared."[31] The telegraph reply from the War Department came the same day, referring Brisbin to the headquarters of the Department of Dakota, where Colonel Gibbon confirmed the propriety of Doane's application. However, Brisbin did not wait for Doane's erstwhile business partner to save him from punishment. On November 20 the major assigned the lieutenant an especially dreary detail, again sending him down the Yellowstone River—this time not to rescue abandoned potatoes but to haul telegraph poles, insulators, and wire for the construction of a line from Fort Ellis to Fort Custer.[32] The job threatened to keep Doane in the field beyond the date of his leave's commencement and to interfere with his plans to take Mary to the altar.

Although it looked very discouraging at the time, Brisbin's attempt to punish Doane led indirectly to another ambitious exploration scheme for the lieutenant, arguably the most desperate of his career. The officer Doane had been ordered to confer with regarding the telegraph construction was 1st Lt. Adolphus W. Greely of the Fifth Cavalry, temporarily assigned to the United States Signal Corps. Greely had been interested in Arctic exploration since 1876, the year he met Capt. Henry W. Howgate, an official in the army's Signal Corps headquarters in Washington, D.C. Howgate formed a close relationship with Greeley while lobbying Congress to finance a polar expedition scheme. Even Doane had met the captain when he had visited Washington to interest Secretary of War Belknap in the Nile expedition in 1875. When Doane met Greely in the lower Yellowstone Valley that November, the two men discussed their mutual interests in exploration as much as the task of building the Fort Custer telegraph line. Soon enough Doane had another reason for impatience in awaiting the commencement of his furlough. He wanted to get to Washington in order to convince Howgate to add his name to any possible Arctic expedition.

While on the telegraph detail, Doane once again exceeded his orders. Instead of turning back after reaching Kaiser's Store on the Yellowstone, he went with Greely all the way to Fort Custer, where he sent a hopeful message to Mary, indicating that he would be in Helena for their wedding day on December 15.[33] Once he arrived back at Fort Ellis, however, Doane learned that Brisbin's attempts to interfere with the leave application had been partially successful. After General Terry returned to St. Paul and relieved Colonel Gibbon as temporary commander of the Department of Dakota, he ordered Doane to remain on duty until at least Christmas, unless his services could be "sooner spared by commanding officer, Fort Ellis."[34] Terry's decision was based on Brisbin's unsubstantiated allegation that Doane's leave had been applied for without the knowledge of his company commander. When Captain Ball confirmed the opposite and said that he had forwarded the request in accordance with standard military procedure, Brisbin claimed an unidentified third party had told him that Doane inappropriately applied for the leave. After Doane threatened to write a letter to department headquarters demanding that Brisbin name the mysterious informant, the major got orders to send Doane on a court-martial detail.

2nd Lt. Lovell H. Jerome had served in the Second Cavalry since his 1866 graduation from West Point, but his lackluster record reflected his continuous bout with alcoholism. He had signed numerous pledges to refrain from drinking; but in July 1878 he again indulged, this time in Doane's company when the two were traveling back to Fort Ellis from Fort Custer. Doane filed charges, which Brisbin had dutifully forwarded to department headquarters. Doane had been called as a witness at Jerome's trial in St. Paul, Minnesota, and Brisbin ordered Doane to report there by a circuitous route through Helena and then down to the Union Pacific railroad station at Ogden, Utah Territory.[35] The required travel to Minnesota would further delay the start of Doane's leave, but by stopping in Helena to get married he could at least take his new wife along.

The wedding took place in the home of Thomas P. Fuller, the Internal Revenue collector for Montana, conducted by the Reverend Clark Wright and witnessed by the territorial governor, Benjamin F. Potts. Guests at the affair included Mary's parents, who had made the long ride from Hunter's Hot Springs, and her sister, Lizzie Kate, who would be married herself within a year to Bozeman freighter Frank Rich. The newlyweds departed on the overland stage the next day on the start of a dreary, four-day journey to the railroad, a trip that would tax Mary's endurance but not dampen her happiness. After all, her new husband had told her: "I love you more and more fondly from day to day." She felt sure he would never want to leave her side.[36]

CHAPTER 9

"I am almost wild at the thoughts of your being willing to leave me"

The Centennial Tent and the

Howgate Arctic Expedition

With the winning of his teenaged bride and the successful evasion of Major Brisbin's authority, Doane had every reason to slip into a comfortable lull in his career. He could do nothing to get a promotion because he would have to wait for a vacancy to occur within the regiment, and he had received the generally favorable notice of his superiors in official reports regarding the 1876 and 1877 campaigns. Doane could not be contented, though. Just as Abraham Lincoln's law partner once described the president's drive, Doane's ambition was the little engine that knew no rest; and he continued to look for ways to establish his reputation as an innovator and explorer. In his consuming quest for recognition neither his new spouse nor his own life would deter Doane. He would risk losing both in his final desperate attempts to gain the "paragraph in the encyclopedia of the human race" that he so earnestly wanted.

Following their Helena wedding, Doane and Mary made their way to the Union Pacific station at Corrine, Utah, to begin their honeymoon journey. Their first stop was St. Paul, Minnesota, where

Doane had to testify in the court-martial trial of Lieutenant Jerome. Doane had filed formal charges against Jerome in 1878 for the alcoholic lieutenant's failure to repay a loan from an enlisted man, so his testimony was crucial for the prosecution.[1] Duly convicted on the strength of Doane's evidence, Jerome eventually resigned. Doane left St. Paul before the verdict, when he received permission to commence his previously approved leave.

The couple next went to Washington, D.C., and rented rooms at a comfortable home in the latter part of January 1879. Regardless of the romantic allure of sharing the attractions of the capital city with her new husband, Mary quickly discovered that her honeymoon was actually a business trip for Doane. For the next few weeks he called on influential people to promote his exploration credentials and his "Centennial Tent" invention. Mary was certainly aware of his efforts to sell the tent idea, but subsequent evidence suggests that she had no idea her husband also called on Capt. Henry Howgate at the Signal Corps office to discuss Arctic exploration opportunities. Doane successfully concealed his intention to undertake another expedition by spending long hours at home, sketching out his tent design and composing lengthy detailed specifications for its construction. On February 20 he sent a copy of the specifications to the Board of Equipments of the Quartermaster General's office, along with a remarkably audacious cover letter. In it Doane apologized for having no model of the tent for inspection and then boldly asked to be returned to duty, ordered to the federal arsenal at Philadelphia, and authorized to spend the army's money to supervise the sewing of a prototype of his tent. In exchange, Doane promised to allow "said tent to belong to the United States when finished, free of all liability for royalty," a meaningless offer considering that he had not yet even patented the design.[2]

Doane's gambit worked, because within two weeks of making his request he received orders restoring him to duty and sending him to Philadelphia.[3] He returned to Washington on March 24 with the model tent and proudly had it pitched on the grounds in front of the Quartermaster General's office. Now that he had actually produced a prototype of his invention, Doane secured the services of an attorney at the Scientific American Patent Agency, who assured him he would have no trouble obtaining approval of the design. Doane felt sure he stood on the brink of success and wrote to Colonel Gibbon on March 28, sending along a copy of his specifications and the receipts for his expenses in filing for the patent. While waiting for Gibbon's reply, the inventor eagerly showed his tent to the Quartermaster General's equipment board, which recommended adopting the Centennial Tent on March 31.[4] Doane next approached the surgeon general for his endorsement of the design as beneficial to the health of soldiers in the field.

Colonel Gibbon reacted to Doane's excitement with measured commendation. Since Doane had reminded Gibbon of their 1876 contract agreeing to split all expenses and profit for the Centennial Tent, the colonel naturally worried that the lieutenant would be asking for capital to start up their own manufacturing company. "I supposed our arrangement had expired by limitation long ago," Gibbon remarked pensively, and he insisted he would be a "poor hand" at judging the merits of any manufacturing firm that they might choose to produce the tents.[5]

"The idea never entered my mind of abrogating our agreement," Doane wrote back, explaining that his field service had prevented him from pressing the issue of patenting and marketing the tent idea until now.[6] Doane explained that they stood to profit not from directly making the tents but from collecting a royalty from the army when the quartermaster made purchases from independent contractors. The lieutenant then presented Gibbon with several ideas for furthering their prospects. He wanted Gibbon to use his influence to convince the secretary of war to order Doane to visit various state militia headquarters to demonstrate the tent, explaining that "this will enable me to go with the endorsement implied of the War Department by granting the detail."[7] Doane also asked the colonel to advance five hundred dollars to cover the traveling expenses to be incurred while demonstrating the tent. Finally, he requested that Gibbon write articles for the various military service journals, pay to have them reprinted, and mail hundreds of copies to line officers throughout the army.

For a brief moment all indications seemed to point toward success for Doane. The patent office sent formal notice that the Centennial Tent had been approved on April 11, and the assistant surgeon general of the army, Charles H. Crane, wrote a letter endorsing the design on May 3.[8] Doane made preparations to go to New York and meet with Brinkerhoff, Turner and Company, to arrange the details of the tent's manufacture and the royalty attachment for each one he hoped the War Department would buy in the coming year. Before Doane could leave for New York, however, the entire scheme started to unravel. Colonel Gibbon, in sending his $55 check for the patent fees, had to inform his partner that "unfortunately I am in no condition to advance money at this time and see no prospect of being able to do so." Gibbon could offer no more encouragement than his suggestion that Doane call on two of his old Civil War comrades who currently held positions in the Connecticut and Wisconsin militia units to see if their respective state governments would begin purchasing the Centennial Tents. Although he agreed to write an article for a service journal, Gibbon naturally balked at the idea of purchasing hundreds of offprints for direct mail distribution.[9]

Doane may have been willing to use his own money for an advertising tour and mailing, but the whole business collapsed before he could have made such a rash move. George W. McCrary, the secretary of war, never ordered Doane to demonstrate his invention to anyone, and the animosity of the army's commanding general, William T. Sherman, contributed to McCrary's ultimate decision to reject the Centennial Tent. Doane had realized all along that Sherman's approval for the tent design would be necessary and had correctly predicted to Gibbon that "the trouble, if any, will come from there."[10] Sherman reviewed the equipment board's recommendation and promptly refused to approve the design, much to Doane's bewilderment.

The reason why Doane failed was really quite simple. The inventor had unknowingly picked the very worst time for selling General Sherman on the merits of a design improvement for tents. In a case quite similar to Doane's prior to the Civil War, Capt. Henry H. Sibley had also invented a conical tent design, the "Sibley Tent," which he duly patented in 1856. In 1858 Sibley formed a partnership with another officer, Capt. William Wallace Burns, who had a staff commission as Commissary of Subsistence and used his office to promote the adoption of the Sibley Tent. When the Civil War broke out, the Union army purchased thousands of Sibley Tents. Burns then successfully argued that royalties on those purchases should be paid entirely to him, because Sibley had defected to the Confederacy. Burns had been battling the government for his money ever since and finally won a Supreme Court decision that resulted in two special bills for payment in United States Congress. By the summer of 1879, when Doane tried to market his own tent, Burns stood to gain thousands of dollars from his lengthy legal fight.[11] General Sherman's disgust with the slow-moving legal process that promised to enrich Burns naturally extended to Doane's similar idea. As a result, Sherman stonewalled the adoption of the Centennial Tent, and all of Doane's subsequent pleas to Secretary McCrary proved fruitless.

Defeated and embittered, Doane terminated his honeymoon leave by reporting back to the Department of Dakota headquarters at St. Paul on June 2. There he received orders to report to a new post being constructed in northern Montana Territory, Fort Assinniboine. The site for the fort had been picked out in part to guard the nearby Canadian border from encroachment of northern Indian tribes, including Sitting Bull's Sioux; but the work of actually constructing the barracks and officers quarters had just begun the summer the Doanes arrived. A massive tent city had been pitched to house two companies of the Second Cavalry, eight companies of the Eighteenth Infantry, and scores of workmen hired to construct the substantial brick buildings. The Doanes established themselves in a pair of wall tents and set up housekeeping with ration boxes for furniture while waiting for their new home to be erected. Although living conditions were initially crude, Mary would soon move into the finest home she had ever known, on a post that would eventually be considered the best in the entire western region.[12] The absence of Major Brisbin, who had not been transferred to Fort Assinniboine, was an added benefit as far as Doane was concerned.

Mary tried to assuage her husband's disappointment, but Doane allowed his resentful anger to grow into a dangerous rage. The situation reached a head when a newspaper story quoting Doane's acerbic Yellowstone report to Major Brisbin appeared in a Washington, D.C., newspaper in February 1880. Brisbin had told Doane that he would not forward the report because of the lieutenant's personal attacks on the Yellowstone National Park superintendent Philetus Norris, but the major obviously had done so anyway. Angered, Doane took a newspaper clipping that garbled the contents of his report, along with a copy of the altered version of his original that Brisbin had edited, and composed a lengthy letter to the adjutant general proving that Brisbin had sent a forgery to Washington. "It is not pleasant to serve, and be continually obliged to watch for the results of falsehood, treachery, and discredit, of which the details herein given show, but are an example of many practiced by Major James S. Brisbin," he concluded in his preliminary draft. Doane had second thoughts about actually sending the letter, however. Perhaps Mary's influence in healing his bitterness over failure had begun to take hold, or, just as likely, he began to reflect on the career consequences of retaliating against Brisbin. He drafted a new conclusion to the letter that suggests both possibilities. He assumed the pose of one whose concern for the welfare of Yellowstone National Park, "in the enduring grandeur of its mighty mountains, its resplendent canyon, its glorious lakes and waterfalls, its thousands of thermal springs and its wondrous geysers," had compelled him to write the letter. He still accused the major as an example of those who attempted to achieve "fictitious reputations in connection" with Yellowstone, implying that his own association with the park differed completely and should be recognized as such.[13]

After he finished his accusation of Brisbin's treachery, the possibility of again achieving fame as an explorer began to dominate Doane's thoughts. Exploration of the Arctic had captured the nineteenth-century American imagination as a moon launch would enthrall a later generation, and Doane saw the chance to capitalize on that interest. Men who braved the exotic environment of the far north seemed particularly heroic to an increasingly urbanized population, especially by the 1880s, when the territory of the continental United States seemed so thoroughly mapped. Added to the mystique of Arctic geography was the mysterious fate of its best-known explorer. Sir John Franklin, a British naval officer searching for a sea route across the top of North America, had disappeared with his entire command in 1847. During the next decade some forty expeditions had been launched to find him. Even as late as the 1860s American explorer Charles Hall still made headlines for an ill-advised "rescue" operation for the missing Franklin party. In addition to these quixotic expeditions were those based primarily on nationalistic chauvinism, with daring adventurers willing to risk all to be the first to plant their country's flag at the North Pole. Doane realized that Arctic exploration had tremendous potential for creating instant celebrity: American expeditions had been "consistently characterized by the individuals who led them rather than the stated objectives."[14] It is little wonder that Doane had turned his intentions northward and had approached Captain Howgate with his ambitions while still in Washington trying to sell the Centennial Tent idea.

English-born Henry W. Howgate had served in the Union Army during the Civil War and subsequently as the postmaster of a small Michigan town. He reentered the service with a commission as captain at the Washington, D.C., office of the Army Signal Corps and became the property and disbursement officer under Brig. Gen. Albert J. Myer. Aside from embezzling thousands of dollars, which he allegedly lavished on prostitutes and a mistress, Howgate spent much of his time in Washington advancing an idea for polar exploration by means of permanent colonies in the northern latitudes. Howgate argued that such bases would be able to take advantage of seasonal changes in the northern ice pack for further exploration and could easily be resupplied by annual shiploads of provisions. Tirelessly petitioning Congress for funding the plan, Howgate had gathered a few powerful opponents during the 1870s, including General Sherman, who denounced the entire idea of military participation in Arctic exploration. Among those who helped promote Howgate's vision were many in the international scientific community. Karl Weyprecht, an Austrian army officer, had been instrumental in calling for a worldwide cooperative effort in investigating the Arctic. At an 1875 conference in Gratz, Weyprecht prepared the groundwork for the first International Polar Year, an agreement between eleven nations to establish observation posts in the far north for simultaneous recording of weather and atmospheric data.[15] Howgate's proposed colony at Lady Franklin Bay on Ellesmere Island off the northwest coast of Greenland dovetailed perfectly with Weyprecht's proposal, and during the winter of 1879–80 it appeared that congressional approval would be forthcoming.

While Howgate worked to advance his dream, Doane got a reminder of the potential for fame residing in any connection to the Arctic. 1st Lt. Frederick Schwatka of the Third Cavalry had begun a career as an explorer that would quickly surpass Doane's modest accomplishments. Schwatka, an intellectually gifted West Point graduate, had served on the plains under the command of Gen. George Crook and, in addition to gaining a credible combat record, had also managed simultaneously to qualify as both a physician and a lawyer. Unlike Doane, Schwatka wasted no time hoping for government sponsorship of exploration activities and instead actively courted the popular press for opportunities. In 1878 he presented his credentials to James Gordon Bennett, editor of the *New York Herald*, after reading that the newspaper intended to finance yet another Franklin search in the Arctic. Impressed with the talented lieutenant's credentials, Bennett convinced Secretary of War McCrary to grant Schwatka a leave of absence to lead the expedition. Bennett also assigned *Herald* reporter William H. Gilder to go along. Although the expedition had yet to be heard from during the time when Doane spent his first winter at Fort Assinniboine, the *Herald* made sure American readers did not forget about the intrepid men Bennett had sent to the Arctic.[16] The obvious lesson for would-be heroes to seek private sponsorship for their expeditions did not occur to Doane, and he continued to hold out for a journey officially sanctioned by the government.

When Howgate wrote to Doane in September 1879 with the information that a ship had been purchased for his planned Arctic colony, Doane eagerly telegraphed in reply that he would be available for duty.[17] "I'm pleased to learn that matrimony has not cooled your ardor for Arctic exploration," Howgate wrote back. "At present I do not need you as I am only in the early stages of organization. I have bought a steamer and am collecting supplies, but propose to have Congress authorize the detail of the necessary officers and men of the expedition."[18] It is not clear when Doane finally told Mary of his plans as they spent their first anniversary in their comfortable Fort Assinniboine home, but events soon pushed the issue to the forefront. The bill authorizing expenditures and military assignments for Howgate's polar colony slowly made its way through Congress and by March of 1880 seemed certain of passage. Howgate sent two telegrams to Doane reminding the lieutenant of his need to provide the names of men willing to volunteer for the expedition. Doane quickly complied, suggesting the names of Sgt. Fred Server and every other member of the 1876 Snake River expedition. Because service at the proposed polar colony called for a three-year commitment from all the volunteers, orders would have to come directly from the secretary of war, a formality that Howgate assured Doane would be easily arranged.[19]

In his consuming desire to lead another expedition, Doane apparently gave little thought to Mary's feelings on the matter. Inconsolable over her husband's plans to leave her for three years, Mary wrote, "I am almost wild at the thoughts of your being willing to leave me . . . it seems like such an impossible thing for you to do."[20] But tears from his young bride could not dissuade Doane from taking chances any more than the frozen waters of the Snake River had in the winter of 1876. Willing to gamble his life and his future marital happiness in order to be recognized as an explorer, he stubbornly made preparations for Mary to stay with her parents in Bozeman by selling off their household goods and otherwise settling financial affairs. If Mary thought her husband irrational for his willingness to sacrifice everything for such a trip, she might have considered that so many others shared his reckless courage. When three of the soldiers Doane suggested for the expedition declined the appointment, dozens of men volunteered to take their place, even offering money to purchase a vacancy from those who had been successful. "It is ever so, no matter how difficult the service, nor what may be the prospective hardships and dangers," Doane reflected later on the volunteers. "The enlisted men of the regiments on the frontier show a spirit of enterprise and adventure only paralleled in the records of the Spanish Conquests."[21]

As winter gave way to spring, Howgate pressed forward with his plan and, as promised, secured the official orders for the men's participation from the secretary of war. Howgate purchased a Scottish steam frigate, the S.S. *Gulnare,* probably with money he had embezzled from the army. To anyone who asked, Howgate claimed that the money for his ship came from a legacy he had inherited from his aristocratic English family, and he had the *Gulnare* brought to Washington for its final preparation. Unfortunately, Howgate had purchased the ship without adequately examining its features. The expedition would pay dearly for his haste in its selection. Fretting over the timing to get the expedition underway, Howgate finally got the official orders for Doane telegraphed on May 8 and then followed up with messages, urging the lieutenant to hurry to Washington. Doane could only move as fast as the army would allow in releasing him for duty, and he did not receive written permission to leave Fort Assinniboine until May 17. Mary rode along with him to Fort Benton, where they waited for a steamboat that would take Doane and his men down to the railhead at Bismark, Dakota Territory. Mary's reaction the next day when Doane put her on the stagecoach to Bozeman must have been traumatic. He admitted later: "The separation for a period which promised at that time to be of such long continuance was a trial to both of us which was far more severe than any hardships, either anticipated or subsequently encountered."[22]

As the steamboat *Helena* churned its way downstream to Bismarck, Doane recorded his experiences with a detail that would assist the composition of his future report and his present obligation to write frequently to Mary. Both husband and wife realized the exchange of their letters would come to a sudden halt once the expedition actually got underway, so they wrote with an almost urgent frequency. "I feel quite bewildered yet at our separation," he wrote a few hours after he had parted from Mary, "and begin to realize a sense of loneliness which is quite new and strange."[23] A few days later when they arrived at Fort Buford, he sent her another letter detailing all the financial arrangements he had hastily made, closing with the somewhat empty assurance: "I would give the world to have you with me."[24] Once Doane arrived at Bismarck his progress to Washington was more rapid, but he continued to send Mary brief letters from stations they stopped at, not necessarily to reassure her but more to express his anxiety over the possibility that other members of the expedition would arrive in Washington before him. He need not have worried. The *Gulnare* would be going nowhere until it passed an inspection by the naval board, an outcome that even Howgate began to doubt once he had a good look at the ship himself.

On May 30 Doane arrived in Washington and sent the enlisted men to nearby Fort Whipple while he himself checked into the Ebbet House Hotel across from the treasury building, eagerly anticipating the coming adventure. When he reported to Captain Howgate the next day, however, Doane received the first disappointment of the expedition. Unknown to the lieutenant, Howgate had promised the leadership of the polar colony to several officers, including his protégé, 1st Lt. Adolphus W. Greely. When Doane arrived Howgate told him that Greely would be appointed commander because the secretary of war himself had ordered it. So desperate to go on the expedition, Doane did not balk at having to serve under an officer two years his junior and offered to waive his seniority. "I volunteered to serve under Lt. Greely with a private understanding that I would have charge of the advance exploration work, while he would remain at the proposed station at Lady Franklin Bay in command of the colony," Doane explained.[25]

The first week of June the inspectors sent by the navy board closely examined the *Gulnare* at the shipyard in Alexandria, Virginia. The *Gulnare* proved to be shockingly decrepit, and the board flatly refused to accept responsibility for the vessel. After issuing the condemnation order on June 9, secretary of the navy Richard W. Thompson followed up with another letter to Captain Howgate, asserting that "entering the ice in her present condition the *Gulnare* would be crushed as easily as an egg shell."[26] Lieutenant Greely, who had gone to New York to purchase supplies, had enough sense to withdraw from the expedition, but Doane and 1st Lt. William H. Low, another officer Howgate had seduced into volunteering for Arctic service, became all the more determined to see the project through. Even though the two officers were willing to risk their lives, the War Department decided not to risk the lives of the enlisted men of the detachment and ordered all of the volunteers back to their respective western posts. "The bitter disappointment of these tried and faithful soldiers was painful to witness," Doane recorded. "They used all honorable means to affect [*sic*] an arrangement by which they might go on the vessel, in a private capacity; but all having failed, went back to their stations, to hope and wait."[27]

At least one person received the news of the expedition's troubles with relief. "Your telegram was received this morning and I am delighted," wrote Mary from Bozeman. "I infer from it that you do not know whether you are going or not and if you do not know at this time there is no doubt in my mind but that it will fall through and I am so hopeful this morning."[28] Mary had not counted on her husband's all-consuming drive for fame. Fortunately for Doane, Captain Howgate proved just as stubborn in the face of adversity. He announced to the local press that he had spent too much of his own money to give up on the project and would outfit the *Gulnare* as a private expedition. Doane and Low immediately applied for a leave of absence to accompany a hastily gathered replacement crew and began preparations for continuing with the colonization plans. The *Gulnare* underwent superficial repairs to its machinery. Howgate, fearing the lateness of the season, ordered supplies loaded with reckless speed. The haphazard results of the haste told fearfully in the coming voyage.

Howgate appointed Doane to command the reorganized expedition, a rather empty gesture because he would only be accompanying the *Gulnare* as far as its intended destination to unload the supplies and then return to the United States. Doane had received only three months leave, while Lieutenant Low, who managed to get an entire year away from active duty, would command the colony once established on shore. Capt. Henry C. Palmer would be in charge of the *Gulnare* during the voyage, so Doane's status for most of the trip was little more than that of a high-ranking passenger on an Arctic cruise. Other members of the expedition had hopes of remaining with the proposed colony for periods even longer than Low's commitment. Henry Clay, grandson and namesake of the famous Kentucky politician, joined the expedition as secretary. Slight of build and as hungry for fame as Doane, Clay resigned his elected position as prosecuting attorney of Louisville to lend his famous name to Howgate's expedition. A more headstrong member of the group could be found in Dr. Octave Pavy, an American-born Frenchman who had unsuccessfully tried several times to finance his own expeditions to the Arctic. Pavy's obsession with exploration had cost him his fortune, his family, and, briefly, even his sanity.[29] The doctor considered himself the expedition's resident expert and looked with scorn on anyone else who would presume to lead, especially an ambitious cavalry officer like Doane.

Pavy's attitude would likely have presented no problem had Doane remained with the *Gulnare* to assert his authority, but the ship left Washington on June 21 without him. Doane and Low both decided to rendezvous with the ship at Halifax, Nova Scotia, traveling there by train in order to finish up personal business before actually embarking for the Arctic. Doane's route took him through Boston, where he spent three days and may have visited Hattie Reed, the widow of his old California Hundred commander, James Sewall Reed. Low visited family in New York before arriving in Halifax on June 29, and Doane met him there the next day. The local press reported favorably on the arrival of the two American officers and predicted great success for the proposed expedition. The only thing missing to start the great adventure was the *Gulnare*.[30]

The ship's misfortunes began before it even left sight of land. Once it passed beyond the mouth of the Potomac River and anchored off Fort Monroe, Virginia, on June 22, Captain Palmer discovered the ship's compass was defective and had to send ashore for a new one. The *Gulnare* continued its voyage north on the June 24 under a good head of steam, but the hasty manner in which it had been loaded prevented the crew from making good use of the ship's sails. Lighter cargo had been stowed deep in the hold, while more heavy items were piled on top. To add to the imbalance, an entire load of lumber intended to be used for constructing the Arctic colony's buildings had been lashed to the deck, making the whole vessel dangerously top-heavy. On June 28, while Doane traveled through Maine on his way to Halifax, the boiler of the *Gulnare* almost exploded. The crowns on all three furnaces had collapsed due to overheating from a heavy salt deposit, which the engineers had failed to notice. Without steam pressure the ship essentially floated helplessly in a dense fog off the coast of Nova Scotia.[31] The bumbling engineers reported to Captain Palmer that the ship lacked even the most basic tools for emergencies, and Doane later reported in disgust to Howgate that "there was not even a monkey wrench on board."[32] Dr. Pavy convinced Palmer that operating the top-heavy vessel under sail would be too dangerous for an attempted landing at Halifax and that the *Gulnare* should proceed to St. John's, Newfoundland, which had been their intended last stop before heading to Lady Franklin Bay. By the time the *Gulnare* had been towed into the harbor at St. John's on July 7, Pavy had asserted himself as the expedition's leader and spoke to the local press with an assumed authority.[33] The doctor began telegraphing Howgate, demanding to make his appointment official, and immediately ordered an inspection of the boilers with an eye to contracting for their repair. The two engineers who had been responsible for the boiler resigned before Palmer could discharge them, and they caught a mail packet back to Halifax.

Doane and Low, initially unaware of the *Gulnare*'s troubles, waited anxiously in Halifax during the first two weeks of July and sent telegrams to Howgate asking if he had heard anything from the ship. On July 14 the mail packet from St. John's arrived carrying the *Gulnare*'s former engineers. Instead of questioning the wisdom of even proceeding in the enterprise, Doane's first concern was that Pavy would complete the repairs and leave St. John's before he and Low could reach him. Even after the two engineers got drunk and told Doane in detail how shabbily the repairs at Alexandria had been done, he anxiously telegraphed Howgate to order the ship held until they could get there. Howgate telegraphed Pavy to authorize no more purchases until Doane could get to St. John's and then sent a message to Doane telling him to discharge the troublesome doctor if he felt the need.

When Doane and Low arrived at St. John's on July 22 the workmen had just finished the expensive repairs. The ship performed satisfactorily on a five-mile test cruise outside the harbor, but Canadian authorities would not allow the ship go any farther. Aside from the repair bill, Pavy had run up expenses exceeding $4,450, using the authority of the United States consul Thomas N. Molloy to make contracts. Molloy had wired Howgate for the money to cover the costs. Exasperated at the delay, Howgate wired the funds with an urgent concern that the expedition proceed before the short Arctic summer had ended. Unfortunately, Molloy had committed a few financial irregularities of his own during his residence in Newfoundland, and once Howgate's credit line arrived at the local bank the cashier promptly withheld $2,750 to cover Molloy's personal debts. Doane, feverishly engaged in having the *Gulnare*'s cargo reloaded and purchasing last minute supplies, had to go to the bank with Henry Clay, whose experiences as an attorney were suddenly of tremendous value to the expedition. Seated in the cashier's office, Clay pointedly asked the official "if he really considered it legal to impound money entrusted to his care by a third party for settling the debts of a first party who owed him."[34] The cashier calmly replied that he not only considered it legal but proposed to hold everything he could get his hands on in a similar manner. As the two men were ushered out the door, Doane remarked to Clay that "flowers would speedily bloom above a bank cashier who would attempt such tricks in the Rocky Mountains."[35] The delay continued until the last day of the month, when, at a meeting of the bank directors, Consul Molloy finally got the money released by promising to settle his own indebtedness promptly.

The *Gulnare* put to sea ten hours after the delivery of its papers, but no one had great hopes for the coming voyage. During the long delay the expedition members had ample time to endure the derisive comments of every crew at the port regarding their ship's utter uselessness for travel in the Arctic seas. The *Gulnare*'s propeller, claimed the local sailors, would break the instant the ship encountered real ice, and the leaks that required pumping out the bilge every day threatened to sink the vessel should the steam pressure fail. Even though he would not consider abandoning the voyage, Doane had to admit his doubts in a letter to Howgate written before the departure. "Please do not imagine that I write this in a spirit of discouragement or dissatisfaction," he said after detailing the *Gulnare*'s shortcomings. "I simply all state what appears to be the facts. We must not deceive ourselves, and next year must profit by the dear bought experiences of this. We will run the old ship as far as she will go and may be successful. If we do make a success of it, it will be luck and imprudence that will do the business."[36]

The members of the expedition began to seem as ill selected as the ship they traveled on. Dr. Pavy and another member of the expedition, Dr. Leonard Rohe, had a violent quarrel about their respective status within the group before leaving St. John's. By the time the problem had been brought before Doane for mediation both doctors had ceased speaking to one another, and Rohe ended up resigning rather than accepting the lukewarm apology that the lieutenant managed to force from Pavy. The expedition's secretary displayed his own petulance by holding himself aloof from everyone. Henry Clay complained in a letter home that his comrades were a hard, independent, and harsh set of misfits without a Christian among them, a criticism that included their commander. As for Doane himself, his own suitability as an Arctic explorer came into question as soon as the *Gulnare* left the harbor and he fell victim to uncontrollable seasickness. "It did not affect me violently with subsequent relief," he would recall, "but with a vile nausea compelling me to lie on my back night and day and utterly paralyzing the digestive functions, so that I wasted away as if starving to death. Added to this was a headache and bewilderment of ideas as if one's brains were stirred up with a ladle, leaving prominent but one desire, to get on shore, and but one propensity—to revile the sea and every-thing pertaining to it."[37]

While Doane languished in his cabin below deck, things worsened for the crew of the *Gulnare* above. On the afternoon of August 2 as the ship churned north toward Greenland a storm overtook the vessel that grew worse by the hour. The overloaded ship strained and pitched all night long; although the engineers managed to keep the ship under steam enough to maintain its balance the sea constantly broke over it. The calking of the deck began to work loose, and down in the engine room the firemen and engineers became drenched with showers of icy water. The lumber stacked on the deck became water soaked and heavy, while a crack in the stern of the *Gulnare* (which daylight showed through in calm weather) now let in flood of water every time a wave struck. To complicate the situation, the steam pumps began to fail. When the *Gulnare* had been fitted out at the Alexandria naval yard, the bilge of the vessel had been left full of chips and shavings. These shavings choked up the pumps, and the engineer had to shut down every few minutes to clear the valves as the ship tossed about on the angry sea.

The seams burst on the coal sacks, allowing the floating lumps to grind around the propeller shaft, making the freezing water a filthy, gritty soup that numbed the limbs of the engine crew and covered their hands with slime.

After twenty-four exhausting hours, the storm showed no sign of abatement, and the waves washed away one of the lifeboats. The water that had filled the hold began to come dangerously close to the furnace doors. Everyone knew that if the engine stopped the ship would instantly flounder. When one of the panic-struck firemen began saying his prayers, the chief engineer cursed him with a bellowing of German-English profanity, which struck some of the hysterical crew as uncontrollably funny. The humor escaped Captain Palmer, who had no intention of sacrificing his life for a hare-brained attempt to establish an Arctic colony. He announced his decision to throw the entire deck-load of lumber overboard. The desperate gamble worked, and the ship became perceptively easier to manage the instant the 10,000 feet of waterlogged pine boards swept away into the waves.

Doane heard it all from his cabin as he wretched helplessly in the darkness. About 2 A.M. on the morning of August 4 the gale suddenly abated. "It blew to the last minute as if determined to send us to the bottom," recalled Doane. "The ship appeared to glide into smoother water as if into a harbor and we at once resumed our course. We had drifted to within a few miles of Cape Farewell, South Greenland, and were drifting rapidly in that direction when the gale stopped blowing. . . . Had the storm continued two hours longer we would have struck the rocks of Cape Farewell, or in less time perhaps would have been rushed against one of the grand icebergs. As it was we survived the gale and were all very glad of it."[38]

The battering the *Gulnare* took in the storm convinced Captain Palmer to head for the first port he could find; and on August 8 the ship reached Godhavn on Disko Island, halfway up the west coast of Greenland. Godhavn, an ancient village established by the Danes in the seventeenth century, had a small harbor, 10 inhabitants, and 131 Eskimo villagers, all overseen by a Danish inspector appointed by the country's trading monopoly. When the *Gulnare* pulled into the harbor alongside a Danish ship, some of its crew began pointing excitedly at the starboard side of the expedition vessel. A translator came on board and explained that the sailors had seen an obviously rotten nine-foot plank in the side of the *Gulnare* that had been stove in by the rough sea. When Captain Palmer investigated, he found the spongy, rotten wood no more than a quarter-inch thick; only its position, backed against the side of a boiler inside the hull, had prevented it from giving way entirely. As another storm began to rise on the sea outside the harbor, Doane got on shore and reflected soberly on how close they had all come to perishing.

At Godhavn Scottish whalers whose vessel had been crushed by the ice in Greenland's Melville Bay the previous June were awaiting transport home on the Danish ship. After Doane met with Godhavn's inspector to arrange for emergency repairs, the Scotsmen told him that the ice this season had been much worse than anyone expected and that no ship could expect to reach Lady Franklin Bay this summer. While digesting that intelligence, Doane began to realize how the limited resources of Godhavn would further complicate their mission. There were only two oak planks on the entire island, and one of them cracked in two when the village carpenter tried to spring them into place on the *Gulnare*'s damaged hull. Nails had to be hand made by the Godhavn blacksmith, and the few pine boards that remained below deck had to be appropriated to sheathe the makeshift repairs, leaving none to build housing for the proposed colony even if they did reach their objective. Doane needed more coal to continue their journey and hoped to be able to secure workers who would be willing to mine a nearby deposit and transport the fuel to Godhavn, but no available boats could handle the job. The *Gulnare* would have to steam several miles to the coal banks and anchor offshore while the hired men loaded the coal one a sack at a time. Considering the quality of the coal obtained and the time consumed, Doane estimated that they gained only one day's fuel at the cost of ten navigable days. As if these factors were not enough, on August 17, while Doane tried to estimate how much longer the brief Arctic summer would last, an eight-inch snow fell in Godhavn. He reluctantly made up his mind to abandon the expedition.

Doane spent a great deal of time writing his observations on the geology, flora, and fauna of Greenland, trying to compose a descriptive narrative that would compare favorably to his Yellowstone report. He recorded information that he felt might be of use in a future attempt to establish a polar colony, describing in detail the habits and customs of the Eskimos that might someday be used at Lady Franklin Bay. Consistent with his views on all Native peoples, Doane had little faith in the Eskimos' abilities, either as guides or in providing labor for a colony once it could be established. "They are mild, sneaking, treacherous, watchful and suspicious, like all other Indians," he wrote. "They are also improvident, shiftless, dishonest, and untruthful . . . all the sentimental writings extant in relation to them are of a class with the Cooper declinations of other Indian characters."[39]

Dr. Octave Pavy and Henry Clay certainly did not share Doane's disparaging view. Excited about the opportunity of learning from the Eskimos, both men decided to remain in Greenland after the lieutenant announced he would abandon the expedition. Pavy in particular wanted to learn the techniques of dog sledging, while Clay had his own reasons for wishing to prove his worth as a descendant of his famous grandfather by wintering in Greenland. Doane had both men sign a statement confirming their voluntary decision to remain in the country and took them to Ritenbenk, the settlement just north of Godhavn on August 21. There the two disembarked with a healthy load of supplies, temporarily setting up their headquarters with the Danish officer in charge of the village. Time would not suppress Pavy's quarrelsome nature, however, and before long he and Clay would grow to hate one another and end up living at opposite ends of Disko Island.

It took until the end of August to load the minuscule amount of low-quality coal onto the *Gulnare,* and on September 1 the ship returned to Godhavn. Before they could begin the journey home, Captain Palmer decided that the ship needed extra ballast to settle the vessel against the gales he knew awaited them. So another eight-day delay occurred while a crew worked to bring a load of rock on board. The precaution proved justified, for the *Gulnare* battled a few squalls during the seventeen-day voyage back to St. John's, one of which blew the ship dangerously close to the coast of Labrador. On September 24 the ship reached St. John's, a rapid homeward run in spite of the fact that the sails had been relied upon as much as possible in order to conserve fuel. Just before they crew made ready to put into the harbor, a heavy wind struck, which made it necessary to reduce the sail. It seemed as if nature was trying one last attempt to destroy the *Gulnare.* The fuel was so low that Captain Palmer seriously considered opening a barrel of salt pork and tossing it into the firebox to get sufficient steam to enter the harbor. Fortunately the ship swung under the lea of a point of land and managed to reach safety just as the sun set. Doane could recall little of the previous few days. "I was seasick as usual during the whole of the return voyage," he said, "and so weak from starvation as to be scarcely able to walk on arrival at St. John's. As may be supposed, I lost no time in getting on shore. The moment terra-firma was reached my appetite returned. There is a colored man who keeps a restaurant in St. John's. He doubtless remembers me notwithstanding that I paid my bill."[40] Doane had to telegraph the news of his failure to Howgate, a task made all the more difficult by having to inform the captain that the *Gulnare* needed more money to purchase coal. Irritated, Howgate wired back that he had no money left and ordered Doane to tell Palmer he would have to sail back to Washington, which the captain flatly refused to do. Doane let the two continue the argument by telegraph while he and Low caught the next ship for Halifax.

On arrival at the mainland the officers got additional news that only added to their humiliation over having to cancel the expedition. Just two days before the *Gulnare* reached St. John's another ship from the Arctic had landed at New Bedford, Massachusetts, bearing Lt. Frederick Schwatka and *New York Herald* reporter William H. Gilder. The telegraph wires immediately began to hum with the triumphant news that the intrepid explorers had returned with solid evidence of the Franklin party's fate and that the other accomplishments of the Schwatka expedition had exceeded everyone's expectations. Schwatka had completed the longest dog-sledge journey on record, 3,124 miles over a period of eleven months and twenty days. He had also proven that white explorers could, by adopting the ways of the Eskimos, successfully adjust to life in the Arctic and "prosecute any projects that their superior intelligence may dictate or their ambition may desire."[41] By the time Doane and Low got their hands on a newspaper during the train trip back to Washington, D.C., Schwatka was already well on his way to becoming a national hero.

In far-off Bozeman, Mary got the news that Doane had returned safely from a mutual friend, who advised her to be ready to go to Washington while her husband explored the possibility of a permanent transfer to the signal corps. Even if Doane could convince Howgate to give him another chance to go on an expedition the next year, Mary would definitely have something to say about it. "I could not sleep last night for thinking of you and how dreadful it would be for you to make any agreement for another horrible trip," she wrote. "I cannot believe you would willfully break your word with me . . . . I have regretted a thousand times my folly in staying here and letting you go. I will never do so again, for many reasons, which I shall tell you when I see you."[42] Selfishly, Doane refused to heed his wife's warnings and lingered in Washington, ostensibly to work on his report but also flirting with the idea of continuing his association with Howgate's proposed polar colony. Sensing her husband's motives, Mary wrote again with considerably more force. "I can tell you one thing," she said seriously. "You can go just wherever you please and I shall not say a word, so long as you take me along. But I am going with you from now on, just as sure as you live. I am as determined on that as I can be and you can rest assured I mean to put it into execution just so sure as I live to finish this letter, which is not at all doubtful. I don't keep telling you this for to be mean, but for you to make your arrangements accordingly."[43]

Doane had little choice but to accept her ultimatum, so he requested his leave be cancelled and orders be issued to return him to his regiment. At least he got permission to go to Fort Ellis for the rest of the winter and complete his report on the ill-fated expedition, a prospect made more palatable since Major Brisbin no longer commanded the post. When he returned to Montana, Doane had the crushing experience of reading a best-selling book written by William Gilder based on his articles for the *New York Herald* and giving details of Schwatka's triumph. Doane sadly realized as he set down to record his own journey that his own failure looked even worse in comparison to the success of Schwatka. At an American Geographical Society meeting in October 1881, the membership declared that "Lieutenant Schwatka has . . . performed a journey unparalleled in the history of Arctic travels . . . never once faltering in the direct purpose of his journey and, above all, by the proper exercise of a natural gift of command, he has won a splendid victory and added his own to a long list of illustrious names connected with this Arctic search, names which the world will not willingly let die."[44] Much as Hayden had trumped Doane's early reconnaissance of Yellowstone, Schwatka had obliterated any memory that another American expedition had even been sent north.

Mary once again helped Doane accept his fate. "I shall make home so happy for you that you will never regret the failure of this dreadful expedition," she wrote. "We have but a few years at the best and let us stay together those few and be happy. I can make your home pleasant enough to counterbalance all the disappointments this failure has been."[45] Evidence that Mary's influence began to help Doane accept his lot in life can be found in the contents of his completed report to Captain Howgate. Aside from the usual grandiose prose and periodic references to his 1870 Yellowstone expedition, the document Doane wrote reflected something that had been totally lacking in all his previous military writings: a healthy dose of self-depreciating humor. Enough of his old bitterness still showed through in a few points, especially in a jealously sarcastic reference to the Franklin party cenotaph Schwatka reported having erected; but for the most part Doane tailored his composition to offering information that would be of use to a future expedition, delivered with more than a few sarcastic remarks at his own expense. "We raised no flags, converted no natives, killed none," he wrote. "We did not see anything half so grand, half so sublime, nor half so beautiful there as can be seen in the Yellowstone National Park and a dozen other localities at home." Doane also expressed a sentiment that had been lacking in his previous essays, a genuine concern for the welfare of others. He prefaced his report with the plea: "Hoping that no more small appropriations may be made by the government to outfit Arctic Expeditions, to be followed by large ones for the purpose of rescuing the same, the following is respectfully submitted."[46]

The report's words turned out to be unfortunately prophetic. Just four months after Doane mailed it to Washington, Captain Howgate sent out another expedition to Lady Franklin Bay, this time under the command of Lt. Adolphus Greely. Following Doane's recommendations to charter a vessel rather than purchase one, Greely's party sailed from St. John's on July 7, 1881, stopping first at Godhavn, where they picked up the feuding Dr. Pavy and Henry Clay. Having been amply warned by Doane, Howgate should have informed Greely of Pavy's combative ego, but the lieutenant had to find out himself once the expedition reached its destination. There

Pavy demanded that Clay be sent home or he would resign himself, and Greely chose to send the Kentucky attorney back on the chartered supply ship rather than lose the expedition's only physician.

During the following two years at their isolated station, Pavy refused to recognize Greely's authority and attempted to incite mutiny among the enlisted men. Greely had problems far more severe than Pavy's insubordination, however. Two resupply attempts to reach the colony failed, and Greely decided to abandon the colony in September of 1883 to travel south and try to find a relief ship. The party got no farther than Cape Sabine, a lonely promontory on the east coast of Ellesmere Island, where nineteen of the twenty-five men, including Dr. Octave Pavy, slowly starved before their rescue on June 22, 1884. Ironically, when found, Greely and the survivors were slowly wasting away in a tattered Centennial-style tent.

Howgate had probably disregarded much of Doane's advice when sending Greely out in 1881 because he had other things on his mind. The thousands of dollars he had pilfered from the government treasury could no longer be concealed, and Howgate tried to flee Washington shortly after the Greely expedition shipped north. Arrested on orders of Brig. Gen. William B. Hazen, the army's chief signal officer, Howgate managed to evade prosecution first by jumping bail and then, after his re-arrest, escaping from jail by convincing the warden to allow him a visit home to bathe. He would remain a fugitive for the next thirteen years, and the scandal of his malfeasance created considerable embarrassment for the new secretary of war, Robert Todd Lincoln. Lincoln had always been cool to the Arctic colonization plan, and Howgate's knavery resulted in a particularly hostile attitude being shared by many in the upper levels of the War Department. It should be no surprise that when Doane sent the adjutant general a letter on November 28, 1881, declaring he did not want to be considered for another expedition, Brig. Gen. Robert C. Drum angrily scribbled on the back: "Little likelihood!" A clerk penciled below: "After erasing this remark, I will file."[47]

CHAPTER 10

"I am beginning to think that Whiskey is the enemy most formidable in this campaign"

The Geronimo Campaign

D oane's ill-fated Arctic adventure ended his quest for any further recognition as an explorer. To the end of his life he would bewail that his one triumph, the 1870 Yellowstone expedition, had been purposely overlooked; but he would never again attempt to gain a reputation as a "Pathfinder." Instead of looking for opportunities to build on his past fame, Doane began to turn his attentions toward future comfort in 1880, and that included indulging the demands of his new wife to provide a stable home environment. Defeated and exhausted, Doane sank into a career lethargy that put Mary's well-being above his own, a sacrifice that would cost him the one thing he had worked for ever since publishing his Yellowstone report. By meeting Mary's needs for home stability, Doane would place himself beyond the possibility of ever again serving in an official capacity in Yellowstone National Park.

Living down the *Gulnare* fiasco proved very difficult for Doane after his return to Fort Ellis. In welcoming him back to Bozeman the local newspaper remarked pointedly that if Doane had not discovered the North Pole he at least had learned to repeat his prayers in the Eskimo language.[1] Although Mary promised to console her husband over his failure, she made no secret of her gratitude that the expedition had been called off. "I for one am glad that you failed, and I presume that I have the concurrence of a second party," Doane's mother bluntly wrote after exchanging letters with Mary. "I think it folly to suffer so much and gain so little of real consequence."[2] Mary's delight to have her husband back also took a darker turn as he finished his Arctic report in March 1881. Doane's thwarted intentions to spend three years north of the Arctic Circle had thoroughly unbalanced his young wife, and she began clinging to him with an irrational desperation. Mary was contented as long as they remained together at Fort Ellis; but once Doane got orders to report back to Fort Assinniboine in late May 1881 the strain of any separation threatened to unhinge her entirely.

In the months since the Doanes had last made their home at the post, Fort Assinniboine had grown into a small city of brick buildings, including an indoor shooting range, gymnasium, school, and library. The nonmilitary residents had evolved into a tightly knit insular community with a well-defined, or at least well-understood, social ranking. Participation in activities such as elaborate dancing balls, horseback riding excursions, and harvesting produce from the post's vegetable gardens was strictly segregated by rank and social caste as far as the officers' and enlisted men's wives were concerned.[3] Mary's recognition of her place within this complex hierarchy was stymied by the continuing separation anxiety she felt whenever her husband was called into the field to deal with Indian matters.

For the most part the neighboring Gros Ventre, Assiniboine, and Blackfoot tribes remained peacefully confined on their respective reservations, but the soldiers of Fort Assinniboine nevertheless had the constant task of rounding up and returning to Canada starving Cree and Métis people who wandered south searching for buffalo. Although the Crees' homeland for the better part of a century encompassed the plains and mountain areas straddling the border between Canada and the United States, in the late 1870s the desperate Crees frequently came south of the international line in search of sustenance when the buffalo herds grew scarce north of the border. In Montana Territory they came into sharp conflict with the reservation Blackfoot, Assiniboine, and Gros Ventre tribes, who did not appreciate the competition for the rapidly depleting bison herds. U.S. authorities viewed the incursions with increasing alarm. The Canadian government did not share their concern over the Crees' hunting migrations and even mildly encouraged border crossings to lessen their responsibility to issue annuities to the Indians.[4] As the white ranching community of northern Montana Territory began to threaten vigilante-style action against the wandering Crees, however, the United States Army stepped up its policy of forcibly removing all "foreign" Indians to stave off incidents that could lead to full-scale war.

Doane accompanied his first expedition against the Crees almost immediately after arriving at Fort Assinniboine in July and rode out on his second patrol on August 19. Leading Company L as a part of a battalion commanded by Capt. Martin E. O'Brien, Doane traveled far down the Milk River from Fort Assinniboine in an attempt to confront some Crees rumored to be driving a vast buffalo herd north into Canada. Immediately after his departure Mary became ill and sent notes to him by the column's regular courier, making sure Doane knew of her discomfort. For his part Doane tried to reassure her that the whole expedition was a "put up job" by nervous Indian agents at forts Belknap and Browning: "should we find any Indians there are no hopes of our being able to kill any of them."[5] The patrol returned to the fort on September 10, having accomplished little more than the wanton slaughter of the buffalo the soldiers encountered. One day they killed more than forty merely to harvest their tongues.

Doane's patrols against the Cree incursions began to take a toll on both husband and wife during the fall of 1881. Mary's anxiety over her husband's field duties manifested itself in more illnesses and more strident complaining in her frequent letters to him. Doane's reaction to Mary's unhappiness and the frustrating duty he had to perform took a more serious turn—for the first and only time in his professional life he began to drink liquor. The alcohol experimentation happened when Capt. Jacob Kline of the Eighteenth Infantry started on October 8 with a substantial force, including Doane's Company L, on a lengthy mission to the country between People's Creek and the Milk River to remove all Cree and Métis people. Two days later the column reached Fort Belknap, where Doane grumbled in his first letter to Mary that the use of force had been forbidden by Kline and that the Indians would be "rendered more impudent" by the perceived impotence of the soldiers.[6] His tone became more despondent the next day after the column went into camp twenty miles downriver from Fort Belknap. He complained about the monotony of the trip, the cold weather, and the elusive camps they had attempted to find and reported the only casualty of the trip so far to be a man kicked by his horse. "The agent-trader-doctor and a son-in-law came out to see us this morning bringing buffalo mittens and leggings for those who ordered them," he added. "They also brought some bug juice for coloring the Snoots of the United States of America. I drank a whole keg full and am consequently in a deplorable condition."[7]

Even though Doane tried in his letters to downplay the potential danger of his patrols against the Crees he could not alleviate Mary's anxiety or help her adjust to the social environment of Fort Assinniboine. While Doane remained in the field and battled little more than his own boredom, Mary fretted over his safety and expressed her growing dissatisfaction with the Fort Assinniboine social life. "Oh darling, if you were only home," she wrote during a patrol Doane accompanied in March 1882. "I cannot get used to these dreadful separations. . . . We must get to some place where you will be at home for I cannot stand it."[8] Doane did his fair share of complaining in his replies to Mary that spring, once referring to the commander who had sent them out as an "idiot" and confessing that he also hoped for a transfer away from Fort Assinniboine. The disagreeable weather and monotonous service hardened his already harsh views on Indians too. He casually reported burning 100 Cree lodges near Fort Browning on a day as "cold as Greenland" with no more concern for the occupants than he had shown at Heavy Runner's camp on the Marias in 1870.[9]

Mary's troubles at Assinniboine came to a head while Doane was gone during the summer of 1882. She had withdrawn from the garrison's social scene, even refusing to attend a dance organized by the other ladies on July 19, which, she reported with a martyr's flair, included elaborate refreshments of pies and cakes. Obsessed over the well-being of her husband's diet in the field, she had been going to the post garden so often to get fresh vegetables to send him that she was told she had reached her limit. She then turned to the garden maintained by the troopers of Company L and asked a private named Waterbury to continue bringing her produce. Mrs. Randolph Norwood, the wife of Doane's commanding officer, pulled Waterbury aside one afternoon and told him not to pick vegetables for anyone other than her own family and the post chaplain, threatening to put the soldier in the guardhouse if he disobeyed. "I am shut out from the post garden and she is trying to shut me out of the Company garden and I will not stand it," Mary railed to her husband. "I think this is a fine lay out. I wonder when she received her commission? I suppose it will be so after a while that I will have to ask her if I can live in the garrison."[10]

Doane's demoralized experimentation with alcohol had been temporary; but Mary's alienation from the other officers' wives continued, caused in part by her status as having married a divorced man. This would be especially true with women like Mrs. Norwood, who remembered Amelia Doane from the years she had spent at Fort Ellis. While Doane began looking for a way to get transferred from Fort Assinniboine he tried to counsel Mary about her troubles with her neighbors. "Those people are born as they are — they never learn and do not want to," he wrote from the field. "Their ideas are fixed and unchangeable — I feel that they are too uncivilized to worry about and that it is not worth the trouble to be worried about anything they may either do or say."[11] He advised his wife to remain civil with Mrs. Norwood regardless of any perceived insult — not surprising considering the fact that her husband was Doane's commanding officer. Mary remained inconsolable, however, telling her husband that he wasted his career at Assinniboine and that other officers at posts along the Northern Pacific line were gaining distinctions that would never be possible in "this miserable, forsaken command."[12]

To appease Mary and to escape further harsh duty in chasing the Cree Indians, Doane applied for and got a transfer to Company A on September 13, 1882. The couple moved to Fort Maginnis the following month. The post had been completed in late 1881, the last of five Montana installations the army established after the battle of the Little Bighorn. Positioned near the geographical center of the territory near present-day Lewistown, Fort Maginnis consisted of solidly built wooden barracks and officers' quarters that Doane assured Mary were superior in comfort to the brick buildings of Fort Assinniboine. Fort Maginnis was considered an extremely "easy" assignment; the soldiers spent most of their time in routine garrison duties and occasionally rounding up stock rustlers, both white and Indian, for area ranchers.[13] Mary still complained stridently whenever her husband was called into the field. In the summer of 1883 Doane placated her urging by petitioning for duty as a recruiting officer in the "states." He knew that advancement in rank would only occur when a vacancy in his regiment opened, and he could wait as a recruiter without suffering the hardships of frontier service.[14] A post in one of the big eastern cities would allow Doane to be at home with Mary virtually every night too.

To take advantage of a recruiting office vacancy a new field commander for Company A had to be found, because Capt. William P. Clark had a temporary staff assignment in Chicago, leaving Doane the only officer for the unit at Fort Maginnis. Another lieutenant was found to take Doane's place, which allowed Clark to continue his staff duties. Ironically, those duties turned out to be escorting President Chester A. Arthur on a trip through Yellowstone National Park, a detail that occurred just as the paperwork for Doane's recruiting assignment finalized in August 1883.

Mary still fretted over even the briefest separations after they left Montana Territory. Doane's activities as a recruiting officer took him to Milwaukee, Chicago, and St. Louis, along with periodic trips to military installations in Kansas, where he turned over enlistees to their respective regiments. At each separation Mary worried needlessly over her husband's safety. In summer 1884 Doane went to Jefferson Barracks outside St. Louis, leaving Mary at their rented home in Chicago while he got their quarters ready at the post. He arrived at the barracks on July 9 but neglected to telegraph Mary about his safe arrival until July 13, choosing in the meantime to send her daily letters that, as far as she was concerned, took too long. "I was just frantic," she admonished him in a letter. "I laid awake half the night thinking of you and wondering why you did not write."[15]

Other family problems for Doane that year involved renewed contact with his mother, who had begun writing her son with veiled requests for support. James Doane, the youngest brother and, in Doane's opinion, a "trifling scamp," had left the care of Nancy largely to brother George, by that time a confirmed bachelor, with his father's knack for horrible business investments. Nancy and George lived on some leased property in Gilroy, California, where they were joined in late 1882 by another brother, Charles, after his marriage failed. Neither of the two sons seemed particularly adept at earning a living.[16] Doane knew that he would likely have to take the lead in supporting his mother because he alone of the children had a steady income. At least he had the comfort of knowing that his income would increase before his tour of recruiting duty ceased.

Doane's strategy in awaiting a promotion while serving in a comfortable billet paid off on September 22, 1884, when the captaincy of Company A opened up. When Captain Clark died a year after his return from Yellowstone with President Arthur's escort, Doane, as the Second Cavalry's senior first lieutenant, moved into the vacancy. The new captain received his commission at Jefferson Barracks, along with orders to report to his command at the Presidio at San Francisco, California. The transfer seemed ideal to Mary in several ways. The Presidio had excellent officers' quarters; and, as a captain, Doane qualified for more rooms while enjoying a larger salary to furnish them. Also, Mary would be able to take advantage of all the cultural attractions of one of America's most cosmopolitan cities. The transfer had drawbacks as far as Doane was concerned. With Doane and Mary living in a location so near to Gilroy, Nancy Doane could visit her son for the first time after a twenty-year absence and temporarily stay with the couple while George sorted out his financial difficulties. The assignment within the Military Division of the Pacific also put Doane far from Yellowstone National Park, which lay within the jurisdictional boundaries of the Military Division of the Missouri. Just as Congress began considering the feasibility of army administration over the park, Doane found himself at a distinct geographic disadvantage in considering his own appointment to the post.

Waiting at the Presidio while the government debated the feasibility of posting troops to protect Yellowstone proved to be very pleasant. Doane and Mary lived extravagantly, with many dinner invitations to reciprocate and numerous shopping trips into the city, both of which ate away at their income. Without the strenuous physical demands of frontier duty Doane's huge appetite took its toll; he earned the nickname "Fatty" from his intimate friends as he ballooned beyond 250 pounds. He had adequate time to indulge a sedentary lifestyle, finishing off a lengthy narration of his Snake River expedition and, after the well-publicized return of the Greely Arctic expedition survivors, revisiting the draft of his *Gulnare* report. Doane wrote to Sgt. David L. Brainard and Pvt. James R. Frederick for details regarding their horrific ordeal on Cape Sabine and received the somewhat chilling compliment that both men had often wished he had been along on the expedition.[17]

Doane's comfortable routine of dress parades, socializing, and eating at the Presidio seemed destined to continue happily with only one minor irritation. Nancy Doane had temporarily moved in with her son and daughter-in-law, a situation that somewhat strained their marriage. Mary, no longer fearful being separated from her husband, began complaining of illness and fled to Santa Cruz in September 1885 for a lengthy stay at the posh Pacific Ocean House. Once again Doane paid the cost of indulging his wife, incurring great expense while she enjoyed the seaside resort and he remained at the Presidio with his mother. "I wish I was down at Santa Cruz with you," he confided in a letter. "The old lady is more monstrous and stupid than ever."[18] Doane's obvious discomfort in his role as a self-sacrificing provider for his family was offset by his optimism over news regarding Yellowstone National Park that fall.

In August 1885 Congress began to consider changes in the administration of Yellowstone. Adverse publicity regarding the inept civilian management had rekindled congressional interest in the idea of placing military control over the reserve.[19] Supporters of military administration for Yellowstone argued that a company of mounted troops could easily be spared for the detail, and the advantages of shorting the appropriation for the Interior Department also made the idea appealing for politicians. Doane had done his best to agitate for the change. In addition to his scathing 1878 report to Major Brisbin that denounced superintendent Philetus W. Norris, Doane had sent another letter in 1881 to Martin Maginnis (Montana Territory's delegate to Congress), which described the civilian administration's attempts to improve the park as "ridiculous in nature" and urged Maginnis to work toward the goal of stationing troops in Yellowstone to prevent vandalism and poaching.[20] Over the intervening years Doane had made no secret of his qualifications and willingness to be assigned to the Yellowstone detail, and he had every reason to hope that his superiors would consider him an ideal candidate for the job.

Before any change in Yellowstone's administration could be mandated by authorities in Washington, however, the Apaches in Arizona Territory intervened to interrupt Doane's comfortable wait. In spring 1885 a disgruntled Chiricahua Apache known among whites as Geronimo decided he had enough of the regulated life on the San Carlos Reservation and led a small group of like-minded individuals on an extended raid. The reasons for the outbreak were complex, but they included dissatisfaction with the corrupt administration of a few Indian agents and cultural differences with the white authorities, who had no tolerance for long-standing Apache customs. Brig. Gen. George Crook, commanding the Department of Arizona, had initially handled the situation by tracking Geronimo into northern Mexico with Apache scouts; but in late November

1885, when another group of Chiricahua raiders led by Josanie killed two white ranchers and stole horses near Solomonville, Arizona, newspapers agitated for the final subjugation of Geronimo's band.[21] A renewed call for troops from the Military Division of the Pacific came to the Presidio. Doane received a most unwelcome Christmas present on December 27, ordering him, and Company A, to report to Fort Bowie, Arizona Territory, as quickly as rail transport could be arranged.

Mary seemed to endure her husband's Arizona posting with a much calmer demeanor than she had assumed in previous years. When Doane and his company stepped off the train at Bowie Station, Arizona Territory, on January 2, 1886, Mary remained comfortably at home in the Presidio. Now that the captain had been called to the field "in the midst of the most hideous desert wilderness in the world,"[22] Mary distracted herself by entertaining some guests from Montana. George W. Wakefield, a Bozeman banker and old Hunter family friend, had come to San Francisco that winter with his wife and daughter to purchase stagecoaches for an excursion line franchise he had bought out in Yellowstone National Park. Mary kept herself busy going into the city with the Wakefields to attend plays and sightseeing tours, both activities being a radical departure from her self-imposed isolation at Fort Assinniboine. Every day she would dutifully write Doane a letter describing her excursions, keeping him informed about the minutiae of daily life at the Presidio and generally complaining that his replies did not appear in her mailbox with similar regularity.

Without having to worry about Mary's discontent, Doane could indulge in describing his own frustrations in letters home. Hundreds of infantry and cavalry troops temporarily camped at Bowie Station awaiting the orders posting them to distant points; to help them pass the time a scattering of saloons and bordellos had conveniently located nearby. Doane quickly recognized the real threat to his command at Bowie Station and had ample cause to be glad his brief experimentation with alcohol had ended. "The men of both troops are behaving badly," he wrote shortly after arriving with the battalion from the Presidio. "Many [are] drunk."[23] The camp at

Bowie Station provided easy access to whiskey, gambling, and prostitutes, a temptation that many could not resist. "The old strumpets,
white, Mexican, and Negro, follow up the paymasters from camp to
camp in wagons," explained Doane. "They are a hideous lot of
regular cornfed wenches. . . . It is now midnight and the gentle
racket of drunken men is lulled to a low growl of subdued profanity."[24] His report to Mary of the potential trouble in store for his
men was accurate if ill-advised. In his attempt to downplay the Indian menace by describing the demoralizing effect of alcohol and
prostitutes, Doane actually gave his wife two new things to worry
about.

Doane's battalion camped near Bowie Station until January 12,
when they were ordered to establish camps thirty-five miles north
near Ash Springs and Solomonville, the site of the killings during
the Apache raid the previous November. The Indians had long
since returned south of the border, though, and the danger of any
encounter with Apaches that January simply did not exist. "This is
the safest Indian country I was ever in," Doane reassured Mary
before heading to the campsite. "There are about 40 hostiles out
and about 4,000 troops, none of whom ever see Apaches except by
merest accident. Gen. Crook told me that none had been killed by
the troops for a year. . . . The danger and the stampede is all in the
newspapers."[25] He drove home his point by assuring Mary that
southern Arizona was safer than Montana, "or New York — and infi-
nitely more so than Chicago."[26]

The two companies reached their first assigned location on January 15, a pleasant spot along the Gila River east of Solomonville,
which Doane hoped would be far enough to keep whiskey from his
command but still close enough to post daily letters to San Francisco. 1st Lt. Frank U. Robinson, the alcoholic commander of Company K, prepared to lead his men on to Ash Springs, but Doane
demanded he sign an abstinence pledge before leaving. Robinson
refused, and instead gave a verbal promise to his colleague. "I have
no confidence in his keeping it," Doane wrote the next morning
after watching Robinson and 2nd Lt. Alvarado M. Fuller lead their
company off to the southeast. As the column slowly marched away,

many of the enlisted men reeled in their saddles; and some had gotten so drunk the night before that they actually had to be hauled in the teamster's wagons.[27]

While Doane fished, hunted quail, and made friends with Isidor E. Solomon, the local contractor for army supplies, Mary seemed reassured of her husband's safety as well as his distance from the flesh-pots of Bowie Station. "I do miss you so much, although I must confess I have never been so fortunately situated before," she wrote.[28] By staying occupied Mary was able to endure the separation and even enjoy herself. She wrote at length to her husband of an excursion to Chinatown, where she and the Wakefields purchased trinkets and passed through an alleyway lined with prostitutes, a sight that she reported with feigned innocence after reading Doane's description of the Arizona variety.[29] She also requested periodic instructions on which bills to pay and what to tell reporters who sought her out for information on the campaign. Over the years Doane had repeatedly made the same mistake of speaking too frankly in the army, and when he heard about the reporters he intemperately did so again. "The stupidity of what is called campaigning in Arizona is not easily described," he wrote; and he insisted she tell the next reporter that "[t]here is no Indian war in Arizona and has been none . . . more people have been killed by the local papers in a month than by the Indians in five years!"[30]

Doane's assessment was hardly an exaggeration. For the five months following Josanie's successful retreat back across the border, any military action against the Geronimo band would take place hundreds of miles to the south in the mountains of northern Mexico. The sole function of many camps such as Doane's seemed to be the consumption of forage and rations. With so little to do it would be impossible to keep the men from getting into trouble, and Doane reacted bitterly to the realization that his camp near Solomonville had no clear mission and was not likely to receive one from General Crook. "This country is full of tramps, thieves, and ten cent gamblers," he complained. "Both whiskey and water are sold per drink at about the same price at roadside doggeries."[31]

In late March news suggested that Doane's Gila River camp would continue indefinitely. Geronimo, after negotiating a surrender with General Crook near the Mexican border, had a change of heart on the subsequent march north and fled again into the mountains with a handful of die-hard supporters. The botched capture of the renegades and the prolongation of the campaign led to successful demands for Crook's removal from the Department of Arizona and to Doane's conclusion that his quiet camp along the Gila would remain in place for months longer. As a result he sent for Mary to join him and arranged for her to stay at the home of Isidor Solomon, with the provision for her occasionally to stay overnight in camp.

Even as Mary traveled south on the train to join her husband, events occurred that would make her visit frustratingly short. General Crook, smarting under the criticism of his leadership in the campaign, responded to demands that he either concentrate his forces or resign by promptly doing both. Company A's camp on the Gila and Company K's camp at Ash Springs were both terminated, and the soldiers were ordered to return to the vicinity of Fort Bowie. Mary had barely arrived at Solomonville when the orders came, and Doane quickly had to find a new place for her to stay. Fortunately the couple had friends, Albert and Elizabeth Shepard, who lived in El Paso, Texas, and offered Mary a place to stay while the soldiers established a new camp. Shepard worked for the Southern Pacific Railroad, and staying at his home at the border town would allow Mary ready access to the train that could return her directly to her husband in one day's travel.

As Mary settled into the Shepard household in El Paso, Brig. Gen. Nelson A. Miles, Doane's old commander from the Nez Perce War, received his orders to relieve General Crook and assume command of the Department of Arizona. He arrived at Bowie Station on April 11 and exchanged pleasantries with Doane before meeting with the departing Crook. Once again Doane's practice of cultivating influential superiors resulted in his selection for duty, but this time not in a way he would have preferred. "Miles will push things and make short work of it if it can be made," Doane wrote to Mary. "I am pleased with the way he starts in, only would have been glad if he had left us out this time to go home."[32]

Miles had indeed planned to make short work of it, although the task of bringing the Apaches to bay at first seemed especially daunting. He wanted to abandon Crook's policy of using Apache scouts and secure the glory of capturing Geronimo himself; but in order to free up columns of soldiers to march into Mexico he needed all available troops to occupy every available water hole and potential refuge site in southern Arizona. By strategically positioning these semipermanent camps along the Mexican border Miles hoped to cut off any hope of the Apaches to return to their reservation for succor, and he also devised a way to keep those camps in constant communication. Lt. Alvarado Fuller of Company K, whose main duty up to this point had been trying to keep Lieutenant Robinson sober, on April 25 was appointed acting signal officer for the Department of Arizona. The lieutenant would travel from point to point along the length of the entire border, from central Arizona to western New Mexico, establishing heliograph stations at the various camps. The heliograph was a telegraphic signaling device that used the bright desert sun to relay messages instantly across the barren landscape. By strategic positioning of the heliographs Miles could expect to communicate with even his most remote outposts in a matter of hours. Fuller would enjoy a choice duty assignment, allowing him to recruit telegraphers, travel throughout the entire district, and render a service that would add credit and distinction to his record.[33] Given Doane's fascination with gadgetry and his self-promoted reputation as a man capable of becoming familiar with any landscape, it is natural to wonder why Miles did not choose him. Doane would have delighted in constructing the makeshift heliograph devices with pocket mirrors and blacksmith tools as Fuller had done; but Miles had another duty in mind for Doane, one that would have made many of his colleagues envious as they suffered through the stifling heat of the desert that summer.

On the west side of the Dragoon Mountains, a small range of pine-covered heights thirty miles west of Fort Bowie, flowed a seasonal creek fed by a cold spring. The location had been a favorite rendezvous of the Apaches for centuries and the rugged heights above the creek were known as "Cochise Stronghold," named for the legendary chief, whose grave was rumored to be nearby. The creek flowed through a small canyon and emptied into the flat desert valley that formed the drainage of the San Pedro River. At the mouth of the canyon, at an elevation of about 4,800 feet above sea level, stood a huge U-shaped adobe hacienda abandoned by its owner, Albert Tweed, when the Geronimo outbreak first occurred. The location would have to be garrisoned in any case, but the added attraction of the spacious Tweed house made the canyon an ideal place to station troops. Described by Doane as "one of the prettiest places in the world for a camp,"[34] the canyon included a flat area below the house where the soldiers could pitch their tents and safely corral their horses. Twelve miles to the northeast, through the pass where the railroad tracks had cut their route, was Dragoon Summit, a small telegraph station and post office. "I want you to see Cochise's Stronghold," Doane wrote to Mary shortly after his arrival on May 1. "The Stronghold is a wonder of rocky grandeur. . . . The climate is a paradise here where we are."[35]

The active pursuit of Geronimo continued south of the Mexican border, so it seemed as if Cochise Stronghold would be another sleepy camp with little for the soldiers to do. That perception, along with the roomy accommodations and the pleasant temperatures, convinced Doane that Mary could safely rejoin him in the field, and she arrived at the Summit station on May 4. Doane took her to the Tweed house, which he shared with a Mormon family that had temporarily moved into the vacant wing, and they enjoyed a quiet two weeks together. "We lived on the broad porches and enjoyed the beautiful scenery," she remembered years later; "the air was filled with the songs of the mocking birds that infest that country."[36] Doane's second lieutenant, Lloyd M. Brett, handled most of the day-to-day operation of the camp; and the time passed pleasantly enough for Mary, exploring with her husband the spring-fed pools among the rocks in the canyon above the house. Lieutenant Fuller's plum assignment with the heliograph duty may have rankled Doane somewhat, but he at least had been ordered to occupy one of the most desirable locations in the department and had Mary at his side to share it.

The Apaches did not stay below the border as expected. In mid-May Geronimo and his followers had been pressed hard in northern Sonora by several columns of infantry and cavalry that Miles had sent into Mexico. On the night of May 18 a small party of Apaches arrived in the vicinity of Antelope Springs, about twenty-five miles from Doane's camp, where they stole some horses and killed a rancher.[37] The commanding officer of the infantry company camped at Antelope Springs sent a courier to alert Doane's camp of the raid. For the first and only time during his service in Arizona Doane had the opportunity to lead his men into the field with the possibility of seeing real combat, but with Mary's frantic pleadings he could only order Lieutenant Brett out with a detachment to try to head off the Apaches at Dragoon Summit.

If Doane ever resented the circumstances that forced his decision he never expressed them to Mary, although he did exhibit a marked coolness toward his second lieutenant in his subsequent letters. As it turned out, Brett's detachment embarked on an epic chase after Geronimo, earning the undisguised admiration of General Miles, who praised their energy and determination in his summation of the campaign.[38]

The necessity of sending out a subordinate while he remained behind to put Mary back on the train to El Paso robbed Doane of an opportunity for notice. The prestige Brett gained from Miles's citation of the Geronimo pursuit certainly helped advance his career, and he would eventually rise to the rank of major general, commanding a division of the American Expeditionary Forces in World War I. Ironically, Brett's other major achievement in his later career turned out to be the thing Doane wanted most in his life: an appointment as acting superintendent of Yellowstone National Park in 1910.

After the brief excitement of Lieutenant Brett's pursuit, another dangerous enemy arrived at Cochise's Stronghold that summer, one much more deadly than the Indians. Company A had not been visited by the paymaster during their stay at the isolated Gila River camp; but now that they were conveniently located near the railroad both the money and opportunities to spend it could be delivered with more regularity. Whiskey peddlers arrived to relieve the men of their pay just as soon as they received it, and for those inclined to temperance an unsavory assortment of prostitutes offered an alternative form of recreation. Most "doggeries" that plied their trade around the various military camps had been regulated by General Crook in a semiofficial system of registration. When General Miles assumed command of the Department of Arizona he allowed the practice to continue in spite of the danger to his force's morale. Now Doane had to deal with the results of the policy and its effect on his wife's contentment.

The heat of midsummer in El Paso, and an offer from the Shepards to accompany her back to San Francisco, convinced Mary to return to California on June 24. She made arrangements to stop at Dragoon Summit that night to say good-bye to her husband. The following morning, just as Doane was helping her into her car, she viewed with distress two disreputable-appearing women getting off the westbound train. A letter that caught up with her in Santa Ana, California, a few days later confirmed her suspicions. "The old girls who got off came down here and are here now," Doane wrote. "There are three in all and have no men at all with them. Are running the business alone. There was a terrible caterwaul amongst them today about a missing $20.00 piece which one accused the other of stealing."[39]

The carousing at the doggeries only got worse, especially after the men got paid again on July 12. "The usual drunk is imminent and the old hens and the doggery keepers begin to swarm," Doane complained; but he insisted that other than keeping out "tinhorn gamblers" he could do nothing to end the unsavory trade.[40] The worst of the purveyors always seemed to have licenses, and without an imminent Indian threat Doane could not banish the "seedy scallywags."[41] Mary reacted to the news of the siege at her husband's camp by writing anxiously to Doane about her fears for the enlisted men's health and her husband's fidelity. The strain of the onslaught had begun to show, for Doane dismissed her distress with crude jocularity. "What do you suppose I would have to do with those hideous old sluts that are humping soldiers out in the brush in reliefs?" he asked. "If you could see their performances by moonlight once or hear their howls and jokes with the men at a distance of a few hundred yards as I am compelled to night after night you would probably be at least as disgusted as I am."[42]

In spite of his defensive outburst, Doane had to agree with Mary's concerns. "I am beginning to think that Whiskey is the enemy most formidable in this campaign," he sadly admitted.[43] Alcohol certainly turned out to be deadly for his own command at Dragoon Spring that summer. On the Fourth of July a Mexican laborer from nearby Humphrey's Ranch reported that Pvt. Daniel Munger, the oldest enlisted man in Company A, had suddenly died while on picket duty. Lieutenant Brett and the doctor went to fetch the body and returned to confirm the worst; the first casualty of Doane's contingent during their entire Arizona tour of duty had been caused by a heart attack aggravated by a bout of extended drinking. The captain announced his idea of constructing an elaborate tomb for the deceased and holding a funeral with full military honors. The men labored for days putting together a fitting monument for their fallen brother, hauling a huge granite slab to a site above their camp. Doane himself led the funeral service, with the hope that Munger's fate would sober his bored soldiers. The hard labor seemed to have a beneficial effect. Doane next detailed the enlisted men to dig a huge well, ten feet in diameter and twenty-six feet deep. Summer had dried up the spring that fed the small creek from which the camp drew its water, and the "mudhole of urine" that the Mormon family in the Tweed house used for a well had been declared unfit for the soldiers by their physician.[44] The work on Doane's well, hot and difficult, kept up for weeks in the intense heat of July and August, but the activity finally gave the camp a reliable source of water and kept the men from investing too much of their pay at the doggeries.

The heliograph messages from Fort Huachuca, thirty-three miles to the southwest, rarely brought much in the way of substantive news. Either the entire system had done its intended job of surveillance by keeping Geronimo's band south of the border or the establishment of the heliograph system happened by chance to coincide with the Apaches' choice to stay in Sonora. In any case, the messages Doane usually received at Cochise Stronghold passed on information of no greater import than current weather conditions. The exception occurred on September 7, 1886, when the news flashed that Geronimo had surrendered to General Miles and was a prisoner in the Fort Bowie guardhouse, facing deportation to Florida the next day. Not only would Geronimo be banished from Arizona but, according to Miles's orders, every man, woman, and child of the entire Chiricahua and Warm Springs bands of Apaches would also share Geronimo's fate, including the scouts who had helped the army finally locate and capture the renegade Indians.

Doane could not begrudge the soldiers who finally brought in Geronimo what little glory the achievement held. The betrayal of the Apaches in their mass deportation from Arizona may not have caused much of a public outcry at the time, but future observers would universally condemn the outcome that indiscriminately punished Chiricahua allies and enemies.[45] Doane could afford to have his peripheral association with the episode overlooked, but he had much more difficulty accepting another outcome of his Arizona service. On August 6, 1886, the secretary of the interior notified the secretary of war that without a congressional appropriation for salaries it would be necessary to call on troops for the administration of Yellowstone National Park. If anyone in the army's upper echelon gave Doane a second thought for the job, the economics of the situation argued against such a prospect. Gen. Philip H. Sheridan picked a company of cavalry stationed geographically closest to the park and ordered them to proceed to the vicinity of Mammoth Hot Springs to establish a camp for the summer season. Accordingly, Capt. Moses Harris and Company M of the Sixth Cavalry left Fort Custer and arrived at the Park on August 20, inaugurating a 32-year military occupation that Doane had predicted and desperately wanted to lead himself.[46]

Instead of heading to the cool environs of the northern Rockies, Company A was ordered to abandon the Cochise Stronghold camp on September 12 and march overland to Fort Lowell, a permanent post outside of Tucson, Arizona. Doane had to make all the preparations himself, because Lieutenant Brett had been granted leave and a new West Point graduate had yet to arrive to take his place. Mary rejoined her husband at Fort Lowell for a month while the cumbersome process of demobilizing an army continued and the Second Cavalry contingent awaited its turn to board the trains for a return to the Presidio. During the stay at Fort Lowell, Doane's new second lieutenant, William Heebner Bean, joined the troop. A wealthy young man from Norristown, Pennsylvania, Bean quickly gained Doane's trust by demonstrating talent, enthusiasm, and an implied promise of eastern political connections. When he was first informed the young lieutenant would be joining the company, Doane mistakenly thought Bean to be the son of Arizona Territory's delegate to Congress, Curtis Coe Bean. That turned out not to be the case, but Doane had to admit that the Pennsylvanian seemed to be a very well connected young man and of potential great use.

The two companies of the Second Cavalry returned to the Presidio on October 19, and the Doanes resumed their comfortable routine of the urban garrison life. Although he was once again enjoying the mild climate of San Francisco, Doane's feelings of entitlement for the Yellowstone National Park command would not allow him to rest completely. Lieutenant Bean became fascinated with his captain and listened with eagerness to Doane's plans for someday returning to the park he always claimed to have discovered. Based on their experience of moving a company of cavalry from Arizona to California, the two officers devised an elaborate plan documenting the expenses involved in an overland march from the Presidio to Yellowstone National Park. The financial advantages of moving troops from a Montana post to the park had been the stated justification for choosing Captain Harris's company in 1886, and Doane did not intend to have the money argument used against him when the time came for a change in the park's administration. He did not have long to wait. At the beginning of 1889 Harris's term as acting superintendent was rumored to be ending. Doane saw the opportunity of a lifetime. Bean applied for and got a leave of absence to go back east and try to lobby personally for his company's assignment to the park. With such a trusted subordinate on the scene at Washington, D.C., Doane planned the final great campaign of his life.

CHAPTER 11

"By right of discovery"

The Yellowstone Superintendency Campaign

After Doane returned to the Presidio in 1887 he devoted himself to recapturing his Yellowstone fame by using his reputation to win the position of acting superintendent. His career choices since returning from Greenland in 1880 had been made primarily to satisfy the needs of his young wife and to avoid harsh field service. Although Mary had finally found contentment when the couple took up residence in San Francisco, the Geronimo campaign proved particularly arduous for Doane and a major blow to his ambition. While wasting his time in the deserts of southern Arizona, Doane paid dearly the cost of seeking his marital and physical comfort when he was overlooked for consideration as Yellowstone's first military overseer. Doane determined not to repeat his past mistakes if the time ever came for the army to consider a replacement for the superintendent of the park. As a result he would pursue the Yellowstone command with an intensity and singleness of purpose that eventually proved lethal to him.

In his Arizona letters in August 1886 Doane did not express any reaction to the army's announcement that Capt. Moses Harris would be posted to Yellowstone, although his subsequent writings hint that the news must have been a terrible blow. Once back in the comfortable Presidio, Doane also left no written reaction to the January 1887 newspaper coverage of the "first winter expedition" through Yellowstone National Park to be led by Lt. Frederick Schwatka. Already famous for his Arctic explorations, Schwatka announced his intentions to take photographer F. Jay Haynes snowshoeing through the frozen beauty of a Yellowstone winter for the "first time," a claim that completely ignored Doane's earlier struggle down the Snake River in 1876. As it turned out, Schwatka was unable to complete the journey due to poor health, but Haynes and the other members of the expedition managed to come back with spectacular photographs as well as praise from the popular press that Doane coveted.

Although he could no longer seriously entertain the thoughts of physical challenges like a winter's snowshoe trip through Yellowstone, Doane felt his past accomplishments alone should justify his placement as the next superintendent when Captain Harris's assignment ended. Doane found an enthusiastic supporter for his ambitions in his lieutenant, William H. Bean. Ever since the return of Company A from Arizona the two officers had increased their cooperative relationship, with the younger Bean thriving on the wide latitude of freedom that Doane granted him. When the lieutenant asked for leave in the spring of 1888 to investigate the possibility of a staff appointment with the Pennsylvania National Guard, Doane supported his application. The possibility that Bean would be of use in gaining the Yellowstone detail contributed to Doane's preferential treatment of his subordinate, which he confirmed when he decided to go to Yellowstone himself in the summer of 1888. Doane wrote an apology to Bean for the necessity of recalling the lieutenant from Pennsylvania to command Company A at the Presidio temporarily and bluntly asked for help in lobbying influential politicians in Washington. "My dear Captain, I would feel more than sorry if you had not asked me," Bean replied en route to California. He promised to "see to it" that Doane would get the

Yellowstone appointment within a year.[1] The possibility that Bean might be overestimating his potential influence does not seem to have occurred to either man, and Doane traveled to Montana that summer full of hopes for the future.

While Mary stayed with her family in Bozeman and renewed old friendships, Doane spent several weeks in the park, ostensibly to make "scientific observations" on the thermal phenomena but in reality to gather anecdotal information on the management of Capt. Moses Harris. No shortage of opinions on that point seemed to exist. Ela C. Waters, the local manager for the Yellowstone Park Association, which ran the hotels, told Doane about some clashes with the superintendent and how Harris had reprimanded Waters for pouring soap into geysers to hasten their eruption for some impatient railroad executives.[2] Other complaints regarding the primitive state of the park's road system and the alleged arrogance of enlisted men who guarded the various tourist attractions reached Doane's ears. If Doane spoke directly with Harris during his visit he may also have learned that the superintendent had recently been toying with the idea of asking for a transfer from the Yellowstone duty.

When Doane returned to the Presidio that fall he had gathered enough information to begin his personal campaign, but his success depended on the outcome of another campaign being contested on the national front. The presidential election of 1888 put Benjamin Harrison into the White House, and the Republican victory ensured a change in the cabinet positions so crucial to Doane's future. President Grover Cleveland's secretary of war, William C. Endicott, had posted Harris to Yellowstone in 1886 with the acquiescence of Philip Sheridan, then commanding general of the army. Maj. Gen. John Schofield had since replaced Sheridan, and rumors about President Harrison's choice for a new secretary of war mentioned Russell G. Alger, a former governor of Michigan. The changes in the army's administration gave Doane great hope: Alger was a personal acquaintance of Lieutenant Bean, and Doane had served with General Schofield's brother Charles at Fort Ellis during the mid-1870s. With Charles acting as his brother's aide in Washington, Doane had every reason to believe that for once in his life he had the right friends in the right place at the right time.

While waiting for President Harrison's inauguration and appointment of his cabinet, Doane published a pamphlet entitled "Memorandum" that he planned to use in lobbying for help in his bid for Yellowstone's superintendency. "The Yellowstone National Park is an Empire of Wonders at the apex of a great Continent," began his ponderous essay, which went on to discuss the natural features in a combination of descriptive hyperbole and scientific jargon. Doane's effort to present himself as a scientist and geographer obscured his more subtle point: that the park desperately needed visionary management to introduce visitors properly to features currently bypassed by the existing roads and tour itineraries. "Only a beginning has been accomplished," he argued, using access to the Yellowstone Lake as his major example of road building oversight. "Energy, confidence, encouragement, enthusiasm, a realization of great ends to be achieved, a disposition to push things, rather than to place obstacles in the way of enterprise, these are needed, and needed badly now." Doane implied the mismanagement of the park as subtly as possible while simultaneously expressing his own sense of entitlement: "To harmonize the conflicting interests which cluster about this new field of development; to endeavor so to control the current of each enterprise involved, that all may have a general trend towards results of public benefit; to labor for additions to the sum of human happiness and of human knowledge, in a land to which one has some claim by 'right of discovery' at least, is regarded as an object of legitimate ambition and of reasonable desire."[3]

Doane began the first wave of his assault by mailing his pamphlet out to people of influence, especially in Montana, where he asked the state legislature to circulate a petition urging his appointment as Captain Harris's replacement. The mayor of Bozeman, John V. Bogert, started another petition on Doane's request and got every municipal officer and prominent citizen to sign their names. Both petitions were sent to Senator Thomas Carter, and Doane asked him to present the documents after the inauguration. With the solicitation of all these key people Doane then waited for Bean to speak to secretary-designate Alger in Washington, intending that the petitions and personal letters would arrive simultaneously at the War Department.

Had Russell Alger been appointed as the new secretary of war Doane might very well have succeeded. Unfortunately, Benjamin Harrison took the oath of office on March 4 and the next day announced his cabinet choices after months of carefully guarded secret negotiations. Redfield Proctor, a wealthy Vermont capitalist and former governor, received the nod for the War Department and immediately brought to the office a businessman's sense of economy.[4] Bean, whose confidence up to now had been great enough to suggest which subordinates to take to Yellowstone, suddenly found that he had little influence at the War Department at all and confessed that he felt he had to "move discretely [sic]" in the matter.[5] Bean instructed Doane to prepare his application papers and promised to have the president's son, Russell Harrison, speak to the new secretary of war. Russell Harrison had formerly lived in Montana Territory, where he worked at the federal land office in Helena, but his selection as an emissary to Secretary Proctor may not have been the best timing. Just a few days after Harrison's visit to Proctor the president's son voluntarily submitted to an arrest for a libel charge in New York City.[6] Other allies also proved less than helpful. Charles Gibson, the owner of the Yellowstone Park Association, refused to allow his manager, Ela C. Waters, to go any further than simply urging a change in Yellowstone's administration without explicitly endorsing Doane's application. Even a favorable notice from General Miles had less impact than expected. Just like Doane, Miles had spent his entire professional life cultivating influential people in an obsessive pursuit of advancement and prestige. While sympathetic to Doane's ambitions, Miles was far too involved with his own career to offer effective assistance to any subordinate, and his recent demands for both a promotion and increased funding for pet projects in the Military Division of the Pacific had made him thoroughly obnoxious at the War Department.[7]

On April 4 Secretary Proctor announced to General Schofield that he would not approve Doane's transfer to the park on the basis of the expense involved. He had been told the cost of transferring Company A from the Presidio to Yellowstone would be prohibitive, and his business sense simply could not justify incurring unnecessary expenditures. "It seems impossible that the secretary would regard the $6,000 as an insurmountable obstacle," Bean wrote to Doane, "but he is built that way, from Vermont, and most economically inclined."[8] Recognizing the power of the balance sheet, Doane acted on Bean's next suggestion to compile figures comparing the cost of transferring the company from the Presidio to Fort Walla Walla or Yellowstone. According to popular rumor the two cavalry companies in San Francisco were due to rotate to the Washington state garrison, and if Doane could show it would be cheaper to move the men and horses to the park he could again press his request on Secretary Proctor. Even though he did exactly that, getting an informal bid from his old railroad friend Albert Shepard to move the entire company as far as Camas Station, Idaho, for $2,000, Doane's pleadings gained nothing.[9] Secretary Proctor issued the order for Capt. Frazier A. Boutelle of the First Cavalry at Fort Custer to relieve Captain Harris at Yellowstone on June 2, 1889. "It was a case of not having a long enough pole," summarized Bean.[10]

Doane's disappointment solidified his impression that his right of discovery had been denied, and his bitterness grew accordingly. Bean kept his position with the Pennsylvania National Guard and did not return to the company, even attending law school while on duty to become, in his own words, a "genuine Philadelphia lawyer."[11] The lieutenant knew his usefulness to his captain had all but gone, but he still hoped to provide some assistance to help Doane get the Yellowstone detail in the future. "I remember you quoting to me Dumas' Monte Cristo that everything comes to him who waits (or words to that effect)," Bean wrote. "I have adopted it with an addendum — provided he is a rustler."[12] For his part Doane continued a considerable amount of rustling for the park appointment every chance he got at the Presidio. In his annual report of 1890 he claimed geology and mineralogy, especially that of the Yellowstone region, as special fields of study, "anticipating that some time in life, when the field of exploration is no longer new, that a sense of public justice would call me to a field of labor in the Park."[13]

The army called Doane to a field of labor far from his choice. Instead of enjoying the brisk atmosphere of Yellowstone, Doane got the bad news in spring 1890 that Company A would be returning to the stifling heat of Arizona Territory. Mary reluctantly packed their household goods and abandoned their comfortable home in the Presidio to join her husband on the long railroad journey south on June 7. Companies A and K had been assigned to Fort Bowie, and on the night of June 9 they arrived at Bowie Station. As the soldiers began unloading their horses and equipment in the quiet moonlight, Doane arranged for Mary to go ahead to the fort, fifteen miles south of the station. Forty years later she would recall with painful clarity the disappointment of her journey to her new home. "I hope I may be able to convey in a measure the situation as it appeared to me that night," she wrote, describing her arrival at the deserted fort. "No one to meet us to direct, no lights, no dinner, no supplies, no beds, no home. Not a place to sit down, not a place to lay our heads, just a number of big empty houses staring at us. We were sad even to tears."[14] Mary claimed that the troops who had previously occupied the fort left in frenzied haste, fearing that their orders might suddenly be canceled.

The Doanes were assigned their standard two rooms and a kitchen in one of the duplex married officers' houses and set up housekeeping. The stark adobe complex had only a few stunted trees, but Fort Bowie could boast a good reliable spring and a climate that (at 4,900 feet above sea level) was not as hot as the lower surrounding desert. However, the Arizona duty would not allow Doane a leisurely wait for the next vacancy at Yellowstone National Park. Incredibly, one last "outbreak" of Apaches occurred in the summer of 1890, even though the Geronimo band had been banished by General Miles four years earlier. A group of outlaws from the San Carlos reservation, said to be the followers of a former army scout known as the "Apache Kid," had been responsible for three killings in the Globe, Arizona, area and were thought to be making their way to Mexico. Though far from the scale of the Geronimo campaign, the chase organized to capture the Kid and his followers was serious enough to call Miles back to Arizona in July and to reestablish the system of heliograph stations across the entire border district. Doane and a detachment from Company A were sent to a camp high in the Chiricahua Mountains a few dozen miles to the southeast of Fort Bowie to man one of the stations. Just as the heliograph station at Cochise Stronghold had been a boring encampment with no clear purpose, Doane's position in the Chiricahuas turned out to be a two-month bivouac that contributed nothing to the pursuit of the Kid and his band.

In far-off South Dakota another Indian "outbreak" required the army to mobilize troops in large numbers that falsely raised Doane's hope for a Yellowstone assignment. A Paiute shaman named Wovoka gained notoriety as the messiah of a new spiritual movement among western tribes popularly known as the Ghost Dance religion. At the Pine Ridge agency the Lakota Sioux had embraced the Ghost Dance and alarmed local ranchers and government officials, who called for troops in the fall of 1890 to contain the perceived threat. General Miles, who had just achieved his long-sought promotion to major general and transfer to command the Military Division of the Missouri, now had jurisdiction over North and South Dakota and assembled a mighty force to deal with the situation. Among the troops he called up were those of the garrison at Yellowstone National Park. They remained away from the park even after the massacre of a large band of Sioux at Wounded Knee on December 29, 1890.

"I met Mr. Charles Gibson at the Arlington and he told me that all the troops from the Park had been ordered away because of the Indian trouble," Bean excitedly wrote to Doane at the end of December. "He suggested that this might be your opportunity. . . . I called on Senator Power, who said if Miles would request by wire or otherwise that another troop be sent and suggest yours, he [Powers] on being informed would see it to Proctor and Schofield."[15] Doane, hopeful that the Indian trouble would keep troops in the field for months to come, sent a telegram directly to Miles, asking that Company A either be requested to replace the park's detail at

once or at least be transferred to South Dakota so they could participate in the current campaign. "You who have succeeded in many
things can appreciate my feelings in this matter," Doane wrote tell-
ingly and then proceeded to reactivate his network of friends to
pressure Secretary of War Proctor.[16]

Doane had miscalculated on several matters as he embarked on
his letter-writing campaign. He thought the secretary of the interior
would immediately contact Proctor to replace the absent troops at
Yellowstone, but that did not seem to be the case. Charles Schofield
in the War Department sent Doane a brutally frank assessment of
the situation. "I find upon inquiry that the Secretary of the Interior
has decided not to call for troops for the Park until spring," he
wrote. "The outfit that was there last summer and which is now in
the Badlands to witness the coming of the new Messiah, may be sent
back. . . . I have an idea from what I have heard that the Secretary
has his eye on one or two particular men for the detail."[17] Doane
refused to believe that his right to the Yellowstone detail would be
denied again. Figuring that the Miles call for troops had already
eliminated Proctor's earlier economic objection of the transfer,
Doane speculated to Schofield: "I know of nothing else that could
stand in the way but political or personal influence. Do you? Have I
any enemies or calumniators? I do not know of any or of any reason
for any."[18]

Doane may have had no enemies in Washington, but his friends
there were completely ineffective in helping him achieve what he
wanted. On January 15 Bean sent his captain a telegram informing
him that not only had the secretary of the interior unexpectedly
called for the troops after all but Secretary Proctor had immediately
appointed Capt. George S. Anderson as the new acting superintendent of Yellowstone National Park. An 1871 West Point graduate,
Anderson had returned to teach at the Military Academy early in his
career as a professor of natural philosophy. He had an imposing
physical appearance to complement his polished social skills and
deeply impressed Secretary Proctor as a gentleman, scholar, and
soldier.[19] Essentially a man in the right place at the right time, Anderson received orders to transfer from Fort Myer near Washing-

ton, D.C., to a company of the Sixth Cavalry and to proceed with his new command to Fort Yellowstone on February 15, 1891. In his matter-of-fact assessment of the decision Charles Schofield told Doane: "I don't think you have any enemies here or elsewhere. My impression is that both secretaries wanted Anderson and that settled it."[20]

That did not settle the matter for Doane by any means. Once again he felt he had been arbitrarily passed over for the Yellowstone detail and reacted with a rage that overwhelmed any sense of precaution. In a letter to Senator Wilbur F. Sanders of Montana, Doane used a particularly insensitive argument, considering the recent events at Wounded Knee. "I want command of the Yellowstone National Park," he railed. "If I have not deserved it justice is a mockery, merit a scandal, gratitude a farce and liberty a lie. I remember the day when we slaughtered the Piegans, how it occurred to me, as I sat down on the bank of the Marias and watched the stream of their blood, which ran down the surface of the frozen river over half a mile, that the work we were then doing would be rewarded as it has been."[21]

When it became obvious that Senator Sanders would be of little help in the matter in Washington, Doane wrote with even more force to James K. Clark of the Montana House of Representatives in Helena. In a letter similar to those he sent to every member of the legislature that he knew, Doane demanded their assistance by again insisting his participation in the 1870 massacre of the Piegan camp entitled him to Montana's support. "If the Montana Legislature will pass on a joint resolution, asking of the President my detail, it will throw a bombshell into the federal camp," Doane wrote, "which will open the eyes of some of those staid old Eastern Christians, who prefer a howling savage to a Western farmer, and an effeminate dude to a pioneer."[22] The joint resolution never passed, although nearly every member of the Montana legislature did sign a petition on March 3, 1891, asking that the federal government appoint Doane superintendent of Yellowstone. By the time the petition arrived at Fort Bowie it was too late to do any good, however. The form letter sent to all of Doane's advocates from the War Department explained with terse finality that "to comply would involve the transfer of this officer with his troop of cavalry from his present station at Fort Bowie, Arizona Territory, to the Park, and it was consequently not deemed advisable to order him on this duty."[23] Bean, in writing to assure Doane he had fought for the park assignment even though the odds were one out of a hundred, told Doane he would be returning to Company A in April and that "long before retiring time comes I hope and expect to see the 'right of discovery' honored and the Park yours."[24] Despite the young lieutenant's assurances, Doane's letters to Mary show that he bitterly felt the disappointment, and the physical toll of the rejection also began to show.

Doane's health had been deteriorating ever since his first tour of duty in Arizona in 1886, but now he started to decline rapidly. A hernia in his right side became so inflamed that he could no longer wear a belt with a pistol or sword, and he began suffering a numbness in his legs, which incapacitated him after being on his feet for several minutes. As a result he could neither walk more than a few hundred yards nor ride a horse much longer than a few miles. Instead of receiving the medical treatment he needed, Doane got another assignment that merely hastened his physical degeneration. In late March Company A got the unwelcome news that it would be posted to the San Carlos Indian Reservation until further notice, and from the milder climate of Fort Bowie's high elevation Doane would go to spend the summer at the barren flat along the Gila River. "San Carlos proved to be virtually a hole in the ground on the edge of the desert," Mary exaggerated years afterward. "There were no homes, just tents. The thermometer registered 107 on the day of our arrival and it was never below that during our stay of [four] months. It was often 112 at midnight."[25] While conditions at San Carlos could not have been as hellish as Mary remembered, the place was bad enough to cause her to leave when summer arrived in full force. She returned to Fort Bowie with a supply train in July and from there purchased a train ticket for Bozeman. There she would wait for her husband to seek retirement from the army and eventually join her.

Once Mary had fled southern Arizona, Doane began disposing

of all their property while planning to use his medical reports to get an early retirement. His anger over his failed attempt to gain the Yellowstone command led to his conviction that the army owed him a substantial debt. In addition to seeking a statement of disability from the San Carlos agency doctor, Doane worked on another plan for retirement income that he felt he deserved. Gen. John Gibbon had written that troops sent from his department to Wounded Knee that winter had been equipped with "walled Sibley tents," which were essentially copies of the Doane Centennial Tent design. These tents had been used in the field during a winter encampment, so Gibbon suggested that Doane poll the officers involved on what wall height they had found most efficient. The information could be innocently gathered for the purpose of reporting on proper winter shelter for troops, Gibbon said, but the same evidence could be used to sue the government for patent violations.[26] Doane then produced a form letter that he mailed to the company commanders of every regiment that had participated in the campaign or that was rumored to have been supplied with the tents and carefully gathered the responses all through the summer. To Doane it seemed like one more entitlement he had been denied, and with Gibbon's help he hoped at least to realize some gain from the perceived injustice. Optimistic that the general would be able to press the suit in Washington, Doane wrote to Mary: "If he succeeds we may be able to build a stone house next year and have it paid for."[27]

Company A returned to Fort Bowie in November 1891, and Doane immediately applied for a hearing before the Army Retirement Board. His application itemized all of the ailments that had plagued him in the past summer, from the hernia in his side to indigestion and piles. Ignoring his two recent attempts to be posted to Yellowstone based on the park's need for a superintendent of "energy and vision," he concluded: "I can no longer depend upon my physical condition in any emergency which may require exposure, hard fare, or prolonged exertion."[28] After sending in the application, Doane acted as if his retirement would be approved without any trouble and continued to dispose of whatever furniture he could sell to other officers. His commanding officer gave the retirement application a boost by stating on the annual efficiency report that Doane was unfit for active service, and the retirement board for the Division of the Pacific scheduled a hearing for his case in December. "Do not imagine I will delay an hour after receiving orders that will set me at liberty," he assured Mary.[29]

On December 12, 1891, Doane made his appeal to the retirement board in Los Angeles, California. Curiously, his personal statement said almost nothing about his physical condition. Distraught over a lifetime of failure, Doane used the document to itemize the injustices he felt he had endured, beginning with the denial of his request to go to Africa in 1874. Henry Stanley had accomplished the plan Doane designed, he claimed, and the papers to prove it were on file in the War Department. He admitted the 1879 honeymoon trip he had taken to Washington, D.C., had been made solely to demonstrate the Doane Centennial Tent to the War Department and then accused the government of afterward infringing on his patent. The 1888 trip to Yellowstone had been made to "pursue scientific studies in the Yellowstone National park, a locality which I discovered in 1870 and brought to the notice of the world." He also proudly reiterated his action at the Marias River massacre, giving the body count of Indians on the field and insisting that the fight had entirely subjugated other tribes that had been "hostile." Doane concluded his tirade with a statement both defiant and resigned. "I have applied for retirement because I know that I am physically unfitted to continue such work as I have done, believing that a cavalry officer who cannot lead his troop prejudices the interests of the Government by remaining in command of it," he summarized. "If by my service I have not earned retirement I shall not be able to earn it in the future, and if my service has been such as not to deserve retirement, I have been in too long already."[30] Unfortunately for Doane, in 1891 the War Department had in place a policy of specifically limiting the number of officers who could retire for reasons other than age and length of service, and the only way a vacancy could occur for disability retirement would be the death of another pensioner. As a result of this stringent policy, the officers of the Los Angeles board found an excuse to deny Doane's appeal and sent him back to Arizona.

Doane never recovered from the shock of the final setback of his life. His doomed attempts to gain the Yellowstone command and the denial of the retirement board crushed his spirit and destroyed what vibrancy remained of his health. On his return to Fort Bowie he wrote to Mary, allowing the agony of his defeat a voice that heretofore he had always suppressed in his letters to her. "The result of my trip was the usual one with me," he wrote, "a miserable failure." The doctors on the board had taken little notice of Doane's complaint about his legs, and he jealously described two other applicants' success as having gone "through with flying colors but I was rejected. . . . The medical officers even took the ground that I had never been on sick leave as a presumption against me!" In the depths of self-pity, Doane could not even try to conceal his depression, describing himself as "dazed and crushed" by the setback. Although he resolved to continue pressing for the retirement by writing to Washington, the defeat had totally destroyed his faith. "As it is my affair I do all this without expectations and without hope, simply because there is nothing else to do," he said. "I shall try and work a sick leave out of the doctor here and join you, but do not depend on it. Rather expect that it will fail also."[31]

Despite his pessimism, Doane did manage to get a six-month medical leave that allowed him to return to Bozeman in mid-February 1892. Bozeman would have been a fine place to retire. The invigorating climate, the strong local economy, and the thriving cultural institutions made it a desirable place for anyone, but for Doane it had something more. Here he was a hero, or at least a local celebrity, and universally recognized for the one thing in his life that he always wanted: to be known as the man who discovered Yellowstone National Park. Living at his in-laws' house, Doane made the most of his situation by telling everyone other than a few close friends that his full retirement had been approved and making hints that he would be buying a home as soon as he found one that suited Mary. Too many contingencies had to be met in order for the couple to plan for the future, however. The outcome of General Gibbon's halfhearted lawsuit over the tent patent infringement would establish their income; the results of Doane's next application to the retirement board in six months would decide their residence; and ultimately, the consequence of the influenza epidemic of 1891–92 would determine if they had any future together at all.

Doane had written to Mary from Fort Bowie in November when he first read of the sickness in San Francisco, wondering if the epidemic had reached Bozeman. He told her he had learned that it had been very fatal and that "the danger is lung or heart troubles afterwards."[32] Although he had contracted what he thought had been the "grippe" after returning from Los Angeles, Doane's sickness at that time was more spiritual than physical. Now in late April the disease came to the Hunter household in Bozeman, and it struck Doane hard. He languished for days and developed pneumonia after the first week. His weakened constitution entirely spent itself fighting the infection until, in the early morning hours of May 5, 1892, Gustavus Cheyney Doane died in his sleep from heart failure.

The funeral arrangements were handled by the local Grand Army of the Republic post and attended by hundreds of mourners, who accompanied the body to the local cemetery. There was not much of an estate to settle, but Doane's bitter sense of denied entitlement certainly passed on to those who remained. The circumstances of his death had outraged one friend, who knew about the botched retirement application and wrote angrily to the local paper: "Had Captain Doane been allowed to proceed north as he requested three months before he was finally granted leave he would not now be cold and rigid in death; he is simply another victim to army red tape and the worse than asinine stupidity of a medical doctor that in all probability would have starved to death in civil practice for want of employment."[33]

Epilogue

Mary Doane shared in her late husband's sense of injustice, although it would take decades for the seeds of entitlement to germinate fully. Doane's salary had never been enough to provide for the couple's tastes while he lived, and after he died Mary had only a meager widow's stipend and an aged mother to care for. In the spring of 1902 she became desperate enough to petition Senator William A. Clark to introduce a special bill for an increase of her pension. The requested sum of thirty dollars a month may not seem especially extravagant to modern readers, but Mary needed it enough to send additional pleading letters to congressmen Robert Adams of Pennsylvania and Eugene Loud of California, men her husband had known in years past. Her persistence in this small campaign paid off, and after the bill passed the congressional hurdles Mary received a steady income.

As the years slipped by Mary settled into a quiet role as Bozeman's dowager of Montana history, increasingly frustrated by her lack of funds and the scant recognition history had afforded her husband. It would be tempting to compare her with America's most famous military widow, Elizabeth Bacon Custer, who also tried to profit from her husband's memory as she struggled through six decades of widowhood. Elizabeth Custer had a talent for writing, however, and received a substantial income from the memorial volumes she published about her famous husband, while Mary Doane, by her own admission, was not "a literary light by any sense of the word."[1] Aside from the fact that Captain Doane had not become a national hero through a spectacular battlefield death, Mary's inability to write prevented her from articulating his more modest accomplishment as the "discoverer" of Yellowstone National Park. Not until 1929 did the possibility of emulating the example of Elizabeth Custer arrive for Mary Doane — a possibility ultimately ending in failure and disappointment.

There is no record of the first meeting of Professor Merrill G. Burlingame and Mary Doane. It is likely that once the new history instructor settled into his job at Bozeman's Montana State College someone pointed her out as a local celebrity and the last living connection with the frontier's colorful military past. The relationship developed into one of mutual exploitation. Burlingame recognized the widow's vast collection of military orders, personal correspondence, and handwritten reports as a treasure trove of primary source material for his planned dissertation, while Mary saw in the professor the means finally to achieve the recognition her husband always deserved and to gain some financial benefit from his memory. Burlingame began the gradual process of gaining the widow's trust by agreeing to help Mary in her effort to secure copyright to the 1870 expedition report. The three-page letter that landed on the desk of Congressman Evans in the spring of 1930 hints strongly at Burlingame's composition style. After Mary received the disappointing replies from Washington, he suggested to the widow an additional step she could take in order to capitalize on her late husband's voluminous writings.

Recognizing that Doane's 1870 report itself could not be copyrighted, Burlingame proposed to weave a biographical narrative around the text, including the captain's other reports of less spectacular missions, in order to produce a manuscript that could qualify for intellectual content protection. Once he had a chance to peruse the papers in Mary Doane's possession, Burlingame realized that massive gaps existed, with almost no information on the subject's early life, and that Mary could not shed much light on any of Doane's personal life prior to 1878, the year of their marriage. Because this period coincided precisely with the activities that the proposed biography would center on, Burlingame knew that he needed to fill the gaps in the Doane papers by perusing the official army records.

The relationship between Mary Doane and Merrill Burlingame was formalized in the summer of 1934. In June he drove the widow down to Mammoth Hot Springs, where they presented the Yellowstone National Park library with a typed transcript of the 1876 Snake River journal and met with William H. Jackson, the elderly photographer who had known her husband and been among the first to photograph the Wonderland country.[2] The afterglow of being treated so royally at the home of park concessionaire Jack E. Haynes likely contributed to Mary's decision to sign a contract with Burlingame on August 18, giving him ownership of her late husband's papers for the specific purpose of writing the biography. The contract contained an interesting proviso: "Should Mrs. Doane become incapacitated before publication, Mr. Burlingame is to be in sole charge of publication. Should Mr. Burlingame become incapacitated before publication, all papers and manuscripts are to be returned to Mrs. Doane."[3] With the signing of this document, the literary tontine for Captain Doane's papers had begun.

Unfortunately, Burlingame's limited experience in publishing, along with a tendency to recycle extended portions of his graduate school writings, seriously crippled the effort. The professor used secretarial help at the college to transcribe every lengthy handwritten report in the Doane papers, interweaving page after page from his own master's thesis and doctoral dissertation. While still struggling to tie all these diffuse elements into a coherent narrative, Burlingame began sending outlines of the proposed book with query letters to commercial publishers in the spring and summer of 1938. After a discouraging year of rejected queries, Mary Doane and Merrill Burlingame finally got a response that lifted their spirits. Savoie Lottinville, the director of the University of Oklahoma Press, wrote to Burlingame on May 4, 1939, with the observation that the proposed book sounded as if it would be ideal for a series their press had established on American explorers. Delighted that an editor had actually offered to read the work, Burlingame made the mistake of thinking that his quest for a publisher had reached its end.

Burlingame apparently did not understand how to work with the University of Oklahoma Press. Although Lottinville tried to suggest that a brief historical introduction along with the 1870 Yellowstone report and the 1876 Snake River report would be sufficient, Burlingame insisted on preparing the full biography that Mary wanted. By 1944, after failing to produce a manuscript that the University of Oklahoma Press would contract and receiving rejections from several other publishers, Burlingame abandoned the project entirely and did nothing more with either his manuscript or the original papers in his possession. His failure to fulfill his promise to Mary Doane prompted him to write a biographical article on her and her parents and see to its placement as the very first article in the 1951 first issue of *Montana: The Magazine of Western History*. With only that disappointing essay to show for her years of involvement with Merrill Burlingame, Mary Doane passed away on June 23, 1952, never realizing her dream of seeing her husband's biography in print. Her estate entered into probate court for settlement. Although the personal papers and photographs still in Mary's possession at the time of her death were bequeathed to her attorney's wife, the will made no mention of those materials still stashed away in Burlingame's office.[4] There they would remain for another forty years.

Merrill Burlingame did not become a prolific writer. He spent most of his time administering a growing history department at Montana State College and devoting himself to a number of local heritage projects, such as the establishment of the Museum of the Rockies and the Gallatin County Historical Society. Occasionally Burlingame's involvement with Mary Doane returned to haunt him, especially when researchers sought him out after seeing vague citations from the few historians who had been allowed to access the Doane papers. The transcript of Doane's 1876 exploration journal that Mary Doane deposited with the park during the summer of

1934 remained as a red flag to anyone who cared to look. While Burlingame would occasionally grant "permission" for others to quote from this report, he always followed up his letters with promises that he would again resume work on the biography "as soon as time allowed."[5] This situation likely would have continued indefinitely had not a pair of particularly insistent researchers gotten wind of the material and forced Burlingame to acknowledge his possession of the legacy left him by Mary Doane.

Orrin and Lorraine Bonney, a Houston, Texas, couple with an abiding interest in the Yellowstone region, realized early on that the copyright to the 1870 and 1876 exploration journals rested well within the public domain. They began work on a Doane biography themselves in the mid-1960s and naturally traveled to the Montana State University library at Bozeman to see the original copies of the two reports. Although Burlingame had deposited the 1870 report with the library after his 1967 retirement, he kept the 1876 report locked in his office with the balance of Doane's papers. The professor's subsequent refusal to cooperate with the Bonneys led to an unpleasant exchange of angry letters. Without access to the bulk of Doane's papers, the Bonneys simply used the material that they could find in secondary sources and at the National Archives.

Battle Drums and Geysers: The Life and Journals of Lt. Gustavus Cheyney Doane finally appeared in the late fall of 1970. Ironically, the Bonneys used a format similar to that suggested to Burlingame by Savoie Lottinville in 1944: a biographical introduction and fully edited reproductions of the 1870 and 1876 exploration journals. Considering the vehemence of the argument between Burlingame and the Bonneys, the book contained very little evidence of the conflict. Only two indirect swipes at Burlingame appeared in the book, and they were so heavily veiled that readers would be hard pressed to identify the person in question.[6] Burlingame returned the favor by prudently refusing to review the book when asked by the editors of *Montana: The Magazine of Western History*.[7] The review went instead to W. Turrentine Jackson, a distinguished western historian, who lightly praised the work but criticized its overly heroic presentation of its subject. Jackson lamented, "had they [the Bonneys] spent more time in synthesis and analysis in preparing a definitive biography of Doane, rather than republishing lengthy documents well known to historians and laymen interested in park history, they would have released a book twice as valuable and half as long."[8]

Merrill Burlingame never attempted to finish the Doane biography after the Bonneys "scooped" him. He served Montana State University well and in so doing established over the years a solid reputation as a collegial Montana historian, but he still jealously guarded the material that Mary Doane had placed in his care. Burlingame spent the twilight of his career parceling out all of the manuscripts that he had collected during his academic career in small donations to the Montana Historical Society, the Museum of the Rockies, the Gallatin County Historical Society, and the Montana State University library. His inability to commit to any particular one of these institutions resulted in fragmenting many valuable collections, including the Doane papers, and probably reflected his organizational affinity at any given time. Not until 1992 did the aging professor relinquish his grasp on most of the documents that Mary Doane had given him, donating them after a ceremony that dedicated the Merrill G. Burlingame Special Collections at the Montana State University Libraries. The final scraps of Doane material arrived at the library from Burlingame's filing cabinets shortly before his death in 1994. Not until 2000 did a small cache of Doane letters and documents that the professor had given to the Museum of the Rockies arrive at the repository. The library received another batch of Doane papers from a descendant of Mary Doane's attorney in 2001. Today there are six separate accessions of Doane documents at the university, representing deposits that occurred over a twenty-year period and the legacy of a promise that was never kept.

The twisted trail of Gustavus Cheyney Doane's papers and proposed biography resembles in one way the results of his 1870 expedition through Yellowstone Park. What began as a journey with the potential for Doane's placement among America's most prominent explorers ended with his disappointing recognition at the periphery of the expedition's limelight. If it is true, as one writer suggests, that Doane's reputation "does not loom large on the horizon" of history,[9] the fault does not necessarily lie with his remarkable yet star-crossed career. Like another metaphorical trail, the pathway of Doane's story was paved over by the good intentions of others and arrived at a destination far from the pinnacle of glory that had eluded him in life. Even Doane's tombstone bears mute testimony to his historical obscurity. A typographical error by the stonecutter declared him "Captain, 2nd Cavelry," which remains at his head to this day.

Notes

Chapter 1

1. Doane's 1870 report appeared as an appendix in a pamphlet dealing with the early history of the park two years after Mary's attempt to get publication copyright. See Cramton, *Early History of Yellowstone National Park and Its Relation to National Park Policy,* appendix "M," 113–48.

2. Mary Doane to John M. Evans, February 18, 1930, Fort Ellis and Gustavus C. Doane Collection, 1865–1930, Collection 851, Merrill G. Burlingame Special Collections, Montana State University Libraries, Bozeman (hereafter cited as Fort Ellis Collection).

3. William Brown to John M. Evans, March 6, 1930, Fort Ellis Collection.

4. John M. Evans to Mary Doane, March 7, 1930, Fort Ellis Collection.

5. Mary Doane to John M. Evans, April 20, 1930, Fort Ellis Collection.

6. Utley, *Frontier Regulars,* 19–20.

7. George Doane to Mary Doane, August 2, 1892, Mary Hunter Doane Papers, 1865–1944, Collection 2417, Merrill G. Burlingame Special Collections, Montana State University Libraries, Bozeman (hereafter cited as Mary Doane Papers).

8. Unruh, *The Plains Across,* 119.

9. West, *Growing Up with the Country,* 45.

10. George Doane to Mary Doane, August 2, 1892, Mary Doane Papers.

11. Nancy Doane to Gustavus C. Doane, September 16, 1879, Gustavus Doane Papers, 1860–1939, Collection 2211, Merrill G. Burlingame Special Collections, Montana State University Libraries, Bozeman (hereafter cited as Gustavus Doane Papers).

12. Burns, "The First Half-Century of the College of the Pacific," 28.

13. Ibid., 29. The tuition bond program came back to haunt the school as late as the early twentieth century, when students seeking enrollment presented ancient bond certificates and requested their acceptance at face value.

14. Rockwell D. Hunt, *History of the College of the Pacific, 1851–1951,* 29.

15. Burns, "The First Half-Century," 35.

16. Gustavus Doane, "The Student Bachelors Reverie," Gustavus Doane Papers.

17. Gustavus Doane, "The Changes and Varieties of College Life," Gustavus Doane Papers.

18. Gustavus Doane, "The Beauties of Nature," Gustavus Doane Papers.

19. Gustavus Doane, "The Eloquence of Nature," Gustavus Doane Papers.

20. Gustavus Doane, "The Position and Duties of American Youth," Gustavus Doane Papers.

21. Hunt, *History,* 31.

22. Gustavus Doane, "Familiar Lecture on Geology as Connected with Political Science," Gustavus Doane Papers.

23. Ibid.

24. "To the Archanians," March 11, 1860, Gustavus Doane Papers. Doane wrote on the bottom of this sheet sent by members of the Female Institute: "Testimonial of sympathy and regret sent by the young ladies of the female institute to the Archanians on the breaking up of their society and temporary suspension from college."

25. The files of the *Archanian Clarion* at the University of the Pacific archives contain no issues from 1861 or 1862.

26. *San Jose Weekly Mercury,* June 15, 1865, 2.

Chapter 2

1. Hansen, "The Chivalry and the Shovelry."

2. Mace, "Massachusetts Cavalry from California, 1862–1865," 1–2.

3. McLean, *California Sabers,* 6–7.

4. Mace, "Massachusetts Cavalry," 5; George Doane to Mary Doane, August 2, 1892, Mary Doane Papers.

5. Doane's unofficial status with the California Hundred is confirmed in the reminiscence of George Washington Towle. Although an unnumbered special order in the company record books lists him as "second duty sergeant," Doane's name does not appear in a published roster of the Hundred as it appeared in the *Alta Californian,* December 15, 1862. Doane's service record also confirms that he was not officially accepted into the army until he arrived in Massachusetts in January 1863. Second Massachusetts Cavalry, Descriptive Book, Companies A–E, Book Records of Union Volunteer Organizations from the State of Massachusetts, Rec-

ords of the Adjutant General's Office, Record Group 94, National Archives and Records Administration, Washington, D.C. (hereafter cited as Second Massachusetts Cavalry Descriptive Book); George Washington Towle, "Some Personal Recollections of George Washington Towle," typescript, Bancroft Library, Manuscript Collection, University of California at Berkeley; "The California 'One Hundred,'" *Santa Cruz Sentinel,* December 20, 1862; Rogers and Rogers, *Their Horses Climbed Trees,* 44, 50–51.

6. Towle, "Some Personal Recollections."

7. Samuel Corbett, diary, Bancroft Library, Manuscript Collection, University of California at Berkeley; McLean, *California Sabers,* 7.

8. McLean, *California Sabers,* 7–8.

9. Towle, "Some Personal Recollections."

10. "Further of the Troubles of the California Hundred," *Evening Bulletin,* July 1, 1863.

11. *Alta Californian,* February 13, 1863; Rogers and Rogers, *Their Horses Climbed Trees,* 67–68.

12. Second Massachusetts Cavalry Descriptive Book; Gustavus C. Doane, service record, Compiled Service Records of Union Volunteers from the State of Massachusetts, Records of the Adjutant General's Office, Record Group 94, National Archives and Records Administration, Washington, D.C. (hereafter cited as Doane Service Record, Massachusetts).

13. Towle, "Some Personal Recollections."

14. The Hundred were finally forced to give up their unique hat insignias on May 23, 1863, by a special order from the Second Massachusetts commanding officer, Col. Charles R. Lowell. Rogers and Rogers, *Their Horses Climbed Trees,* 137.

15. McLean, *California Sabers,* 22.

16. "The California Hundred and Their Troubles," *Evening Bulletin,* June 29, 1863.

17. "Further Troubles of the California Hundred," *Evening Bulletin,* July 1, 1863.

18. "The California Hundred," *Napa County Reporter,* June 27, 1863.

19. U.S. War Department, *The War of the Rebellion,* ser. 1, vol. 27 (2), 795 (hereafter referred to as *Official Records;* all references to series 1 unless otherwise stated).

20. *Official Records,* 27 (2), 795–97; "Letter from the Californians in the Army of the Potomac," *Alta Californian,* August 10, 1863.

21. My personal reconnaissance of the battle site with John Hollinger, Elizabeth Williams, and National Park Service historian Robert Crick, Jr., on November 2, 2001, confirmed the orientation of the redoubts and explained why Hargrove would have abandoned such a strong fortification in the face of such superior numbers.

22. Bingham, "We Saved General Lee's Communications with Richmond."

23. McLean, *California Sabers,* 24–25.

24. "Letter from the Californians in the Army of the Potomac," *Alta Californian,* August 10, 1863; Rogers and Rogers, *Their Horses Climbed Trees,* 158–61; *Official Records* 27 (2): 795–97.

25. "The California Hundred," *Evening Bulletin,* September 16, 1863.

26. Towle, "Some Personal Recollections"; "Letter from a Californian in the Massachusetts Cavalry in Service in Virginia," *Alta Californian,* September 28, 1863.

27. Rogers and Rogers, *Their Horses Climbed Trees,* 177.

28. *Napa Register,* November 7, 1863.

29. Towle, "Some Personal Recollections."

30. "Special Order No. 4, Headquarters, 2nd Massachusetts Cavalry, Vienna, Virginia October 16, 1863, Charge and Specifications Preferred against Sergeant Doane," Doane Service Record, Massachusetts. It is interesting to note that "Sergeant Manderson" of Company E, Thirteenth New York Cavalry, is listed as one of the chief witnesses, yet no person by that name appears on the roster of the regiment.

31. John A. Ellet to Alfred W. Ellet, November 3, 1863, Ellet Family Papers, 1839–1968, Collection M698, Department of Special Collections and University Archives, Stanford University Libraries, Stanford, California.

32. Mace, "Massachusetts Cavalry," 63–64; McLean, *California Sabers,* 70–72.

33. Doane Service Record, Massachusetts.

34. Towle, "Some Personal Recollections."

35. *Alta Californian,* April 28, 1864.

36. Hearn, *Ellet's Brigade,* 1–8.

37. Ibid., 77.

38. Bailey, "The Mississippi Marine Brigade," 36; Hearn, *Ellet's Brigade,* 143–44.

39. "[I]t was learned that the Marines had gone into the company quarters of a neighboring regiment, while the men were in their dining room eating supper, and had carried away their red hot stove, pipe and all." Crandall, *History of the Ram Fleet and the Mississippi Marine Brigade,* 257–58.

40. Gen. Charles P. Stone complained that Mississippi Marine Brigade boats returning to Vicksburg from the Red River plundered private property at every landing. Admiral David D. Porter had even more to say about the brigade's activities: "These vessels have already committed a great many arbitrary acts on this river under the cover of performing duty, and have alienated a good many who were disposed to be friends, and I would respectfully recommend that they be not employed on duty that can be performed by the gun-boats; they don't seem to possess the right kind of discretion." *Official Records* 34 (4), 275; 34 (2), 768.

41. Hearn, *Ellet's Brigade,* 224.

42. Crandall, *History of the Ram Fleet,* 386.

43. Ibid., 408–409.

44. Ibid., 409–10.

45. John Linfor to Hanna Durston, April 2, 1864. John Linfor Civil War Letters,

Mss 301, Mississippi Valley Collection, John Willard Brister Library, University of Memphis, Memphis, Tennessee.

46. Crandall, *History of the Ram Fleet,* 410–11; DeCell and Prichard, *Yazoo,* 314.

47. Shea, "Battle at Ditch Bayou," 199.

48. Alfred Ellet to Sarah Ellet, July [10], 1864, Ellet Family Papers, Stanford.

49. Ibid.

50. Hearn, *Ellet's Brigade,* 248–52, 258.

51. *Official Records* 41 (2), 712.

52. Ibid., 39 (2), 319.

53. Ibid.

54. Crandall, *History of the Ram Fleet,* 447–48.

Chapter 3

1. Hearn, *Ellet's Brigade,* 264–65.

2. Annie Doane to Gustavus Doane, May 25, 1865, Gustavus Doane Papers.

3. *Union Gazette* (Bunker Hill, Illinois), February 16, 1866.

4. Bowman, "Reconstruction in Yazoo County," 116–17.

5. Cobb, *The Most Southern Place on Earth,* 49–50.

6. Thomas Van Dorn to wife, July 2, 1865, Thomas J. Van Dorn Papers, Collection Mss S-1319, Western Americana Collection, Beinecke Library, Yale University, New Haven, Connecticut.

7. Annie Doane to Gustavus Doane, May 25, 1865, Gustavus Doane Papers.

8. Thomas Van Dorn to wife, August 20, 1865, Van Dorn Papers, Yale University.

9. "Testimony of several parties in the case of Judge J. J. B. White vs. William Davis, August 9 , 1865," Miscellaneous Records, Mississippi Subcommissioner's Records, Yazoo City, Records of Field Offices, 1865–78, Records of the Bureau of Refugees, Freedmen, and Abandoned Lands, Record Group 105. National Archives and Records Administration (NARA), Washington, D.C.; Bowman, "Reconstruction in Yazoo County," 118; DeCell and Prichard, *Yazoo,* 316; Thomas Van Dorn to wife, October 8, 1865, Van Dorn Papers, Yale University.

10. Nancy Doane to Gustavus Doane, February 19, 1866, Gustavus Doane Papers.

11. Edward Ellet to Alfred W. Ellet, June 10, 1866, Alfred Washington Ellet Papers, 1759–1870, Special Collections, Duke University Library, Duke, North Carolina.

12. Annie Doane to Gustavus Doane, August 19, 1866, Gustavus Doane Papers.

13. DeCell and Prichard, *Yazoo,* 322.

14. D. M. White to A. W. Preston, April 30, 1867, Letters Sent, March 1867 to December 1868, vols. 324 and 325, Mississippi Subcommissioner's Records, Yazoo City, Records of Field Offices, 1865–78, Records of the Bureau of Refugees, Freed-

men, and Abandoned Lands, Record Group 105, National Archives and Records Administration (NARA), Washington, D.C. (cited as Letters Sent, Mississippi Subcommissioner's Records, Yazoo City, RG 105, NARA).

15. Ibid.

16. "Special Orders 41, Headquarters, 4th Military District, Vicksburg, Mississippi, May 18, 1861," Gustavus C. Doane, Service Record, Compiled Service Records of Regular Army Officers, Records of the Adjutant General's Office, RG 94, NARA, Washington, D.C. (hereafter cited as Doane Service Record, Regular Army).

17. *Herald and Mississippian* (Vicksburg), June 7, 1867, clipping in Gustavus Doane Papers. Doane paid to have the entire exchange of letters with Bourne published in the June 7, 1867, issue as an advertisement.

18. Ibid.

19. *Herald and Mississippian* (Vicksburg), June 12, 1867.

20. *Official Records* 24 (1), 720.

21. *Herald and Mississippian* (Vicksburg), June 12, 1867.

22. Allen P. Huggins to A. W. Preston, June 30, 1867, Letters Sent, Mississippi Subcommissioner's Records, Yazoo City, RG 105, NARA.

23. Post Returns, Yazoo City, July–September 1867 (National Archives Microfilm Publication M617, roll 1550); "Returns from United States Military Posts, 1800–1916," RG 94, NARA.

24. D. M. White to A. W. Preston, April 24, 1867, Letters Sent, Mississippi Subcommissioner's Records, Yazoo City, RG 105, NARA.

25. Allen P. Huggins to A. W. Preston, August 30, 1867, Letters Sent, Mississippi Subcommissioner's Records, Yazoo City, RG 105, NARA.

26. Gustavus Doane, "Republican Speech Addressed to the Working Men of the South," Gustavus Doane Papers.

27. Daniel Hitchcock to Mayor D. Jones, September 21, 1867, Letters Received, March 1867–March 1870, Office of Civil Affairs, Department of Arkansas and 7th Army Corps and 4th Military District, Geographical Divisions and Departments and Military (Reconstruction) Districts, Records of United States Army Continental Commands, 1821–1920, RG 393, NARA, Washington, D.C. (hereafter cited as Letters Received, Office of Civil Affairs, RG 393, NARA).

28. D. M. White to U. R. Williams, Acting Assistant Inspector General, 4th Military District, October 17, 1867, Miscellaneous Records, Mississippi, Subcommissioner's Records, Yazoo City, RG 105, NARA.

29. U. R. Williams to James W. Sutherland, Acting Assistant Adjutant General, 4th Military District, October 21, 1867, Letters Received, Office of Civil Affairs, RG 393, NARA.

30. U. R. Williams to Merritt Barber, AAAG, Subdistrict of Mississippi, 4th Military District, December 12, 1867, Miscellaneous Records, Mississippi Subcommissioner's Records, Yazoo City, RG 105, NARA.

31. Edward C. Ellet, "Recollections of Edward C. Ellet, ca. 1910," Ellet Family Papers, Stanford.

32. O. D. Green to Gustavus C. Doane, January 4, 1868, Doane Service Record, Regular Army.

33. Gustavus Doane to John Tyler, AAAG, 4th Military District, March 6, 1868, Letters Received, Office of Civil Affairs, RG 393, NARA.

34. Nathaniel Vancleave to John Tyler, AAAG, 4th Military District, March 28, 1868, Letters Received, Office of Civil Affairs, RG 393, NARA.

35. R. B. Mayes to John Tyler, AAAG, 4th Military District, April 3, 1868, typescript in Mayes-Dimity-Stuart Family Papers, Collection Z69, Mississippi Department of Archives and History, Jackson, Mississippi.

36. Gustavus Doane, to John Tyler, AAAG, 4th Military District, April 6, 1868. Letters Received, Office of Civil Affairs, RG 393, NARA.

37. J. B. Mayes to John Tyler, AAAG, 4th Military District, April 14, 1868, Letters Received, Office of Civil Affairs, RG 393, NARA.

38. DeCell and Prichard, *Yazoo*, 325–26.

39. Ibid.

40. Ellet, "Recollections," Ellet Family Papers, Stanford.

Chapter 4

1. Randall and Donald, *The Civil War and Reconstruction*, 537–38.

2. Utley, *Frontier Regulars*, 15.

3. Ibid., 37, n. 13.

4. Doane Service Record, Regular Army.

5. Ibid.

6. Ibid.

7. Commanding officer, Fort McPherson, Nebraska, to George Douglas, August 25, 1868, Fort McPherson, Nebraska, Letters Sent, 1867–1886, Records of Posts, 1820–1940, United States Army, Records of Continental Commands, 1821–1920, RG 393, NARA, Washington, D.C.

8. Ruggles, "Statement of Campaigns, Expeditions, and Scouts Made in the Department of the Platte during the Year Ending September 30, 1868," 27.

9. Ellet, "Recollections," Ellet Family Papers, Stanford.

10. Brackett, "A Trip through the Rocky Mountains," 334.

11. Ellet, "Recollections," Ellet Family Papers, Stanford.

12. Utley, *Frontier Regulars*, 188–91.

13. Clarke, "Sketch of Malcolm Clark," 261.

14. U.S. Secretary of War, *Piegan Indians*, 2–4.

15. Ibid., 32.

16. Ibid., 15.

17. Ege, *Tell Baker to Strike Them Hard*, 42.

18. Gustavus Doane, "Lieutenant Doane's Report," in Rodenbough, *From Everglade to Canon with the Second Dragoons,* 552–53.

19. Ibid.

20. Ege, *Tell Baker to Strike Them Hard,* 43; Bennett, *Death, Too, for the Heavy Runner,* 116.

21. Doane, "Lieutenant Doane's Report," 553.

22. Ibid.

23. Starr's accusation was recalled in the 1920s by William White, who out of respect for Doane may have intentionally garbled the particulars. White said that Starr only identified the man giving the order to execute the prisoners as the "officer of the guard" and that the murders took place during the return march of the soldiers to Fort Shaw. None of the prisoners accompanied Baker's command on the return march, however, so the only evening the alleged incident could have taken place was the night of January 23, when Doane was the sole officer left in the captured Piegan village. White, *Custer, Cavalry & Crows,* 33.

24. Eugene Mortimer Baker, "Piegan Affair — Col. Baker's Report," in Rodenbough, *From Everglade to Canon,* 552; U.S. Secretary of War, *Piegan Indians,* 73.

25. U.S. Secretary of War, *Piegan Indians,* 70.

26. Ibid., 73.

27. Utley, *Frontier Regulars,* 191. The only exceptions to the prohibition against army officers serving as Indian agents occurred among the Sioux in 1876 and 1877.

28. *New North West* (Deer Lodge, Mont.), February 11, 1870, 2.

29. U.S. Secretary of War, *Piegan Indians,* 74.

30. Langford, *The Discovery of Yellowstone Park,* xxxiv.

31. Ibid., xix–xx.

32. Doane, letter to H. D. Washburn, August 12, 1870, Samuel Thomas Hauser Papers, MC 37, Box 31, folder 6, Montana Historical Society, Helena, Montana (hereafter cited as Hauser Papers).

33. Winfield S. Hancock, letter to John Gibbon, August 15, 1870. Fort Ellis, Montana, Letters Received, 1867–1886, Records of Posts 1820–1940, U.S. Army, Records of Continental Commands, 1821–1920, RG 393, NARA (hereafter cited as Fort Ellis, Letters Received).

34. Langford, *Discovery,* 7–8; Warren Caleb Gillette, diary, entry of August 22, 1870, Warren C. Gillette Papers, 1865–1912, Collection SC 243, Montana Historical Society, Helena, Montana.

35. Gustavus Doane, "Report of Lieutenant Gustavus C. Doane, Dec. 15, 1870," entry of August 26, Collection 492, Merrill G. Burlingame Special Collections, Montana State University Libraries, Bozeman (hereafter cited as Doane Report, 1870).

36. Langford, *Discovery,* 29.

37. Doane Report, 1870, entry of August 31.

38. Langford, *Discovery,* 29.

39. Ibid., 74. Langford claimed that he had Pvt. Charles Moore sketch the prostrate Smith as well. The drawing attributed to Trumbull appears without citation in Bonney and Bonney, *Battle Drums and Geysers,* 239.

40. Langford, *Discovery,* 51; Doane Report, 1870, entry of September 4.

41. Langford, *Discovery,* 51.

42. Ibid., 50–51.

43. Bonney and Bonney, *Battle Drums and Geysers,* 312–13.

44. Everts, "Thirty-seven Days of Peril."

45. Doane Report, 1870, entry of September 13.

46. Hedges, "Journal," 388–89.

47. Gillette, diary, entry of September 17.

48. Doane Report, 1870, entry of September 18.

49. Langford, *Discovery,* 106.

50. Burt, "Where's the Canyon?" 150.

51. Schullery and Whittlesey, "Yellowstone's Creation Myth."

52. For a full discussion on the development and tenacity of the "campfire myth," see Schullery and Whittlesey, *Myth and History in the Creation of Yellowstone National Park.*

53. Langford, *Discovery,* 119.

54. O. D. Green to John Gibbon, November 17, 1870, Fort Ellis, Montana, Letters Received.

55. The draft that Doane retained is the copy presently at the Merrill G. Burlingame Special Collections, Montana State University Libraries, Bozeman, Montana.

56. Hayden et al., *Fifth Annual Report,* 8.

57. Gustavus Doane, "Personal Recollections — Two Yellowstone Expeditions," in Rodenbough, *From Everglade to Canon,* 405–406.

Chapter 5

1. "The New Wonder Land," *New York Times,* October 23, 1871, 4.

2. Rodenbough, *From Everglade to Canon,* 411.

3. Eugene Mortimer Baker to AAG, Department of Dakota, February 12, 1871, Fort Ellis, Montana, Letters Sent, 1867–1886, Records of Posts 1820–1940, U.S. Army, Records of Continental Commands, 1821–1920, RG 393, NARA (hereafter cited as Fort Ellis, Letters Sent).

4. J. H. Gilman, receipt, July 10, 1871, Gustavus Doane Papers.

5. Hayden, *Fifth Annual Report,* 9.

6. Quoted in Merrill, *Yellowstone and the Great West,* 152.

7. Jackson, *The Pioneer Photographer,* 119.

8. Gustavus Doane, "Journal of Exploration of the Snake River," ca. 1888, 77, Gustavus Doane Papers.

9. Ibid., 89. In recounting Hayden's published insistence that Bridger Lake did not exist, historian Aubrey Haines has remarked: "This is such a patent misstatement when applied to a body of water over a mile in length that one suspects the geologist of not wanting the lake to exist." Haines, *The Yellowstone Story*, 1:119.

10. *Avant Courier* (Bozeman, Mont.), October 26, 1871.

11. William Henry White, personal interview with Merrill G. Burlingame, summer 1936, cited in "Captain Doane of the Second Cavalry," unpublished manuscript, Merrill G. Burlingame Papers, 1880–1990, Collection 2245, Merrill G. Burlingame Special Collections, Montana State University Libraries, Bozeman (hereafter cited as Burlingame Papers).

12. "Special Orders 142, Headquarters, Department of Dakota, July 17, 1872," Letters Received, 1872, Records of the Adjutant General's Office, RG 94, NARA.

13. Gibbon, "The Wonders of the Yellowstone."

14. Special Agent Simmons to Jasper A. Viall, December 5, 1871, Letters Received, 1824–1907, General Records, Records of the Bureau of Indian Affairs, 1824–1880, RG 75, NARA.

15. Vestal, *Warpath*, 137.

16. Bradley, *The March of the Montana Column*, 56.

17. Barlow, "Report," 6–7.

18. Brown, *Plainsmen of the Yellowstone*, 200; Barlow, "Indian Interference," 7.

19. Barlow, "Indian Interference," 7.

20. Ibid.

21. Vestal, *Warpath*, 142–43; Utley, *The Lance and the Shield*, 108–109.

22. Bradley, *The March of the Montana Column*, 62.

23. Peter Koch to Laurie Koch, September 7, 1872, Christian D. Koch Family Papers, 1829–1912, Collection 202, Special Collections, Louisiana State University Library, Baton Rouge, Louisiana.

24. John Gibbon to AAG, Military Division of the Missouri, August 19, 1872, Letters Received, 1872, Military Division of the Missouri, United States Army, Records of Continental Commands, 1821–1920, RG 393, NARA.

25. Gustavus Doane, "Report on the Navigation of the Yellowstone River," January 12, 1873. Fort Ellis, Letters Sent (transcribed copy in Burlingame Papers).

26. David P. Hancock, endorsement of January 21, 1873, Doane Report, January 12, 1873.

27. James H. Foy to Gustavus Doane, February 21, 1873, Doane Service Record, Regular Army.

28. Kappler, *Indian Affairs, Laws and Treaties*, 2:1008–10; U.S. Secretary of the Interior, *Annual Report of the Secretary of the Interior for the Fiscal Year 1869*, 733.

29. U.S. Secretary of War, *Annual Report of the Secretary of War, 1871*, 24–28; *Annual Report of the Secretary of War, 1872*, 35–42; Eugene M. Baker, report, October 18, 1872, Fort Ellis, Letters Sent.

30. U.S. Secretary of the Interior, *Annual Report of the Secretary of Interior for the Fiscal Year 1873,* 385.

31. Gustavus Doane, "Report to the Commissioner of Indian Affairs, Department of the Interior, February 19, 1874," Records of the Bureau of Indian Affairs, Record Group 75, NARA (transcribed copy in Gustavus Doane Papers).

32. Ibid.

33. Ibid.

34. Ibid.

35. Ibid.

36. Cone, "A Trading Expedition among the Crow Indians, 1873–1874," 420.

37. Doane Report, February 19, 1874.

38. Ibid.

39. Ibid.

40. Ibid., Appendix "F."

41. Ibid.

42. Ibid.

43. Ibid.

Chapter 6

1. Felix R. Brunot to Gustavus C. Doane, March 18, 1874, Doane Service Record, Regular Army.

2. Lovell H. Jerome to Post Adjutant, July 18, 1875, Fort Ellis, Letters Received.

3. Doane letter quoted in Bonney and Bonney, *Battle Drums and Geysers,* 150.

4. Ibid., 152.

5. Ibid., 154.

6. Ibid., 46.

7. White, *Custer, Cavalry & Crows,* 39–40.

8. Strong, *A Trip to the Yellowstone National Park in July, August, and September 1875,* 43.

9. Ibid., 48.

10. Ibid., 54.

11. White, *Custer, Cavalry & Crows,* 41.

12. Strong, *A Trip to the Yellowstone National Park,* 51. Evidence suggests that Doane actively exaggerated his role as the "discoverer" of Yellowstone National Park to anyone of importance. Francis V. Greene, an official with the government's Canadian boundary survey, also visited the park in 1875 and wrote that Doane had told him that the Mammoth Hot Springs terraces "had entirely changed shape since he first saw them five years ago." This was a deliberate misstatement on Doane's part, because he entirely overlooked the area in 1870. Francis Vinton

Greene to "Dear Parents," August 25, 1875, Western America Collection, Beinecke Rare Book and Manuscript Library, Yale University (microfilm copy available in Burlingame Papers).

13. Warner, *Generals in Blue*, 45.

14. White, *Custer, Cavalry & Crows*, 28–29.

15. Bradley, *The March of the Montana Column*, 42.

16. Ibid., 48.

17. John Gibbon to Gustavus Doane, October 28, 1876, Gustavus Doane Papers.

18. Bradley, *The March of the Montana Column*, 121.

19. Ibid., 87.

20. Gustavus C. Doane, report to AAG, Department of Dakota, July 11, 1876, Gustavus Doane Papers.

21. U.S. Secretary of War, *Annual Report of the Secretary of War, 1876*, 474.

22. Doane, "Journal of Exploration of the Snake River," 15, Gustavus Doane Papers.

23. White, *Custer, Cavalry & Crows*, 102.

24. Doane, "Journal of Exploration of the Snake River," 40, Gustavus Doane Papers.

25. White, *Custer, Cavalry & Crows*, 103.

26. Fred E. Server, Diary, 1877, Collection 507, Merrill G. Burlingame Special Collections, Montana State University Libraries, Bozeman, Montana.

27. Doane, "Journal of Exploration of the Snake River," 50–51, Gustavus Doane Papers.

28. White, *Custer, Cavalry & Crows*, 104.

29. Doane, "Journal of Exploration of the Snake River," 83, Gustavus Doane Papers.

30. Ibid.

31. Ibid., 91.

32. Quoted in Bonney and Bonney, *Battle Drums and Geysers*, 549.

33. White, *Custer, Cavalry & Crows*, 107.

34. Ibid.

35. Ibid., 109.

36. James Brisbin to A. H. Bainbridge, December 17, 1876, Fort Ellis, Letters Sent.

37. John Gibbon to Gustavus Doane, October 28, 1876, Gustavus Doane Papers.

38. Server, Diary.

39. Betts, *Along the Ramparts of the Tetons*, 136.

40. Doane, "Journal of Exploration of the Snake River," 106, Gustavus Doane Papers.

41. Brisbin quoted in ibid., 119.

42. Server, Diary.

43. White, *Custer, Cavalry & Crows*, 110.

Chapter 7

1. Gustavus C. Doane, letter to Mary Lee Doane, February 18, 1892, Gustavus Doane Papers.

2. Zimmer, *Frontier Soldier*, 12–28.

3. Nelson A. Miles to James Brisbin, April 12, 1877, Gustavus Doane Papers. In the winter of 1877–78 Doane requested official copies of all correspondence to and from the District of the Yellowstone to document his activities carefully. All are certified by the headquarters as "true copies" and compare favorably with original records that I examined at the National Archives and Records Administration, Washington, D.C.

4. "General Order Number 6, Headquarters, Battalion Second Cavalry, in Camp on Yellowstone," April 12, 1877, Gustavus Doane Papers.

5. White, *Custer, Cavalry & Crows*, 116.

6. Susan Hunter to Mary Lee Hunter, November 18, 1878, Mary Doane Papers.

7. White, *Custer, Cavalry & Crows*, 117.

8. Gustavus Doane to Post Adjutant, Tongue River Cantonment, May 22, 1877, Gustavus Doane Papers.

9. Gustavus Doane to Post Adjutant, Fort Ellis, Montana, May 22, 1877, Gustavus Doane Papers.

10. *Avant Courier* (Bozeman, Mont.), May 24, 1877, 3, May 31, 1877, 3.

11. Gustavus Doane to AAAG, Yellowstone Command, June 13, 1877, Gustavus Doane Papers.

12. Ibid.

13. Smith, *The View from Officers' Row*, 178.

14. Ibid., 172.

15. Gustavus Doane to AAAG, Yellowstone Command, June 13, 1877, Gustavus Doane Papers.

16. Ibid.

17. Ibid.

18. Gustavus Doane to AAAG, Yellowstone Command, June 22, 1877, Gustavus Doane Papers.

19. Nelson A. Miles to Gustavus Doane, June 9, 1877, Gustavus Doane Papers.

20. White, *Custer, Cavalry & Crows*, 199–120.

21. Gustavus Doane to Adjutant General, U.S. Army, January 20, 1878 (transcription in Gustavus Doane Papers).

22. Ibid.

23. Phinney, *Allen-Isham Genealogy*, 3–84.

24. Ibid., 83.

25. White, *Custer, Cavalry & Crows*, 125.

26. Ibid.

27. Gustavus Doane to Adjutant General, U.S. Army, January 20, 1878, Gustavus Doane Papers.

28. Ibid.

29. Ibid.

30. Gustavus Doane to AAAG, Yellowstone Command, July 13, 1877, Gustavus Doane Papers.

31. Greene, *Yellowstone Command*, 223.

32. *Avant Courier* (Bozeman, Mont.), July 12, 1877, 3.

33. Miller, *Charles C. DeRudio*, 31; Special Orders 99, Yellowstone Command, August 6, 1877, Gustavus Doane Papers.

34. Scott, *Some Memories of a Soldier*, 54.

35. Ibid., 59.

36. Hugh L. Scott, "Foreword," in White, *Custer, Cavalry & Crows*, 8.

37. George W. Baird, AAAG, Yellowstone Command to Gustavus Doane, August 2, 1877, Gustavus Doane Papers.

38. Nelson A. Miles to Gustavus C. Doane, August 3, 1877, Gustavus Doane Papers.

39. Gustavus Doane to George W. Baird, AAAG, Yellowstone Command, August 3, 1877, Gustavus Doane Papers.

40. George W. Frost to Gustavus Doane, August 25, 1877, Gustavus Doane Papers.

41. George W. Baird, AAAG, Yellowstone Command to Samuel Sturgis, August 11, 1877, Gustavus Doane Papers.

42. George W. Baird, AAAG, Yellowstone Command to Gustavus Doane, August 11, 1877, Gustavus Doane Papers.

43. E. A. Garlington to Gustavus Doane, August 14, 1877, Gustavus Doane Papers.

44. Gustavus Doane to John Gibbon, August 21, 1877, Gustavus Doane Papers.

45. Hugh L. Scott [remarks at the 1929 Bear Paw Battlefield monument dedication], *Chinook Opinion* (Chinook, Mont.), October 3, 1929.

46. Phinney, *Allen-Isham Genealogy*, 96.

47. John Gibbon, telegram to Gustavus Doane, August 27, 1877, Gustavus Doane Papers.

48. After the end of the 1877 campaign, John Gibbon wrote that his order to Doane specifically authorized his march up the Yellowstone River as far as the Baronett's toll bridge inside the National Park, "to feel for the enemy," but there is no record of any such order being issued while Doane was at Fort Ellis. John Gibbon, "Report of John Gibbon, Col. Seventh Infantry Commanding, to Assistant Adjutant-General, Department of Dakota, Oct. 18, 1877," in U.S. Secretary of War, *Annual Report of the Secretary of War, 1877*, 523.

49. Samuel Sturgis to Gustavus Doane, August 29, 1877, Gustavus Doane Papers.

50. Ibid.

51. Scott, *Some Memories of a Soldier,* 62.

52. Charles C. Gilbert to Gustavus Doane, August 31, 1877, Gustavus Doane Papers.

53. Gustavus Doane to AAAG, Department of the Columbia, September 1, 1877, Gustavus Doane Papers.

54. Gustavus Doane, note to Charles C. Gilbert, September 2, 1877, Gustavus Doane Papers.

55. Scott, *Some Memories of a Soldier,* 68.

56. Ibid.

57. Phinney, *Allen-Isham Genealogy,* 98.

58. Oliver Otis Howard, "Report of Brigadier General O.O. Howard," September 1, 1877, in U.S. Secretary of War, *Annual Report of the Secretary of War, 1877,* 625.

59. Ibid., 625.

60. Samuel D. Sturgis, "Report of Colonel Samuel D. Sturgis," December 5, 1877, in U.S. Secretary of War, *Annual Report of the Secretary of War, 1877,* 508.

61. Ibid.

62. Scott, *Some Memories of a Soldier,* 68.

63. Frank Baldwin, ADC, District of Yellowstone to Gustavus Doane, September 13, 1877; Gustavus Doane to AAAG, Yellowstone Command, September 28, 1877, Gustavus Doane Papers.

64. Gustavus Doane to AAAG, Yellowstone Command, September 28, 1877, Gustavus Doane Papers.

65. Peter Leary, AAG, Department of the Columbia to Gustavus Doane, October 11, 1877, Gustavus Doane Papers.

66. George W. Frost to Nelson A. Miles, Yellowstone Command, September 10, 1877, Letters and Telegrams Received, September 1877–April 1878, District of the Yellowstone, Records of Districts 1841–1920, U.S. Army, Records of Continental Commands, 1821–1920, RG 393, NARA, Washington, D.C. (hereafter cited as Letters Received, District of the Yellowstone, RG 393, NARA).

67. George W. Frost to AAG, Department of Dakota, October 6, 1877, Gustavus Doane Papers.

68. James Brisbin to AAG, District of Montana, October 7, 1877, Gustavus Doane Papers.

69. George W. Frost to James Brisbin, October 10 , 1877, Letters Received, District of the Yellowstone, RG 393, NARA.

70. James Brisbin to AAAG, Yellowstone Command, October 21, 1877, Letters Received, District of the Yellowstone, RG 393, NARA.

71. James S. Brisbin to AAG, Department of Dakota, October 26, 1877, Fort Ellis, Letters Sent, 1867–1886.

72. George F. Wright, acting post adjutant, Fort Ellis, "Special Orders 216," November 7, 1877, Gustavus Doane Papers.

Chapter 8

1. Susan C. Hunter, "Reminiscence," ca. 1912, Mary Doane Papers; Mary Doane, untitled speech, February 22, 1931, Mary Hunter Doane Collection, 1881–1950, Collection 292, Merrill G. Burlingame Special Collections, Montana State University Libraries, Bozeman (hereafter cited as Mary Doane Collection).

2. *Avant Courier* (Bozeman, Mont.), November 23, 1871.

3. Hunter, "Reminiscence," Mary Doane Papers.

4. Bender, "The Very Atmosphere Is Charged with Unbelief," 19.

5. Amelia Link Doane to Gustavus Doane, December 21, 1877, Mary Doane Papers.

6. Gustavus Doane to Mary Lee Hunter, August 1, 1878, Mary Doane Papers.

7. Gustavus Doane to Post Adjutant, Fort Ellis, November 18, 1877, Gustavus Doane Papers.

8. George F. Wright, Acting Post Adjutant, Fort Ellis, to Gustavus Doane, November 23, 1877, Gustavus Doane Papers.

9. Special Orders No. 231, Fort Ellis, Montana, November 27, 1877, Doane Service Record, Regular Army.

10. Nelson A. Miles to AAG, Department of Dakota, December 18, 1877, Doane Centennial Tent Company Records, Rutherford B. Hayes Library, Fremont, Ohio.

11. George W. Frost to E. A. Haugh, Commissioner of Indian Affairs, December 8, 1877, Letters Sent, 1869–1879, Records of the Montana Superintendency, Records of the Bureau of Indian Affairs, 1793–1989, RG 75, NARA, Washington, D.C.

12. Nelson A. Miles to AAG, Department of Dakota, February 9, 1878, Gustavus Doane Papers.

13. George W. Frost to Nelson A. Miles, February 12, 1878, Letters Received, District of the Yellowstone, RG 393, NARA.

14. James Brisbin to AAG, Department of Dakota, February 17, 1878, Fort Ellis, Letters Sent.

15. Gustavus Doane to George W. Frost, March 1, 1878, Fort Ellis, Letters Received.

16. George P. Buell, endorsement on letter of Gustavus Doane, May 13, 1878, Gustavus Doane Papers.

17. James Brisbin to AAG, District of Montana, May 31, 1878, Fort Ellis, Letters Sent.

18. James Brisbin to AAG, Department of Dakota, June 4, 1878, Fort Ellis, Letters Sent.

19. James Brisbin to AAG, Department of Dakota, June 5, 1878, Fort Ellis, Letters Sent.

20. Ibid.

21. George D. Ruggles to Nelson A. Miles, June 12, 1878, Gustavus Doane Papers.

22. William T. Sherman, endorsement on communication, June 24, 1878, Fort Ellis, Letters Received.

23. Gustavus Doane to James Brisbin, July 21, 1878, Fort Ellis, Letters Received.

24. Ibid.

25. James Brisbin to Gustavus C. Doane, July 23, 1878, Gustavus Doane Papers.

26. Ibid.

27. Gustavus Doane to Mary Hunter, August 1, 1878, Mary Doane Papers.

28. Mary Doane, interviewee, "St. Vincent's Academy," notes prepared by Merrill G. Burlingame based on an interview dated January 10, 1950, Mary Doane Collection.

29. Mary Hunter to Gustavus Doane, October 13, 1878, Mary Doane Papers.

30. Gustavus Doane, untitled poem to Mary Hunter, ca. August 1878, Mary Doane Papers.

31. James Brisbin, telegram to Adjutant General, U.S. Army, November 18, 1878, Doane Service Record, Regular Army.

32. James S. Bribin to Gustavus Doane, November 20, 1878, Gustavus Doane Papers.

33. Gustavus Doane to Mary Hunter, December 2, 1878, Gustavus Doane Papers.

34. George D. Ruggles to Gustavus Doane, December 6, 1878, Gustavus Doane Papers.

35. Fort Ellis, Special Orders No. 210, December 11, 1878, Gustavus Doane Papers.

36. Gustavus Doane to Mary Hunter, December 2, 1878, Gustavus Doane Papers.

Chapter 9

1. Johnson, "Solved"; James Brisbin to Lovell H. Jerome, July 20, 1878, Fort Ellis, Letters Sent.

2. Gustavus Doane, Centennial Tent Specifications, 1879, Gustavus Doane Papers.

3. E. D. Townsend to Gustavus Doane, March 7, 1879, Gustavus Doane Papers.

4. Joseph P. Sanger, letter to Gustavus Doane, March 31, 1879, Doane Centennial Tent Records.

5. John Gibbon to Gustavus C. Doane, April 10, 1879, Doane Centennial Tent Records.

6. Gustavus Doane to John Gibbon, April 22, 1879, Doane Centennial Tent Records.

7. Ibid.

8. Charles H. Crane to Gustavus Doane, May 3, 1879, Doane Centennial Tent Records.

9. John Gibbon to Gustavus Doane, April 25, 1879, Doane Centennial Tent Records.

10. Gustavus Doane to John Gibbon, April 22, 1879, Doane Centennial Tent Records.

11. United States, Supreme Court, *Cases Argued and Adjudged in the Supreme Court of the United States/Reported by John William Wallace* (Washington, D.C.: W. H. and O. H. Morrison, 1866–76), reprint edition, vol. 79, 388–90; William Wallace Burns Papers, 1848–1910, box 1, folder 9, "Miscellaneous Documents Pertaining to Sibley Tent Lawsuit," Cushing Memorial Library, Texas A&M University, College Station, Texas.

12. Miller and Cohen, *Military and Trading Posts of Montana,* 5.

13. Gustavus Doane to the Secretary of War, February 10, 1880 (two separate drafts), Gustavus Doane Papers.

14. Lopez, *Arctic Dreams,* 361–66.

15. Ibid., 368.

16. Gilder, *Schwatka's Search.*

17. Henry W. Howgate to Gustavus Doane, September 24, 1879, Gustavus Doane Papers.

18. Henry W. Howgate to Gustavus Doane, October 12, 1879, Gustavus Doane Papers.

19. Gustavus Doane, "Howgate Expedition Report," March 16, 1881, 1, Fort Ellis Collection.

20. Mary Doane to Gustavus Doane, June 5, 1880, Mary Doane Papers.

21. Gustavus Doane, "Howgate Expedition Report," 2, Fort Ellis Collection.

22. Ibid., 3.

23. Gustavus Doane to Mary Doane, May 20, 1880, Gustavus Doane Papers.

24. Gustavus Doane to Mary Doane, May 23, 1880, Gustavus Doane Papers.

25. Gustavus Doane, "Howgate Expedition Report," 7, Fort Ellis Collection.

26. Guttridge, *The Ghosts of Cape Sabine,* 33.

27. Gustavus Doane, "Howgate Expedition Report," 9, Fort Ellis Collection.

28. Mary Doane to Gustavus Doane, June 14, 1880, Mary Doane Papers.

29. Apple, "In Search of a Star," 22.

30. Gustavus Doane, "Howgate Expedition Report," 13, Fort Ellis Collection.

31. Henry Clay, "Expedition Notes," August 30, 1880, Gustavus Doane Papers.

32. Gustavus Doane to Henry W. Howgate, July 27, 1880, Fort Ellis Collection.

33. Gustavus Doane, telegram to Henry W. Howgate, July 14, 1880, Gustavus Doane Papers.

34. Gustavus Doane, "Howgate Expedition Report," 23, Fort Ellis Collection.

35. Ibid.

36. Gustavus Doane to Henry W. Howgate, July 27, 1880, Fort Ellis Collection.

37. Gustavus Doane, "Howgate Expedition Report," 32, Fort Ellis Collection.

38. Ibid., 36.

39. Ibid., 54–55.

40. Ibid., 93.

41. "Arctic Meeting at Chickering Hall," 257.

42. Mary Doane to Gustavus Doane, October 5, 1880, Mary Doane Papers.

43. Mary Doane to Gustavus Doane, October 14, 1880, Mary Doane Papers.

44. "Arctic Meeting at Chickering Hall," 258.

45. Mary Doane to Gustavus Doane, June 15, 1880, Mary Doane Papers.

46. Gustavus Doane, "Preliminary Remarks," in "Howgate Expedition Report," Fort Ellis Collection.

47. Gustavus Doane to the Adjutant General, United States Army, November 28, 1881, Doane Service Record, Regular Army.

Chapter 10

1. *Avant Courier* (Bozeman, Mont.), November 18, 1880, 3.

2. Nancy Doane to Gustavus Doane, January 16, 1881, Gustavus Doane Papers.

3. Hardeman, "Brick Stronghold of the Border," 60.

4. Hogue, "Disputing the Medicine Line," 8–9.

5. Gustavus Doane to Mary Doane, August 26, 1881, Gustavus Doane Papers.

6. Gustavus Doane, letter to Mary Doane, October 10, 1881, Gustavus Doane Papers.

7. Gustavus Doane, letter to Mary Doane, October 11, 1881, Gustavus Doane Papers.

8. Mary Doane to Gustavus C. Doane, March 13, 1882, Mary Doane Papers.

9. Gustavus Doane to Mary Doane, March 21, 1882, March 25, 1882, Gustavus Doane Papers.

10. Mary Doane to Gustavus Doane, July 13–21, 1882; Gustavus Doane to Mary Doane, March 13, 1882, Mary Doane Papers.

11. Gustavus Doane to Mary Doane, July 25, 1882, Gustavus Doane Papers.

12. Mary Hunter Doane to Gustavus C. Doane, July 14, 1882, Mary Doane Papers.

13. "Record of Events, January 1883," Post Returns, Fort Maginnis, 1880–1890 (National Archives Microfilm Publication M617, roll 727); Returns from United States Military Posts, 1800–1916, RG 94, NARA.

14. Foner, "The Socializing Role of the Military," 94–95.

15. Mary Doane to Gustavus Doane, July 13, 1884, Burlingame Papers.

16. Gustavus Doane, to Mary Doane, February 4, 1886; Nancy Doane to Gustavus Doane, November 22, 1882, Gustavus Doane Papers.

17. James R. Frederick to Gustavus Doane, September 17, 1884, Gustavus Doane Papers.

18. Gustavus Doane to Mary Doane, September 19, 1885, Mary Doane Papers.

19. Hampton, *How the U.S. Cavalry Saved Our National Parks,* 73–80.

20. Gustavus Doane to Hon. Martin Maginnis, January 14, 1881, Letters Received Concerning Superintendents, 1872–1886, Appointments Division, Records of the Department of the Interior, RG 48, NARA, Washington, D.C.

21. Faulk, *The Geronimo Campaign,* 57–71.

22. Gustavus Doane, postcard to Mary Doane, January 1, 1886, Gustavus Doane Papers.

23. Gustavus Doane to Mary Doane, January 11, 1886, Gustavus Doane Papers.

24. Ibid.

25. Gustavus Doane to Mary Doane, January 7, 1886, Gustavus Doane Papers.

26. Gustavus Doane to Mary Doane, January 10, 1886, Gustavus Doane Papers.

27. Gustavus Doane to Mary Doane, January 17, 1886, Gustavus Doane Papers.

28. Mary Doane to Gustavus Doane, January 31, 1886, Gustavus Doane Papers.

29. Mary Doane to Gustavus Doane, January 13, 1886, Mary Doane Papers.

30. Gustavus Doane to Mary Doane, February 6, 1886, February 10, 1886, Gustavus Doane Papers.

31. Gustavus Doane to Mary Doane, January 24, 1886, Gustavus Doane Papers.

32. Gustavus Doane to Mary Doane, April 17, 1886, Gustavus Doane Papers.

33. Fuller eventually achieved the rank of major in the Spanish American War and even published a popular science-fiction novel (*A.D. 2000*). Heitman, *Historical Register and Dictionary of the United States Army,* 439–40; Jeffery, "A Historical Geography of the Heliograph in the Department of Arizona," 71.

34. Gustavus Doane to Mary Doane, May 1, 1886, Gustavus Doane Papers.

35. Gustavus Doane to Mary Doane, May 1, 1886, Gustavus Doane Papers.

36. Mary Hunter Doane, untitled speech, ca. 1930, Mary Doane Collection.

37. Parsons, *The Tombstone Years,* 357.

38. Nelson A. Miles, "The Geronimo Campaign Report of Brigadier General Miles," September 18, 1886, quoted in *Nelson A. Miles,* ed. Pohanka, 159.

39. Gustavus Doane to Mary Doane, July 4, 1886, Gustavus Doane Papers.

40. Gustavus Doane to Mary Doane, July 12, 1886, Gustavus Doane Papers.

41. Gustavus Doane to Mary Doane, August 18, 1886, Gustavus Doane Papers.

42. Gustavus Doane to Mary Doane, July 17, 1886, Gustavus Doane Papers.

43. Gustavus Doane to Mary Doane, August 10, 1886, Gustavus Doane Papers.

44. Gustavus Doane to Mary Doane, July 6, 1886, Gustavus Doane Papers.

45. Faulk, *Geronimo Campaign,* 152–75.

46. Gustavus Doane to Mary Doane, August 13, 1886, Gustavus Doane Papers.

Chapter 11

1. William H. Bean to Gustavus C. Doane, July 1, 1888, Gustavus Doane Papers.

2. Haines, *Yellowstone Story,* 17–18.

3. Doane, *Memorandum,* 3.

4. Bowie, "Redfield Proctor," 4.

5. William H. Bean to Gustavus Doane, March 11, 1889, Gustavus Doane Papers.

6. *New York Times,* April 12, 1889.

7. Wooster, *Nelson A. Miles and the Twilight of the Frontier Army,* 170–71.

8. William H. Bean to Gustavus Doane, April 20, 1889, Gustavus Doane Papers.

9. Gustavus Doane to A. B. Carr, June 10, 1889, Gustavus Doane Papers.

10. William H. Bean to Gustavus Doane, May 25, 1889, Gustavus Doane Papers.

11. William H. Bean to Gustavus Doane, September 25, 1889, Gustavus Doane Papers.

12. William H. Bean to Gustavus Doane, September 7, 1890, Gustavus Doane Papers.

13. Gustavus C. Doane, "Report of Attention Given to Special Subjects," May 1, 1890, Doane Service Record, Regular Army.

14. Mary Hunter Doane, untitled speech, Mary Doane Collection.

15. William H. Bean to Gustavus Doane, December 30, 1890, Gustavus Doane Papers.

16. Gustavus Doane to Nelson A. Miles, January 7, 1891, Gustavus Doane Papers.

17. Charles Schofield to Gustavus C. Doane, January 8, 1891, Gustavus Doane Papers.

18. Gustavus Doane to Charles Schofield, January 13, 1891, Gustavus Doane Papers.

19. Haines, *Yellowstone Story,* 454–55.

20. Charles Schofield, to Gustavus Doane, January 21, 1891, Gustavus Doane Papers.

21. Gustavus Doane to W. F. Sanders, January 7, 1891, Gustavus Doane Papers.

22. Gustavus Doane to James K. Clark, January 27, 1891, Gustavus Doane Papers.

23. William R. Proctor to William W. Morrow et al., January 29, 1891, Gustavus Doane Papers.

24. William H. Bean to Gustavus Doane, February 2, 1891, Gustavus Doane Papers.

25. Mary Hunter Doane, untitled speech, Mary Doane Collection.

26. John Gibbon to Gustavus Doane, January 12, 1891, Gustavus Doane Papers.

27. Gustavus Doane to Mary Doane, December 12, 1891, Mary Doane Papers.

28. Gustavus Doane to Adjutant General, U.S. Army, November 2, 1891, Gustavus Doane Papers.

29. Gustavus Doane to Mary Doane, November 24, 1891, Gustavus Doane Papers.

30. Gustavus Doane, "Statement to Retiring Examination Board," December 16, 1891, Doane Service Record, Regular Army.

31. Gustavus Doane to Mary Doane, December 21, 1891, Gustavus Doane Papers.

32. Gustavus Doane to Mary Doane, December 2, 1891, Gustavus Doane Papers.

33. *Avant Courier* (Bozeman, Mont.), May 7, 1892.

Epilogue

1. Mary Doane to Merrill G. Burlingame, December 17, 1934, Burlingame Papers.

2. Mary L. Doane to J. E. Haynes, September 1934, Jack E. Haynes and Haynes, Inc., Records, Collection 1504, Merrill G. Burlingame Special Collections, Montana State University Libraries, Bozeman.

3. "Contract for the Preparation and Publication of the Biography of Captain Gustavus C. Doane," August 18, 1934, Burlingame Papers.

4. "Final Account and Report of Executor, Petition for Distribution of Estate and for Final Discharge of the Executor," Probate Court file 3674, Gallatin County Clerk's Office, Bozeman, Montana.

5. Merrill G. Burlingame to Agnes Wright Spring, September 20, 1958; Merrill G. Burlingame to Merlin K. Potts, June 1, 1960, Burlingame Papers.

6. Bonney and Bonney, *Battle Drums and Geysers,* 140, 447.

7. Robert G. Athearn to Merrill G. Burlingame, December 1970, Burlingame Papers.

8. Jackson, book review, 82.

9. Calkins, *Jackson Hole,* 107.

Bibliography

Manuscripts

Burlingame, Merrill G. Papers, 1880–1980, Collection 2245. Merrill G. Burlingame Special Collections. Montana State University Libraries, Bozeman.

Corbett, Samuel. Diary. Manuscript Collection. Bancroft Library. University of California at Berkeley.

Doane, Gustavus Cheyney. Papers, 1860–1939, Collection 2211. Merrill G. Burlingame Special Collections. Montana State University Libraries, Bozeman.

———. Report of Lieutenant Gustavus C. Doane, December 15, 1870, Collection 492. Merrill G. Burlingame Special Collections. Montana State University Libraries, Bozeman.

Doane, Mary Hunter. Papers, 1865–1944, Collection 2417. Merrill G. Burlingame Special Collections. Montana State University Libraries, Bozeman.

Doane Centennial Tent Company Records. Rutherford B. Hayes Library, Fremont, Ohio.

Ellet, Alfred Washington. Papers, 1759–1870. Rare Book, Manuscript, and Special Collections Library. Duke University, Duke, North Carolina.

Ellet Family Papers, 1839–1968, Collection M698. Department of Special Collections and University Archives. Stanford University Libraries, Stanford, California.

Fort Ellis and Gustavus C. Doane Collection, 1865–1930, Collection 851. Merrill G. Burlingame Special Collections. Montana State University Libraries, Bozeman.

Jack Ellis Haynes and Haynes, Inc., Records, Collection 1504. Merrill G. Burlingame Special Collections. Montana State University Libraries, Bozeman, Montana.

Koch, Christian D. Family Papers, 1829–1912, Collection 202. Special Collections. Louisiana State University, Baton Rouge, Louisiana.

Mary Hunter Doane Collection, 1881–1950, Collection 292. Merrill G. Burlingame Special Collections. Montana State University Libraries, Bozeman.

Mayes-Dimity-Stuart Family Papers, Collection Z69. Mississippi Department of Archives and History, Jackson, Mississippi.

Server, Fred E. Diary, Collection 507. Merrill G. Burlingame Special Collections. Montana State University Libraries, Bozeman.

Towle, George Washington. "Some Personal Recollections of George Washington Towle." Manuscript Collection. Bancroft Library, University of California at Berkeley.

U.S. Army. Records of the Adjutant General's Office. Compiled Service Records of Union Volunteers from the State of Massachusetts. RG 94. National Archives and Records Administration, Washington, D.C.

U.S. Army. Records of Continental Commands, 1821–1920. Records of Districts 1841–1920. District of the Yellowstone, 1876–77. RG 393. National Archives and Records Administration, Washington, D.C.

—— Geographical Divisions and Departments and Military (Reconstruction) Districts. RG 393. National Archives and Records Administration, Washington, D.C.

—— Records of Posts, 1820–1940. Fort Ellis, Montana, 1867–1886. RG 393. National Archives and Records Administration, Washington, D.C.

U.S. Bureau of Refugees, Freedmen, and Abandoned Lands. Records of Field Offices, 1865–78. RG 105. National Archives and Records Administration, Washington, D.C.

Books and Articles

Adams, Gerald M. *The Post Near Cheyenne.* Boulder, Colo.: Pruett Publishing Co., 1989.

Apple, Lindsey. "In Search of a Star: A Kentucky Clay Goes to the Arctic." *Filson Club History Quarterly* 71, 1 (January 1997): 3–26.

"Arctic Meeting at Chickering Hall, October 28th 1880. Reception of Lieut. Frederick Schwatka and His Associates of the Franklin Search Party of 1878, 1879 and 1880: Addresses by Chief-Justice Daly, Lieut. Frederick Schwatka, U.S. Army, and Dr. Isaac I. Hayes." *Journal of the American Geographical Society of New York* 12, 4 (1880): 237–96.

Backus, Samuel W. *Californians in the Field; Historical Sketch of the Organization and Services of the California "Hundred" and "Battalion," 2nd Massachusetts Cavalry: A Paper Prepared and Read before the California Commandery of the Military Order of the Loyal Legion of the United States, December 1, 1889.* Military Order of the Loyal Legion of the United States. War Paper No. 4. California Commandery, 1889.

Bailey, Anne J. "The Mississippi Marine Brigade: Fighting Rebel Guerillas on Western Waters." *Military History of the Southwest* 22, 1 (1992): 31–42.

Barlow, John W. "Report." In *Letter from the Secretary of War, Transmitting the Report of Major J. W. Barlow, Who Accompanied a Surveying Party of the Northern Pacific Railroad, in Relation to Indian Interference with That Road.* S. Exec. Doc. 16, 42 Cong., 3 Sess. (1872), serial set 1545, 1–19.

Bender, Norman J. "The Very Atmosphere Is Charged with Unbelief: Presbyterians and Higher Education in Montana, 1869–1900." *Montana: The Magazine of Western History* 28, 2 (Spring 1978): 16–25.

Bennett, Ben. *Death, Too, for the Heavy Runner.* Missoula: Mountain Press, 1982.

Betts, Robert B. *Along the Ramparts of the Tetons: The Saga of Jackson Hole, Wyoming.* Niwot: University Press of Colorado, 1978.

Bingham, Robert. "We Saved General Lee's Communications with Richmond." *Civil War Times Illustrated* 5, 8 (September 1966): 22–25.

Bonney, Orrin H., and Lorraine Bonney. *Battle Drums and Geysers: The Life and Journals of Lt. Gustavus Cheyney Doane, Soldier and Explorer of the Yellowstone and Snake River Regions.* Chicago: Sage Books, 1970.

Bowie, Chester Winston. "Redfield Proctor: A Biography." Ph.D. dissertation. University of Wisconsin–Madison, 1980.

Bowman, Robert. "Reconstruction in Yazoo County." *Publications of the Mississippi Historical Society* 7 (1907): 115–30.

Brackett, Albert. "A Trip through the Rocky Mountains." *Contributions to the Historical Society of Montana* 8 (1917): 329–44.

Bradley, James H. *The March of the Montana Column: A Prelude to the Custer Disaster.* Ed. Edgar I. Stewart. Norman: University of Oklahoma Press, 1961.

Brown, Mark H. *The Flight of the Nez Perce.* New York: G. P. Putnam & Sons, 1967.

———. *Plainsmen of the Yellowstone.* New York: G. P. Putnam & Sons, 1961.

Burns, Robert E. "The First Half-Century of the College of the Pacific." M.A. thesis. College of the Pacific, 1946.

Burt, Struthers. "Where's the Canyon?" *Saturday Evening Post* 202, 2 (July 13, 1929): 150.

Calkins, Frank. *Jackson Hole.* New York: Alfred A. Knopf, 1973.

Clarke, Helen P. "Sketch of Malcolm Clark." *Contributions to the Historical Society of Montana* 2 (1896): 255–68.

Cobb, James C. *The Most Southern Place on Earth: The Mississippi Delta and the Roots of Regional Identity.* New York: Oxford University Press, 1992.

Cone, Carl B. "A Trading Expedition among the Crow Indians, 1873–1874." *Mississippi Valley Historical Review* 31, 3 (December 1944): 407–30.

Cramton, Louis C. *Early History of Yellowstone National Park and Its Relation to National Park Policy.* Washington, D.C.: GPO, 1932.

Crandall, Warren Daniel. *History of the Ram Fleet and the Mississippi Marine Brigade in the War for the Union on the Mississippi and Its Tributaries: The Story of the Ellets and Their Men, Written under the Auspices of Their Society of Survivors.* St. Louis: Buschart Bros., 1907.

DeCell, Harriet, and JoAnne Prichard. *Yazoo: Its Legends and Legacies.* Yazoo, Miss.: Yazoo Delta Press, 1976.

Doane, Gustavus Cheyney. *Memorandum.* San Francisco: Presidio, 1889.

———. *Report upon the So-Called Yellowstone Expedition of 1870.* S. Exec. Doc. No. 51. 41 Con. 3 Sess. (1871), serial set 1440.

Ege, Robert J. *Tell Baker to Strike Them Hard.* Bellevue, Neb.: Old Army Press, 1970.

Everts, Truman C. "Thirty-seven Days of Peril." *Scribners' Monthly* 3, 1 (November 1871): 1–17.

Faulk, Odie. *The Geronimo Campaign.* New York: Oxford University Press, 1969.

Foner, Jack D. "The Socializing Role of the Military." In *The American Military on the Frontier: The Proceedings of the 7th Military History Symposium, United States Air Force Academy, 30 September–1 October 1976,* ed. James P. Tate, 85–99. Washington, D.C.: Office of Air Force History, 1978.

Fuller, Alvarado M. *A.D. 2000.* Chicago: Laird & Lee, 1890. Reprinted in 1911.

Gibbon, John. "Tents for Armies." *United Service* (October 1879): 517–19.

———. "The Wonders of the Yellowstone." *Journal of the American Geographical Society of New York* 5 (May 1873): 112–37.

Gilder, William H. *Schwatka's Search: Sledging in the Arctic in Quest of the Franklin Records.* New York: C. Scribner's Sons, 1881.

Goetzmann, William H. *New Lands, New Men: America and the Second Great Age of Discovery.* New York: Viking, 1986.

Greene, Jerome A. *Nez Perce Summer, 1877: The U.S. Army and the Nee-Me-Poo Crisis.* Helena: Montana Historical Society Press, 2000.

———. *Yellowstone Command: Colonel Nelson A. Miles and the Great Sioux War, 1876–1877.* Lincoln: University of Nebraska Press, 1991.

Guttridge, Leonard F. *The Ghosts of Cape Sabine: The Harrowing True Story of the Greely Expedition.* New York: G. P. Putnam's Sons, 2000.

Haines, Aubrey L. *The Yellowstone Story: A History of Our First National Park.* 2 vols. Yellowstone National Park: Yellowstone Library and Museum Association, 1977.

Hampton, H. Duane, *How the U.S. Cavalry Saved Our National Parks.* Bloomington: Indiana University Press, 1971.

Hansen, Sandra. "The Chivalry and the Shovelry." *Civil War Times Illustrated* 23, 8 (September 1984): 30–33.

Hardeman, Nicholas P. "Brick Stronghold of the Border: Fort Assinniboine, 1879–1911." *Montana: The Magazine of Western History* 29, 2 (Spring 1979): 54–67.

Hayden, Ferdinand V., et al. *Fifth Annual Report: Preliminary Report of the U.S. Geological Survey of Montana and Portions of Adjacent Territories.* Washington, D.C.: GPO, 1872.

Hearn, Chester G. *Ellet's Brigade: The Strangest Outfit of All.* Baton Rouge: Louisiana State University Press, 2000.

Hedges, Cornelius. "Journal." *Contributions to the Historical Society of Montana* 5 (1904): 370–94.

Heitman, Francis B. *Historical Register and Dictionary of the United States Army.* Washington, D.C.: GPO, 1903.

Hogue, Michael. "Disputing the Medicine Line: The Plains Cree and the Canadian-American Border." *Montana: The Magazine of Western History* 52, 4 (Winter 2002): 2–17.

Humphreys, Charles A. *Field, Camp, Hospital and Prison in the Civil War, 1863–1865.* Freeport, N.Y.: Books for Libraries Press, 1971.

Hunt, Rockwell D. *History of the College of the Pacific, 1851–1951.* Stockton: College of the Pacific, 1951.

Jackson, William Henry. *The Pioneer Photographer: Rocky Mountain Adventures with a Camera.* Yonkers-on-Hudson, N.Y.: World Book Company, 1929.

Jackson, W. Turrentine. Book review. *Montana: The Magazine of Western History* 21, 4 (Autumn 1971): 82.

Jacoby, Harold S. *Pacific, Yesterday and the Day before That.* Grass Valley, Calif.: Comstock Bonanza Press, 1989.

Jeffery, Charles Frederick. "A Historical Geography of the Heliograph in the Department of Arizona." M.A. thesis. Arizona State University, 1980.

Johnson, Barry C. "Solved: The 'Mystery' of Lt. Lovell Jerome." *Montana: The Magazine of Western History* 19, 4 (Autumn 1969): 90–91.

Kappler, Charles J. (comp.). *Indian Affairs, Laws and Treaties.* 7 vols. Washington, D.C.: GPO, 1903.

Langford, Nathaniel Pitt. *The Discovery of Yellowstone Park: Journal of the Washburn Expedition to the Yellowstone and Firehole Rivers in the Year 1870.* Foreword by Aubrey L. Haines. Lincoln: University of Nebraska Press, 1972.

Lopez, Barry. *Arctic Dreams: Imagination and Desire in a Northern Landscape.* New York: Charles Scribner's Sons, 1986.

Mace, Joanne Beer. "Massachusetts Cavalry from California, 1862–1865." M.A. thesis. Humboldt State University, 1967.

Marquis, Thomas, and Thomas H. Leforge. *Memoirs of a White Crow Indian (Thomas H. Leforge) as Told by Thomas B. Marquis.* New York: Century Company, 1928.

McClernand, Edward J. *With the Indian and the Buffalo in Montana, 1870–1878.* Glendale, Calif.: Arthur H. Clark Co., 1969.

McLean, James. *California Sabers: The 2nd Massachusetts Cavalry in the Civil War.* Bloomington: Indiana University Press, 2000.

Merrill, Marlene Deahl. *Yellowstone and the Great West.* Lincoln: University of Nebraska Press, 1999.

Miller, Charles K. *Charles C. DeRudio.* Mattituck, N.Y.: J. M. Carroll Company, 1983.

Miller, Don, and Stan Cohen. *Military and Trading Posts of Montana.* Missoula: Pictorial Histories Publishing Company, 1978.

Morgan, A. T. *Yazoo; or, On the Picket Line of Freedom in the South.* New York: Russell & Russell, 1968.

Parsons, George Whitwell. *The Tombstone Years: Private Journal of George Whitwell Parsons: Volume Two, the Post-Earp Era (June 28, 1882–March 31, 1887).* Ed. Carl Chafin. Tombstone, Ariz.: Cochise Classics, 1997.

Phinney, Mary Allen. *Allen-Isham Genealogy: Jirah Isham Allen, Montana Pioneer.* Rutland, Vt.: Tuttle Publishing Company, 1946.

Pohanka, Brian C. *Nelson A. Miles: A Documentary Biography of His Military Career.* Glendale, Calif: Arthur H. Clark Co., 1985.

Randall, J. G., and David Donald. *The Civil War and Reconstruction.* Boston: Little, Brown, 1969.

Raynolds, W. F. *Report on the Exploration of the Yellowstone River by Bvt. Brig. Gen. W. F. Raynolds; Communicated by the Secretary of War in Compliance with a Resolution of the Senate, February 13, 1866.* S. Misc. Doc. No. 77, 40 Cong., 2 Sess. (1867), serial set 1317.

Rodenbough, Theodore F. *From Everglade to Canon with the Second Dragoons.* New York: D. Van Nostrand, 1875.

Rogers, Larry, and Keith Rogers. *Their Horses Climbed Trees: A Chronicle of the California 100 and Battalion in the Civil War from San Francisco to Appomattox.* Atglen, Penn.: Shiffer Military History, 2001.

Ruggles, George D. "Statement of Campaigns, Expeditions, and Scouts Made in the Department of the Platte during the Year Ending September 30, 1868." In *Annual Report of the Secretary of War for 1868,* H. Exec. Doc. No. 1, 40 Cong., 3 Sess. (1868), serial set 1367, 25–29.

Schullery, Paul and Lee Whittlesey. *Myth and History in the Creation of Yellowstone National Park.* Lincoln: University of Nebraska Press, 2003.

———. "Yellowstone's Creation Myth: Can We Live with Our Own Legends?" *Montana: The Magazine of Western History* 53, 1 (Spring 2003): 2–13.

Scott, Hugh L. *Some Memories of a Soldier.* New York: Century Company, 1928.

Sharp, Arthur G. "War on the River: The Mississippi Marine Brigade; Battle at Lake Chicot." *Civil War Times Illustrated* 21, 6 (1982): 18–23.

Shea, William L. "Battle at Ditch Bayou." *Arkansas Historical Quarterly* 39, 3 (1980): 195–208.

Smith, Sherry L. *The View from Officers' Row: Army Perceptions of Western Indians.* Tucson: University of Arizona Press, 1990.

Strong, William E. *A Trip to the Yellowstone National Park in July, August, and September 1875.* Norman: University of Oklahoma Press, 1968.

U.S. Secretary of the Interior. *Annual Report of the Secretary of the Interior for the Fiscal Year 1869.* Washington, D.C.: GPO, 1869.

———. *Annual Report of the Secretary of the Interior for the Fiscal Year 1873.* Washington, D.C.: GPO, 1873.

U.S. Secretary of War. *Annual Report of the Secretary of War, 1871.* Washington, D.C.: GPO, 1871.

———. *Annual Report of the Secretary of War, 1872.* Washington, D.C.: GPO, 1872.

———. *Annual Report of the Secretary of War, 1876.* H. Exec. Doc. No. 1, pt. 2, 44 Cong., 2 Sess. (1876), serial set 1742.

———. *Annual Report of the Secretary of War, 1877.* H. Exec. Doc. No. 1, pt. 2, 45 Cong., 2 Sess. (1877), serial set 1794.

———. *Piegan Indians: Letter from the Secretary of War in Answer to the Late Expedition against the Piegan Indians, in the Territory of Montana.* H. Exec. Doc. No. 269, 41 Cong., 2 Sess. (1870), serial set 1426.

U.S. War Department. *The War of the Rebellion: A Compilation of the Official Records of the Union and Confederate Armies.* 70 vols. in 128 parts. Washington, D.C.: GPO, 1880–1901.

Unruh, John D. *The Plains Across.* Urbana: University of Illinois Press, 1979.

Utley, Robert M. *Frontier Regulars: The United States Army and the Indian, 1866–1891.* New York: Macmillan Publishing Company, 1973.

———. *The Lance and the Shield: The Life and Times of Sitting Bull.* New York: Henry Holt, 1993.

Vestal, Stanley. *Warpath.* New York: Houghton Mifflin Company, 1934.

Warner, Ezra J. *Generals in Blue: Lives of the Union Commanders.* Baton Rouge: Louisiana State University Press, 1995.

West, Elliott. *Growing Up with the Country: Childhood on the Far Western Frontier.* Albuquerque: University of New Mexico Press, 1989.

White, William Henry. *Custer, Cavalry & Crows, Being the Thrilling Account of the Western Adventures of William White: The Story of William White as Told to Thomas Marquis.* Ed. John Popovich. Fort Collins, Colo.: Old Army Press, 1975.

Wooster, Robert. *Nelson A. Miles and the Twilight of the Frontier Army.* Lincoln: University of Nebraska Press, 1993.

Zimmer, William Frederick. *Frontier Soldier: An Enlisted Man's Journal of the Sioux and Nez Perce Campaigns, 1877.* Ed. Jerome A. Greene. Helena: Montana Historical Society Press, 1998.

Newspapers

Alta Californian (San Francisco, California)

Avant Courier (Bozeman, Montana)

Evening Bulletin (San Francisco, California)

Herald and Mississippian (Vicksburg, Mississippi)

New York Times

San Jose Weekly Mercury (San Jose, California)

Union Gazette (Bunker Hill, Illinois)

Index